Building Peace in Northern Ireland

Building Peace
in Northern Ireland

Edited by
MARIA POWER

LIVERPOOL UNIVERSITY PRESS

First published 2011 by
Liverpool University Press
4 Cambridge Street
Liverpool
L69 7ZU

This paperback version published 2014

British Library Cataloguing-in-Publication data
A British Library CIP record is available

ISBN 978-1-84631-659-3 *cased*
ISBN 978-1-78138-008-6 *paperback*

Typeset in Acta by
Koinonia, Manchester
Printed and bound by
CPI Group (UK) Ltd,
Croydon, CR0 4YY

For
Michael J. Hubbart
1936–2010

Contents

Acknowledgements

This collection owes a debt of gratitude to a number of people, most notably the contributors who have made it possible. Appreciation is due in particular to my colleagues at the Institute of Irish Studies, Marianne Elliott, Diane Urquhart, Lauren Arrington, Kevin Bean, Clare Downham, Huston Gilmore, Maria McCann, Pat Nugent, Frank Shovlin and Andrew Tierney who have provided invaluable support and advice as have Jon Tonge in the University of Liverpool's Politics department and Alison Welsby at Liverpool University Press. Finally, I would like to thank my parents, Alice and Eric, my brother, Claude, and sister-in-law, Andrea, and my nephew, Gabriel for their constant love and encouragement.

Contributors

Nicholas Acheson is Lecturer in Social Policy and a member of the Institute for Social Science Research at the University of Ulster, Northern Ireland, where he was a researcher at the Centre for Voluntary Action Studies from 1997. He currently leads research on voluntary action and civil society with a particular interest in civil society and social cohesion. Recent publications include (with Brian Harvey) *Social Policy, Ageing and Voluntary Action* (2006, Institute for Public Administration, Dublin), 'A Case of Avoiding "Political Mumbo Jumbo": Lessons from Northern Ireland for the Role of Voluntary Associations in Community Cohesion Policies', *Policy and Politics* (2010) and 'Welfare State Reform, Compacts and Restructuring Relations between the State and the Voluntary Sector: Reflections on Northern Ireland's Experience', *Voluntary Sector Review* (2010).

Elham Atashi is Assistant Professor of Peace Studies at Goucher College. She received her PhD from the Institute for Conflict Analysis and Resolution at George Mason University. Her research interests primarily centre on Northern Ireland, post-war reconstruction and peacebuilding, peace processes and transitional justice. She has published on issues relating to transformation of armed groups to political parties, bottom-up approaches to peacebuilding and the role of civil society in reconciliation and conflict transformation. She also works extensively as a practitioner focusing on peacebuilding on the ground. She has worked as a consultant to various international organizations providing training programs and workshops focusing on Northern Ireland, the Middle East, the Balkans, Afghanistan, South and Central Asia.

Kevin Bean is a Lecturer in Irish Politics at the Institute of Irish Studies, University of Liverpool. His research interests include Provisional republicanism, state counter-insurgency strategies and the development of nationalism as a political force in contemporary Europe. His recent publications include *Republican Voices* (co-edited with Mark Hayes) (Monaghan, 2001), *The New Politics of Sinn Féin* (Liverpool, 2007), 'Defining Republicanism: Shifting Discourses of Post-Republicanism and New Nationalism', in M. Elliott (ed.), *The Long Road to Peace in Northern Ireland* (Liverpool, 2007), '"The Economic and Social War against Violence": British Social and Economic

Strategy and the Evolution of Provisionalism', in A. Edwards and S. Bloomer (eds.), *Transforming the Peace Process in Northern Ireland* (Dublin, 2008), and 'The Politics of Fear? Provisionalism, Loyalism and the "New Politics" of Northern Ireland', in G. Spencer and J. McAuley (eds.), *Ulster Loyalism after the Good Friday Agreement: History, Identity and Change* (Basingstoke, 2011).

Sandra Buchanan holds a PhD (2009) from the University of Ulster in conflict transformation, having previously completed a Postgraduate Diploma (1995) and MA (1996) in Peace Studies there. Based on over a decade of peace-building practice in the Border Counties and on a cross-border basis, her PhD research was concerned with analysing the work of a number of transformation tools in this region from a social and economic development perspective in terms of lessons learned, producing practice-based recommendations for other regions emerging from conflict (forthcoming, Manchester University Press). Sandra is a Senior Staff member of Co Donegal VEC's Adult and Further Education Service and is also associated with INCORE, the University of Ulster's UN-affiliated International Conflict Research Institute. A member of the PSAI, IPRA and the CRS, she has published in *Irish Political Studies*, *Political Studies Review* and *The Ethnic Conflict Research Digest*, having also presented her research nationally and internationally.

Ivo Damkat is completing a PhD in Sociology at Queen's University Belfast. In his PhD he explores the development of discourses in cross-border cooperation in Ireland among key stakeholders since the Good Friday Agreement. He holds a Masters in Public Administration from the University of Leiden, with a dissertation examining the implementation structures of the European Union Peace Programmes in Northern Ireland. His most recent publication is 'Sustaining Cooperation? The Public, Private and Civil Society Sectors', in *Crossing the Border: New Relationships between Northern Ireland and the Republic of Ireland*, edited by John Coakley and Liam O'Dowd (Irish Academic Press, 2007). He is also an Assistant Statistician with the Northern Ireland Statistics and Research Agency. He was formerly a research assistant for the Mapping Frontiers, Plotting Pathways project at Queen's University Belfast.

Joana Etchart completed a PhD thesis in 2010 on the history of community relations policies in Northern Ireland (1969-1998) in the Sorbonne Nouvelle Paris 3 where she taught English for three years. She is now a Lecturer in British History at the Sorbonne Paris 4. She is a member of the SOFEIR (French Society of Irish Studies). Her current research interests are centred on the study of public policies and community initiatives in the field of peace-building in Northern Ireland, Ireland. She also studies urban regeneration projects in Irish and British cities. In her work, regeneration projects such as the Titanic Quarter in Belfast serve as an entry point for analysing the complex relationship between power, culture and identity.

Marie Hammond-Callaghan is Associate Professor in the Women's and Gender Studies programme and the History Department at Mount Allison University, Sackville, New Brunswick, Canada. She holds a PhD from the National University of Ireland, Dublin. Her main research interests lie in women's peace movement history in twentieth-century North America and Europe, state surveillance of women's groups during the Cold War period and inter-disciplinary gender analysis of peacebuilding, militarism and war. To date she has published several scholarly articles on women's peace activism in the 1970s in the North of Ireland and Canada, including 'Surveying Politics of Peace, Gender, Conflict and Identity in Northern Ireland: The Case of The Derry Peace Women in 1972' (reprint) in Alan O'Day and N. C. Fleming (eds), *From the Treaty to the Present*, vol. III of The History of Anglo–Irish Relations series (Ashgate, 2008) and 'A Tender Flower … to Be Carefully Nourished': The Northern Irish Women's Peace Movement, Gender Order, State Security and the Cold War, 1970–76', in Diane Urquhart and Gillian McIntosh (eds), *Irish Women at War* (Irish Academic Press, 2010). Also, she is co-editor with Matthew Hayday (University of Guelph) of *Mobilizations, Protests and Engagements: Canadian Perspectives on Social Movements* (Fernwood Press, 2008).

Katy Hayward is Lecturer in Sociology at Queen's University Belfast. Her research on peacebuilding has focused on the topics of cross-border coopera-tion, political discourse and European integration. Her publications in this area include *Irish Nationalism and European Integration* (Manchester University Press, 2009) and *Political Discourse and Conflict Resolution* (co-edited with Catherine O'Donnell, Routledge, 2011), a contribution to the *International Encyclopedia of Peace* (Oxford University Press, 2010) and articles in such journals as *Accord*, *Co-operation and Conflict* and the *European Journal of Political Research*.

Cathal McCall is Senior Lecturer in European Studies in the School of Politics, International Studies and Philosophy, and a member of the Centre for Inter-national Borders Research (CIBR), at Queen's University Belfast. His research interests include investigating how EU involvement in promoting cross-border cooperation in the Irish border region compares with its approach to other 'conflict regions' inside and outside the EU. He is contributing editor (with Thomas M. Wilson) of *Europeanisation and Hibernicisation: Europe and Ireland* (Rodopi, 2010).

Kieran McEvoy is Professor of Law and Transitional Justice at the School of Law, and former Director of the Institute of Criminology and Criminal Justice, Queens University Belfast. He has published over forty academic articles and book chapters and has written or edited six books, including *Paramilitary Imprisonment in Northern Ireland* (Oxford University Press, 2001), *Beyond the Wire: Former Prisoners and Conflict Transformation in Northern Ireland*

(Pluto with P. Shirlow, 2008) and *Transitional Justice from Below: Grass-roots Activism and the Struggle for Change* (ed. with L. McGregor, 2008). He has conducted extensive research on many aspects of the Northern Ireland conflict and transition including paramilitary imprisonment, policing, restorative justice, human rights, the sociology of the legal profession and 'dealing with the past'. His next book, *The Trouble with Truth: Struggles with the Past in Northern Ireland* (2012) is published by Routledge.

Claire McGlynn lectures at the graduate School of Education, Queen's University Belfast, where she directs the Doctorate in Education programme and coordinates internationalisation. She has been teaching in a variety of intercultural education settings in England and Northern Ireland for more than twenty years and was a founder of New-Bridge Integrated College in Northern Ireland in 1995. Her research interests include integrated education, multicultural and intercultural education, education for social cohesion in conflict and post-conflict societies and teacher education for diversity. She has presented widely at international conferences and has published articles in national and international journals. She is the co-editor of *Peace Education in Conflict and Post-conflict Societies: Comparative Perspectives* (Palgrave Macmillan USA, 2009), winner of the 2011 Comparative and International Education Society Jackie Kirk Outstanding Book Award, and *Addressing Ethnic Conflict through Peace Education: International Perspectives* (Palgrave Macmillan USA, 2007). She is the current Convenor of the Peace Education Commission of the International Peace Research Association, a former Chair of the Peace Education special interest group of the American Educational Research Association and a member of the editorial board of the *Journal of Peace Education* and the journal *Education*.

Carl Milofsky is Professor of Sociology at Bucknell University in Lewisburg, Pennsylvania. He was one of the original members of the Program on Nonprofit Organizations at Yale University, where he specialized in community-based organizations. He edited the *Nonprofit and Voluntary Sector Quarterly* (1990–1996). He edited *Community Organizations: Studies in Resource Mobilization and Exchange* (Oxford University Press, 1988), and with Ram Cnaan he edited *The Handbook of Community Movements and Local Organizations* (Springer, 2006). He and Albert Hunter co-authored *Pragmatic Liberalism: Constructing a Civil Society* (Palgrave, 2007) and in 2008 he authored *Smallville: Institutionalizing Community in Small Town America* (University Press of New England).

Maria Power is Lecturer at the Institute of Irish Studies, University of Liverpool, where she began as an ESRC Post-Doctoral Fellow in 2003. She was educated at Royal Holloway, University of London, where she received her PhD in 2003. Her research focuses upon the contemporary history of the conflict in Northern Ireland and religious responses to conflict. Her recent publications include *From Ecumenism to Community Relations: Inter-Church Relationships in Northern Ireland 1980–2005* (Irish Academic Press, 2007) as well as a number of articles in various collections and journals. She is currently working on a history of the British government's community relations policy in Northern Ireland from 1968–present day.

Pete Shirlow is Director of Education in the School of Law, Queen's University Belfast. He began his career as a geography lecturer but over time has moved towards issues such as violence and equality legislation. Most of his work has been dedicated to analysing republican and loyalist violence and in particular the transition out of violence undertaken by these groups. He has studied how the 'Troubles' have impacted upon everyday life in segregated communities throughout Northern Ireland, issues of post-imprisonment among former political prisoners, and the construction of fear with regard to ethno-sectarianism. He has edited two books (*Who are the People?* and *Development Ireland*) and has recently co-authored the books *Belfast: Segregation, Violence and the City* and *Beyond the Wire: Former Prisoners and Conflict Transformation in Northern Ireland*. His next book, *The End of Ulster Loyalism?*, is due for publication in 2012.

Maurice Stringer is Professor of Psychology and Director of the Psychology Research Institute at the University of Ulster. His research interests have been primarily in intergroup contact and intergroup relations, cross-group contact and friendships and group segregation and self-esteem effects on health and social attitudes. His recent publications have included (with others), 'Parental and School Effects on Children's Political Attitudes in Northern Ireland', *British Journal of Educational Psychology* 80 (223–40), 'Increased Self-efficacy Following a Ten-day Developmental Voyage', *Journal of Child and Adolescent Mental Health* 22.1 (63–65) and 'Intergroup Contact, Friendship Quality and Political Attitudes in Integrated and Segregated Schools in Northern Ireland', *British Journal of Educational Psychology* 79.2 (239–57).

Timothy J. White graduated with a BA and MA in Political Science from the University of Missouri and went on to complete his PhD in Political Science at the University of Michigan in 1990. In that year, he accepted a position in the Department of Political Science at Xavier University in Cincinnati, Ohio. He now serves as the senior Professor in his Department at Xavier. Dr White was the Irish-American Cultural Institute's Visiting Professor at the National University of Ireland-Galway in 2000. Dr White regularly teaches courses in Irish Political Culture, the institutional framework of government in Ireland, and a course in Irish Historical Sociology. His more than thirty publications have appeared in *Éire-Ireland*, *New Hibernian Review*, *Irish Journal of Sociology*, *Irish Studies in International Affairs*, *International Studies Perspectives*, *Peace Review* and many others. Dr White served two terms in the past decade as the Social Science Representative for the American

Conference for Irish Studies and is also active in the Political Studies Association of Ireland. He also has served two terms on Xavier University's Peace Studies Committee and organized a seminar for scholars and policy-makers in the summer of 2010 on lessons learned from the Irish Peace Process.

1

Introduction:
Peacebuilding in Northern Ireland

Maria Power

When the Good Friday or Belfast Agreement[1] was signed in 1998, those involved believed that they 'were finally able to bring about peace in Northern Ireland'.[2] The process of implementing the accord and resolving tensions between the various political parties began and on 7 May 2007, the Democratic Unionist Party and Sinn Féin entered government together. Nine years after the Agreement was signed, this 'historic' day was heralded by the British and Irish political classes and the media as the end of the conflict in Northern Ireland. As noted by Blair in his description of that day, this achievement signalled the 'normalisation' of the region's politics to the British and Irish governments through a movement away from division:

> Every time we set foot in Northern Ireland there were protests ... always showing how divided the politics of Northern Ireland was from that anywhere else. That day for the first time there was a protest not about Northern Ireland, but about Iraq. When I saw it, I felt that Northern Ireland had just rejoined the rest of the world.[3]

The British and Irish governments believed that the Peace Process, with its focus on elite political settlement, was complete and it was expected that the rest of society would follow the example set by their leaders and overcome divisions to work together.

However, the resolution of conflict is not simple and, as will be demonstrated later in this introduction, Northern Ireland is not peaceful. Now that the political structures have been implemented, emphasis needs to be placed upon relationships between communities and peacebuilding work focused on dealing with the sectarian divisions within society is required. Mitchell's analysis of Northern Irish society illustrates this:

> It's a deeply divided society, it continues that way. While one can agree on political and security measures, it takes a very long time, generations perhaps, to change people's hearts and minds. So while this is a very important step, no-one should think that trust and love is going to be breaking out tomorrow between the two communities in Northern Ireland. That will take a long time.[4]

Organisations aimed at peacebuilding in Northern Ireland have been in existence as long as the conflict itself. Ranging from the widely reported demon-
strations organised by the Peace People in the mid-1970s to the quiet work
of cross-community groups in local areas, those involved have sought to
present an alternative vision to the polarisation that has dominated Northern
Irish politics since partition in 1921. These schemes functioned by focusing
on relationships between communities and operated in both middle and
working-class areas. They worked towards an improvement in community
relations by enabling participants to understand the perspective of the 'other'
community and accept that differences are not threatening. Such grassroots
engagement with issues connected to community relations is crucial because,
as we shall see, it has the potential to promote political stability and enable
the development of democracy. Thus, if we are to fully comprehend the peace
process in Northern Ireland, the work of peacebuilding organisations and
their role and place within society needs to be understood and analysed.[5] This
collection, the first of its kind, aims to do this by exploring the various forms
of peacebuilding in Northern Ireland as well as the governmental initiatives
that have attempted to support it from the 1970s to the present day.[6] It brings
together an international group of scholars to analyse these ideas from a
number of disciplinary and interdisciplinary approaches including the political and social sciences and history. In doing so, it aims to focus debate upon
the role that peacebuilding at a grassroots level can play in supporting the
continuation of peace in Northern Ireland.

The political context

The accord reached at Stormont was certainly significant, not least for the
participation of republicans in the process eventually leading to the Democratic
Unionist Party and Sinn Féin agreeing to work together in government in 2007,
but whether it finally brought peace is highly debatable. The signing of the
Agreement and subsequent negotiations leading to the Hillsborough Agreement of 2010, created political structures based upon a revised form of consociationalism[7] in Northern Ireland.[8] The benefits of such an arrangement for
areas of conflict have been described thus: 'The consociationalist argument is
that particularly in certain contexts – deeply divided societies, where divisions
are longstanding and when there is intra-group violence – it is more realistic
to accept that different groups will continue to exist than to seek the "decon-
struction" of group ties.'[9] The Agreement enabled Northern Ireland to remain
part of the United Kingdom as long as the majority consented, provided for an
all-Ireland dimension and established a Northern Ireland Assembly elected by
proportional representation and a power-sharing Executive, the membership
of which would be based upon the various political parties' electoral success.
These new institutions were predicated upon the conclusion that the conflict

in Northern Ireland was based upon ethno-national rather than economic concerns.[10] But as Wolff argued, 'defining the Northern Ireland conflict ... as an ethno-national one has important implications for its analysis and for the analysis of attempts to settle it'.[11] Consequently, a form of consociationalism was seen as the solution. The situation would be resolved if the divisions that existed within society were acknowledged and elite-level structures were created that would enable the political accommodation of the ethno-national groups, resulting in 'stability, fairness and democracy'.[12] The Agreement, it was argued by McGarry and O'Leary, did just this.

Stability has been brought to Northern Ireland through the Agreement's role in the cessation of paramilitary violence and decommissioning of weapons by the participant's reaffirmation of 'their commitment to the total disarmament of all paramilitary organisations'.[13] This has seen both republican and loyalist paramilitaries put their weapons 'beyond use' leaving 'relatively little prospect of a significant resurgence in political violence'.[14] Thus, according to McGarry and O'Leary, since 1994, violence has declined by 80 per cent and 'Belfast [is] the world's second safest city for crime', producing a 'peace dividend' that has seen employment rates, until the recent financial crisis struck, rise.[15] Furthermore, whilst not privileging identities over one another, the Agreement provided safeguards for the communities involved by enabling them 'to be protected whether they are majorities or minorities, and whether sovereignty lies with the United Kingdom or the Republic'.[16] Finally, consociationalists believe that democracy has been achieved: those elected to office are 'dependent on democratic support, and voters are free to withhold that support and to vote for other parties instead'.[17] The Agreement, according to this line of reasoning, has therefore facilitated a cessation of the conflict in Northern Ireland by not only addressing the issue of conflict management but also that of resolution through its focus upon equality issues as well as political structures. Thus, the Agreement and subsequent political developments 'had the potential to bring closure to the conflict'.[18]

But, as Rupert Taylor argues, 'far more is required for conflict resolution than consociationalists presume'.[19] Such thoughts are echoed by Ian O'Flynn who states 'it is easier to manage conflict than try to resolve it'.[20] At present, the elite-level political system engrains political identities, allowing little room for alternatives to develop. Through the political structures implemented, which focus upon acknowledging and engraining difference, 'it copper-fastened the importance of groups and in doing so denied not only the heterogeneous nature of Northern Irish society but also the assembly of diverse voices within groups'.[21] However, in order for the conflict to be resolved in Northern Ireland, something more than a consociationalist system is needed, especially as this arrangement does not address the sectarianism which provided the impetus for the conflict and continues to fuel sporadic crime.[22] Relationships between the communities, at a grassroots as well as elite level, need to be ameliorated through peacebuilding rather than managed through complex political arrangements as is currently the case. The Agreement has gone some way towards doing this as it addresses some of the key structural problems, such as inequality, that were some of the causes of conflict. But, as a consequence of the Agreement's focus on ethno-nationalism, it fails to place enough emphasis upon the part that conflicted relationships, division and sectarianism have played in creating tensions between the two communities.

This has been compounded by the development of a governmental policy regarding the issue of peacebuilding or community relations through A Shared Future (launched in 2005) and the Programme for Sharing, Cohesion and Integration (launched in 2010).[23] Peacebuilding policies focused on improving community relations became a victim of the uncertainty surrounding devolved government and according to Duncan Morrow, the Chief Executive of the Community Relations Council, 'devolved government did not like A Shared Future. The fact it was enacted under a British direct rule government was enough to make it an object of suspicion. But agreeing an alternative has proved a hard ask.'[24] These government policies raise many questions regarding issues such as communal separation, shared housing and integrated education but place them within a long-term framework rather than viewing them as a means to solve pressing problems. But as Ruane and Todd suggest, 'if we take seriously the potential and the danger of current processes of cultural change, then these aims are as important as the immediate tasks of tackling interface violence and sectarian incidents. Indeed without programmes that deal with these strategic aims, the immediate problems will continue to be reproduced.'[25] For the critics of the consociationalist approach, this is a demonstration of its failure to understand the basic nature of the conflict and the need for the ethno-nationalism that forms the core of this approach to be eroded before the Northern Irish conflict can by fully resolved.[26] In order for a peace process to be successful and more importantly sustainable, the problems, such as communal division, relating to the conflict must be addressed coherently rather than hoping the example of cooperation at the elite level will eventually trickle down to the grassroots.[27] This collection aims to examine the means through which these issues of communal division and segregation are being directly tackled within communities.

However, peacebuilding in Northern Irish society is hindered by a number of factors. The narrow definition of peace upon which the process in Northern Ireland has been brokered has implications for its development. In most conflict situations, the 'termination of violent acts is often equated with the state of peace'.[28] This issue has been articulated thus:

> In 1999, at a seminar on peacemaking and preventative diplomacy sponsored by the UN Institute for Training and Research, a participant identified two types of peace: the 'no more shooting type' and the 'no more need for shooting type'. The remark captured an essential distinction governing the resolution of conflicts, between ensuring the minimal conditions for peace – ending the fighting between armed factions or

between insurgents and the state – and building peace over the long term, by establishing stable polities that process and deal with conflict without recourse to violence. This latter effort involves an attempt to address at least some of the conditions that led to the conflict in the first place.[29]

In Northern Ireland, the dramatic fall in Troubles-related deaths[30] has been viewed as an end to conflict.[31] However, conflict continues by other means. Instances of sectarian criminal damage have risen by 15 per cent in the past year (2008/9–2009/10) although at 573, this figure is still lower than the 677 incidents reported in 2005/6. However, crime motivated by sectarianism rose by 25 per cent between 2008 and 2009 whilst the numbers of racially motivated incidents are steadily multiplying.[32] Paramilitary-style shootings have increased from 16 in 2008 to 41 in 2009, but this figure is still half of what it was in 2005. In addition, the numbers of paramilitary-style assaults have doubled from 40 in 2008 to 81 in 2009.[33] Furthermore, there is evidence to suggest that Northern Ireland has become more segregated since 1998: the number of peace lines maintained by the Northern Irish Office has grown from 37 in October 2006 to 48 in November 2010.[34] In addition, the Community Relations Council lists 88 segregation and security barriers in Belfast alone,[35] with an application being made to Derry City Council to erect a new interface at Lisnagelvin in March 2011.[36] According to the Northern Irish Justice Minister, David Ford, 'These walls, fences and gates are daily reminders that, despite the political progress we have made over the last decade, we still have a huge challenge ahead to break down the mistrust and separation that exists within our community.'[37] Suggestions have been made on their removal, but such a process would take at least five years to complete, requiring the cooperation and support of local communities and the government.[38] In addition, much social or public housing (which was the epicentre of most of the conflict's violence) remains segregated. The 2001 Census (the most recent available) suggests that 70% of social housing tenants live in areas that are at least 90% Catholic or Protestant.[39] In addition, 37% of the Northern Irish population live in segregated areas and in 2009/10, 114 people asked for housing transfers due to intimidation compared to 62 in 2005/6.[40] Finally, whilst in 2009, 62% of people said they would send their child to an integrated school, only 6.7% actually did. The lack of integration in education is somewhat softened by a trend that has emerged for Catholic parents to send their children to controlled or state schools, whilst a smaller proportion of Protestants are sending theirs to maintained or Catholic schools.[41]

As well as their impact upon community relations in Northern Ireland, these elements of the conflict have financial implications for the region. Research by Deloitte and Touche found that 'the issues of segregation and conflict continue to influence policy decisions, public service provision and hence resource allocation' with the cost of division being estimated at £1.5 billion annually.[42] Thus, work that encourages and enables communities to work together or share resources would also be financially beneficial for the region.

Despite this, popular perceptions of the strength of community relations have improved in the years since the Agreement (although they have fluctuated mainly as a consequence of events, such as the Holy Cross protests in 2001). In 1996, prior to the Agreement being signed, a social attitudes survey demonstrated that 43% of the population thought that relationships between Protestants and Catholics would be improved in five years time,[43] by 2009, these figures stood at 68% for Catholics, 56% for Protestants and 67% for those with no religion. However, these figures are still lower than they were at their peaks in 1995, 1999 and 2007.[44] Furthermore, the disparity between Catholics, Protestants and those with no religion in this regard, demonstrates that a gulf still exists between the communities in Northern Ireland with reference to their attitudes to the normalisation of society and, as Devine et al. note, could raise questions about their belief in the efficacy of the peace process: 'There is little room for complacency. The most recent results appear to indicate that respondents have some concern that relations between the two main communities have become as good as they can get and that further improvement is unlikely – or perhaps undesirable.'[45] Consequently, although it has been argued, in particular by McGarry and O'Leary, that stability and democracy have been brought to the region, such statistics demonstrate that despite the fact that the devolved institutions provided by the Agreement are now working, Northern Irish society is not peaceful. The sectarianism that motivated the conflict still remains. It now manifests itself through crime rather than terrorist activities and needs to be dealt with constructively in a way that will eventually allow the 'no more need for shooting' type of peace to emerge and strengthen the stability brought by the Agreement and ensuring the continuation of democracy.

The contribution of peacebuilding to Northern Irish society[46]

Critiques of the nature of the Agreement and the political settlement in Northern Ireland indicate that additional structures and support need to be implemented in order to underpin the start made in 1998. In the years immediately after the Agreement, some academics and commentators called for public policies to be created which would promote social integration. For instance, Wilford and Wilson argued that 'If political stability is to be won, policy needs to change from "consociationalism" and crisis-management and towards a focus on integration and a strategic commitment to the emergence of a civil society.'[47] Such an idea, it was argued, would lead to the dilution of ethno-national identities in Northern Ireland and create cross-cutting identities, encouraging people to think beyond the politics of the conflict. Whilst embedding 'bread and butter' issues into the politics of the region is one of the ultimate goals of a peace process, the rate at which this should be done and the methods that need to be employed are debateable. This is especially true of Northern Ireland, where

> The legacy of conflict and violence is a long one. This is especially true in those areas where conflict was most acute. Whereas people living in districts where conflict was an unusual, sporadic or distant experience have often embraced the benefits of peace with relief, trust is not easily won in the face of recent memory of bereavement, anger and fear.[48]

Such problems are not easily solved and, as the chapters in this collection demonstrate, need to be addressed at a local as well as national level. Thus, instead of pursuing a policy of integration, in order for the progress towards democracy and stability brought by the restoration of devolved government to be sustained, relationships at the grassroots need to be reconciled and developed. Peace processes stand a better chance of success if the whole of society, rather than just the elite level, is involved and one of the main ways to engage people is through forms of peacebuilding activity.[49] Through such work, stability and democratic participation can be improved if relationships between communities are encouraged by the forms of contact and work discussed in this collection. Through such engagements people are encouraged 'to make a genuine effort to understand the force of [the other community's] views' and 'to reflect seriously on what they have to say, rather than simply treating them as obstacles or enemies'[50] or indeed pretending that they do not exist. However, rather than creating a single public identity for a region that has suffered ethnic conflict,[51] such schemes focus on relationships, removing the fear and mistrust that in many areas helped to generate the conflict. As Lederach argues, 'it is perhaps self-evident but oft-neglected that *relationship* is the basis of the conflict and its long-term solution ... Reconciliation is not pursued by those seeking innovative ways to disengage or minimize the conflicting groups' affiliations, but instead is built upon mechanisms that engage the sides of a conflict with each other as humans-in-relationship.'[52] Such work has the potential to improve community relations, thereby negating the causes of the conflict, and its violence, as well as dealing with the consequences without erasing people's ethnic identities. The forms of peacebuilding discussed in this collection are central to this.

In the years leading up to the Agreement and its immediate aftermath, the role of civil society (the main arena through which grassroots peacebuilding takes place) in the Northern Irish Peace Process attracted some attention.[53] However, there was a tendency in this literature, as in the governmental policy that promotes this work, to see the political process and civil society as two parallel structures which worked alongside each other rather than with one another. So, for example, David Bloomfield rightly commented that in Northern Ireland 'it is noteworthy that two practical approaches exist simultaneously, and appear to operate in different areas of the conflict and to address different concerns, rather than alternating with each other either on the same parts of the conflict or on the conflict as a whole'.[54] However, the negotiations leading up to the Agreement demonstrated the centrality that the peacebuilding or community relations sector had in conflict resolution.[55] In the immediate aftermath of this, civil society organisations offered mass support to political processes through the 'yes' campaign.[56] However, the Agreement also contained 'a framework within which the underlying conditions of the conflict can be addressed ... as a framework for addressing the deeper roots of division, its goal is to generate and channel wide-ranging social changes to secure reconciliation within Northern Ireland and on the island of Ireland'.[57] The means through which such an aim might be realised is one of the main goals of the peacebuilding discussed in this collection.

The potential for such peacebuilding work to contribute to the continuation of peace processes post-Agreement through its focus on relationships has been demonstrated by Varshney.[58] This study shows that inter-communal contact holds the key to the resolution of conflict and more importantly the maintenance of peace by reducing the risk of violence and further polarisation whilst improving community relationships. Whilst everyday contact[59] and associational contact[60] are both important to promoting peace, associational contact is 'sturdier' in its ability to maintain calm in conflict situations. Thus, the pre-existence of such associational contact means that any conflict which occurs can be dealt with peacefully and through negotiation rather than erupting into violence. Where such networks of engagement exist, 'tensions and conflicts were regulated and managed; where they were missing, communal identities led to endemic and ghastly violence'.[61] In addition, associational contact acts as a check on politicians who wish to promote an agenda that would damage relationships. This is because 'vigorous associational life, if inter-communal, acts as a serious constraint on the polarizing strategies of political elites'.[62] Varshney presents two reasons for this: firstly, such inter-communal contact promotes ease of communication as the trust which is a prerequisite for peace is already present. Secondly, associational contact provides an understanding of points of common concern within a community and represents its interests. These concerns can be economic, social or cultural, but they provide a stronger point of reference than everyday interactions thereby strengthening relationships and providing a powerful hindrance for violence as everyone 'would suffer losses from a communal split fight for their turf'.[63] At present, current levels of segregation in Northern Ireland prevent associational contact from operating in the same way. Consequently, grassroots peacebuilding has a role to play in encouraging such associational contact by facilitating and mediating communication. By encountering one another in the associational form encouraged by the peacebuilding discussed in this collection, those involved can reduce 'othering' and enable people to work together on points of common concern without a loss of their own identities to a single public identity. Furthermore, this form of associational engagement can increase stability within previously volatile areas as it promotes the acceptance of the interdependence of different communities.

Peacebuilding also contributes to the strengthening and maintenance of democracy as a result of its concentration upon the whole of society rather than just the elite political class. Such a focus is vital because, as Walzer notes, 'deepening democracy is the responsibility of everyone in society, not simply the responsibility of politicians'.[64] It enables people to join in this process in two key ways: it exposes participants to alternative points of view to their own and it provides members of divided communities with a means to work together to have their needs and concerns addressed through their political structures rather than resorting to violence as has previously been the case. Debate and discussion with those that hold divergent points of view is crucial to democracy. This is especially true in areas where there is ethnic tension: 'if people only engage in discussion and debate with members of their own ethnic group, they may view every issue as an ethnic issue and hence fail to recognise the importance to democracy of exposing themselves to alternative views'.[65] Providing a forum through which people can encounter alternate points of view, peacebuilding organisations support the democratic process by allowing participants to become fully informed when making political decisions regarding, for example, voting choices. Given the need to remove ethnicity as a source of conflict in Northern Ireland, peacebuilding has a significant contribution to make as it enables people to 'engage in discussion and debate' around issues of contention with the support, such as mediation and facilitation, that is necessary to avoid further conflict. The importance of peacebuilding to the maintenance of democracy is further increased by the divisions within Northern Irish society: unless people are willing to communicate with those that oppose them, their exclusivist identities will be reinforced and lead to 'maximalist or uncompromising demands'[66] being made. Such behaviour will move society away from the form of accommodation practiced at the elite political level and hinder the continuation of the process begun with the 1998 Agreement.

Peacebuilding also offers people a political voice, which is especially important to those who have been disenfranchised by the violent and polarised nature of conflict, such as women, thereby promoting the 'maintenance of democracy through the peaceful articulation of the interests of all sections of the community'.[67] Thus,

> Just as it is possible to create institutions that facilitate power sharing between the representatives of different ethnic groups, it is possible to create institutions that facilitate participation and deliberation between ordinary people, both within and across different ethnic groups, and that enable them to effectively channel their views and opinions to government.[68]

The creation of such organisations encourages democratic engagement beyond the political elites, promoting the idea that engagement with those from the 'other' community can be an empowering rather than disempowering process. The importance to this process of the good or improved relationships developed between different groups through this work is clear. It helps society as a whole to move beyond the polarised nature of politics by creating new cross-community cleavages. But possibly more importantly, as has been shown in other conflict zones, 'the local organs of the state function better when there are robust links [between different ethnic groups] in civic life ... An attempt to rebuild or strengthen civic links between [such groups] is a method that, although indirect, is more effective in keeping the state accountable for the life of its citizens.'[69] This is a step towards the 'normalisation' of Northern Irish politics and an acceleration of the biodegradation of ethnic politics that consociationalists hope will occur. Furthermore, as past experience has demonstrated, the grassroots and mid-range leaderships of such organisations have the ability to represent the views of their members to the top-level leaderships. As stated earlier, such behaviour existed during the negotiations leading to the Agreement, so it would be expected that peacebuilding organisations would continue to operate in the same manner post-accord and act as a support to the democratic institutions by enabling people to hold their political representatives to account and to have their views represented beyond the polling booth.

However, the forms of peacebuilding work focused upon in this collection have come under a great deal of scrutiny and criticism from, for example, academics and the media. These critiques range from suggestions that it simply is not needed as the political violence has ceased to those that argue that such work actually prevents Northern Irish society from moving on and becoming 'normal'. This, when combined with the fact that there is no definitive way of measuring the impact and effectiveness of this work, means that its usefulness will always be under question. According to its critics, the problem primarily lies in the lack of debate surrounding it:

> One view (perhaps the prevailing one during the 1980s–90s), that the mere existence of the P/CRO sector has been beneficial regardless of any empirically definable achievements, is unimpressive. It epitomises the woolly liberalism and well-meaning but ultimately ineffectual culture for which the sector has rightly been criticised. Given the amount of public money that has been poured into the P/CRO 'industry' over the last 30 years, its defenders will have to come up with more than a 'better than nothing' advocacy to justify its existence.[70]

Added to this is the argument that peacebuilding work is effectively superfluous to the needs of Northern Irish society. The numbers of conflict-related deaths have fallen dramatically and there is now an acceptable level of violence within the region. Furthermore, according to this reasoning, the evidence regarding divisions in society is impressionistic and can easily be explained away.[71] Indeed, such critics point out that the politics of the peace process focused upon the realpolitik and was spurred on by moments of violence rather than the work of peacebuilding organisations and their ideologies.[72] Closely linked to this is the notion that within Northern Ireland a self-perpetuating 'peace industry' exists which justifies itself in terms of its contribution to the peace process. 'Northern Ireland's dirty little secret is that there is an entire tranche of the population, from euphemistic "community workers", to quangocrats pocketing hundred-thousand pay packets, who rely on Northern Ireland remaining different and on the distant shadow of the gunman and the occasional bomber and riot for their livelihood.'[73] This 'industry' amounts to £1 billion per annum, is Northern Ireland's largest employer and creates a self-sustaining cycle that 'lowers expectations and sends out negative messages'.[74] This communalisation and professionalisation of peacebuilding has the potential to disenfranchise the very people that it is supposed to help by stifling the creativity and spontaneity that is inherent in this form of grassroots action.[75] According to this critique, the economic development of the region is being hindered as the peace industry stifles the inward investment that is vital for the economic rejuvenation needed to tackle the socio-economic depravation that fuels conflict to occur. In addition to the criticisms surrounding the existence of peacebuilding organisations, the work that they undertake has also been the subject of unfavourable commentary. This focuses upon the methods employed and the subjects that are broached. During the conflict in Northern Ireland, suspicion and mistrust dominated everyday interactions, conversation focused on topics regarded as safe. Work aimed at improving relationships between the two communities is often regarded as perpetuating this convention. Thus, those involved are not encouraged to address the 'contentious' issues, a practice which endorses avoidance and 'denial', increasing misunderstandings between those involved and thereby perpetuating conflict. Furthermore, it is often suggested that this work is dominated by middle-class 'do-gooders', rather than the working classes who were most directly affected by the conflict. Despite this, there is a need to understand more clearly the forms that peacebuilding has taken in Northern Ireland.

Chapter overview

This collection presents the work of an international group of scholars and from their contributions several themes emerge which demonstrate the variety of approaches that have been taken in the study of peacebuilding in Northern Ireland. The first centres upon theoretical aspects of this issue. As Acheson, Milofsky and Stringer argue in the opening chapter, a variety of approaches have been taken by scholars seeking to discover why civil society should matter for peace. This chapter discusses the contact hypothesis developed by Allport,[76] the implementation of social capital theory within the

Northern Irish context and Lederach's three-tier model. In doing so, they not only provide a critique of their use but offer a new approach. Whilst the role of civil society in peacebuilding is explored, both implicitly and explicitly, by all of the contributors (with Buchanan and Bean exploring such issues in some depth in their chapters), White particularly focuses upon the nature of its contribution. He adopts the approaches of a number of political scientists, including Darby, McGinty and Wolff, and in doing so demonstrates the political importance of civil society to peacebuilding in Northern Ireland. However, he argues that civil society organisations capable of securing the trust needed to create sustainable peacebuilding efforts in Northern Ireland are lacking as a consequence of the polarising nature of the Agreement.

The next theme focuses upon the contribution of education and religion to the peacebuilding process. The institutions associated with these two areas have frequently been accused of contributing to the continuation of the conflict through their influence in developing identity, but McGlynn and Power consider an alternative view: the contribution made to the healing of divisions in Northern Ireland. McGlynn's chapter on integrated education examines its long-term contribution to peace as well as highlighting the challenges that it still faces in an increasingly diverse society. She argues that a key concern is how identity is addressed and that integrated education has the potential to be most effective when dealing with this issue. Power, in her chapter on churches and peacebuilding, also focuses on identity and its relationship to peacebuilding. She discusses the role that the leaders of the Protestant and Catholic churches played in promoting peacebuilding. This chapter concludes that religious leaders tried to engage in efforts in peacebuilding by renouncing violence and supporting local initiatives but that their main contribution was their work in explaining their religious perspectives to one another.

The involvement of groups such as women, ex-combatants and members of sections of the nationalist community is considered in the chapters by Hammond-Callaghan, McEvoy and Shirlow, Etchart and Bean. Hammond-Callaghan investigates the role played by women in peacebuilding in the 1970s. Locating the work of such women within the twentieth-century international women's peace movement, this chapter explores the means through which the conflict shaped women's community involvement and asks if their political marginalisation affected the form that this took. This analysis is achieved through an examination of the work of the Peace People, Women Together for Peace and the Derry Peace Women. Her conclusion not only demonstrates the importance of women's involvement within communities but also the need for their incorporation into macro-political processes. In recent years, politically motivated former prisoners and ex-combatants have become active in developing new forms of peacebuilding. McEvoy and Shirlow's chapter demonstrates the role that politically motivated former prisoners have played in the promotion of peace. It begins with a discussion of the process of transformation and reintegration that politically motivated former prisoners go through in order to engage in such work before demonstrating the schemes and methods used by this group. This chapter aptly demonstrates the challenges inherent in peacebuilding and conflict transformation. Etchart's chapter presents a case study of two specific schemes created by loyalists in the aftermath of the Agreement. She further explores the motivations and methods of ex-paramilitaries who work in the areas of peacebuilding and conflict transformation. She argues that in a post-conflict society, leadership and membership of peacebuilding groups provides loyalist leaders with continued status within their communities as well as a means of political expression. Bean's chapter offers an exploration of the development of community organisations and civil society within the nationalist community. He, thus, continues the theoretical discussion begun by Acheson, Milofsky and Stringer and White and places it within the sphere of community development. He argues that the historical experiences of the nationalist community have profoundly shaped the definition of peacebuilding and that community organisations have often acted as power brokers between nationalists and the state.

The final theme emphasises the influence (or lack) of government policy and funding upon peacebuilding. Acheson, Milofsky and Stringer discuss this briefly, but Buchanan in her study of the policy framework of the British and Irish governments, from 1986–2006, demonstrates just how ad hoc their approach has been. She argues that the lack of long-term planning and sustainability as well as the conceptual misunderstandings inherent in the approaches taken by, for example, the International Fund for Ireland, Europe (through Peace I, II and III) and the two governments led to avoidable difficulties. She concludes that such problems are preventing conflict transformation and peacebuilding from succeeding. Her chapter employs cross-border cooperation as a case study and this is further highlighted by Hayward, McCall and Damkat. The North/South dimension provided one of the foundation stones of the Agreement whilst the European Union's Peace Programmes also placed emphasis upon this as a means of peacebuilding. This chapter investigates the impact that the cross-border elements within the Agreement have had upon its practice and concludes that sustainability is one of the key issues facing not only cross-border cooperation but also peacebuilding. Atashi's chapter empirically examines public perceptions of the European Peace and Reconciliation fund through the use of interviews with people living in interface areas and community relations workers. This chapter argues that the marginalisation experienced by interface areas is also apparent in the distribution of funding with the main benefactors being the middle classes and those able to deal with the bureaucracy inherent in the system. It concludes that rather than helping to build peace, funding schemes are deepening the conflict as competition for scarce resources increases. Each of the chapters that address this issue argue that the governments (both British and Irish) lack the long-term commitment necessary to ensure that peacebuilding schemes achieve their aims and enable an improvement in relationships between communities in Northern Ireland.

This collection does not aim to quantify the impact or effectiveness of this work. Instead, whilst not exhaustive in the forms of such endeavours that it analyses, it aims to present the first collective assessment of the efforts towards peace that have been occurring within and between communities from the 1970s onwards. In doing so, it seeks to raise questions regarding the approaches to and sustainability of such work as well the contributions that peacebuilding has to make to the future of Northern Ireland.

Notes

1 Hereafter known as 'the Agreement', see http://www.nio.gov.uk/agreement.pdf (accessed 11 July 2010).
2 J. Powell, *Great Hatred, Little Room: Making Peace in Northern Ireland* (London, 2008), 309.
3 T. Blair, *A Journey* (London, 2010), 199.
4 Senator George Mitchell, speaking on 26 March 2007, cited in John McGarry and Brendan O'Leary, 'Power Shared after the Deaths of Thousands', in Rupert Taylor (ed.), *Consociational Theory: McGarry and O'Leary and the Northern Ireland Conflict* (Abingdon, 2009), 15–84 (15).
5 The forms of peacebuilding discussed within this collection work within civil society in Northern Ireland, whilst they do not make up all of civil society or indeed even adhere to the ethos of some of it, they do have a crucial role to play in the peace process. For a discussion of the negative impact that some elements of civil society can have on peace processes, see M. Cox (ed.), *Social Capital and Peacebuilding: Creating and Resolving Conflict with Trust and Social Networks* (Oxford, 2009).
6 One of the issues regarding the study of peacebuilding, civil society and conflict transformation in Northern Ireland is the lack of agreed definition of any of the terms. Rather than creating a standard definition for the purposes of this collection, it has been decided to allow each contributor to form their own. For a full discussion of this issue see Buchanan's essay in this volume.
7 Tonge defines the classic features of consociationalism as power sharing, proportionality in government, mutual vetoes and bloc autonomy. J. Tonge, *Northern Ireland* (Cambridge, 2006), 26. See also Donald L. Horowitz, 'Explaining the Northern Ireland Agreement: The Sources of an Unlikely Constitutional Consensus', *British Journal of Political Science* 32 (2002), 193–220 (194).
8 J. McGarry and B. O'Leary, *The Northern Ireland Conflict: Consociational Engagements* (Oxford, 2004), 262–63.
9 J. McGarry, 'Political Settlements in Northern Ireland and South Africa', *Political Studies* 46.5 (1998), 853–70 (860).
10 J. McGarry and B. O'Leary, *The Politics of Antagonism: Understanding Northern Ireland* (London, 1996), 4, and *Explaining Northern Ireland: Broken Images* (Oxford, 1995), 306.
11 S. Wolff, 'From Sunningdale to Belfast, 1973–98', Jorg Neuheiser and Stefan Wolff, *Peace at Last? The Impact of the Good Friday Agreement on Northern Ireland* (Oxford, 2002), 1–24 (1).
12 McGarry and O'Leary, 'Power Shared', 47. This article provides a full outline of the case for the success of the Agreement.

13 The Agreement on Decommissioning.

14 McGarry and O'Leary, 'Power Shared', 47.

15 McGarry and O'Leary, 'Power Shared', 47.

16 McGarry and O'Leary, *The Northern Ireland Conflict*, 280.

17 McGarry and O'Leary, 'Power Shared', 80.

18 Tonge, *Northern Ireland*, 189.

19 R. Taylor, 'The Injustice of a Consociational Solution to Northern Ireland', in Taylor (ed.), *Consociational Theory*, 309–329 (310).

20 I. O'Flynn, 'Progressive Integration (and Accommodation Too)', in Taylor (ed.), *Consociational Theory*, 264–278 (278).

21 P. Shirlow and B. Murtagh, *Belfast: Segregation, Violence and the City* (London, 2006), 5.

22 *Belfast Newsletter*, 9 March 2011 or *Belfast Media*, 8 March 2011, http://www.belfastmedia.com/home_article.php?ID=2333 (accessed 16 March 2011).

23 *A Shared Future – Policy and Strategic Framework for Good Relations* (Belfast, 2005), http://www.ofmdfmni.gov.uk/index/equality/community-relations/a-shared-future-strategy.htm (accessed 31 January 2011) and *Programme For Cohesion, Sharing And Integration* (Belfast, 2010), http://www.nidirect.gov.uk/reformatted_final_print_version_csi_-_26.07.10.pdf (accessed 31 January 2011).

24 *Irish Times*, 25 October 2010.

25 J. Todd and J. Ruane, *From 'A Shared Future' to 'Cohesion, Sharing and Integration': An Analysis of Northern Ireland's Policy Framework Documents* (Joseph Rowntree Charitable Trust, 2010), 17.

26 For an example of this argument, see Rupert Taylor, 'Northern Ireland: Consociation or Social Transformation?', in J. McGarry (ed.), *Northern Ireland and the Divided World, Post-Agreement Northern Ireland in Comparative Perspective* (Oxford, 2001), 37–52.

27 See, for example, McGarry and O'Leary, 'Power Shared', 68.

28 O. Ramsbotham, 'The Analysis of Protracted Social Conflict: A Tribute to Edward Azar', *Review of International Studies* 31.1 (2005), 109–126 (114).

29 C. J. Arnson and D. Azpuru, 'From Peace to Democratization: Lessons from Central America', in J. Darby and R. MacGinty (eds.), *Contemporary Peacemaking: Conflict, Violence and Peace Processes* (Basingstoke, 2003), 197–211 (197).

30 In 2007–9, there were five Troubles-related deaths compared to 253 in 1989–91 (Paula Devine, G. Kelly and G. Robinson, 'An Age of Change? Community Relations in Northern Ireland', *Ark Research Update* 72 [January 2011]). Troubles-related deaths are those that can be directly attributed to the political conflict.

31 For example, in a recent broadcast of 'Thinking Allowed' on BBC Radio 4, Laurie Taylor commented that most of his listeners would be surprised to hear that paramilitary punishment beatings were still a feature of life in West Belfast ('Thinking Allowed', broadcast 19 January 2011, http://www.bbc.co.uk/iplayer/console/b00xhj80/Thinking_Allowed_19_01_2011 [accessed 31 January 2011]).

32 Office of the First Minister and Deputy First Minister, *Good Relations Indicators 2010 Update* (Belfast, January 2011), http://www.ofmdfmni.gov.uk/index/equality/equalityresearch/research-publications/gr-pubs.htm (accessed 31 January 2011), Priority Outcome 1.

33 Office, *Good Relations Indicators*, Priority Outcome 3. For a discussion of the causes of such attacks and the increases, see H. Hamill, *The Hoods: Crime and Punishment in Belfast: Crime and Punishment in West Belfast* (New Jersey, 2010).

34 These are located in Belfast, Derry, Portadown and Lurgan. Office, *Good Relations Indicators*, Priority Outcome 3, lists this figure as 48 for November 2010 and comments that 'No further physical security measures have been erected by NIO

since the last update in November 2009.'

35 Such barriers include (but are not limited to) physical structures such as walls and fences, security gates designed to enable areas to be closed off and buffer zones of derelict land or brownfield sites at an interface or at the boundary of a marked residential area. Community Relations Council, *Towards Sustainable Security: Interface Barriers and the Legacy of Segregation in Belfast* (Belfast, 2008), 11–20, http://www.conflictresearch.org.uk/cms/images/stories/daniel/pdfs/iwg%20publication2.pdf (accessed 7 July 2010).

36 *Belfast Telegraph*, 4 March 2011.

37 David Ford speaking on 16 February 2011, Community Relations Council, 'Peacelines Remain Obstacle to a Shared Future', http://www.community-relations.org.uk/about-us/news/item/671/peacelines-remain-obstacle-to-shared-future-ford/ (accessed 17 February 2011).

38 T. Macauley, *A Process for Removing Interface Barriers: A discussion Paper Proposing a Five Phase Process for the Removal of 'Peace Walls' in Northern Ireland* (Belfast, 2008), http://cain.ulst.ac.uk/issues/segregat/docs/macaulay200708.pdf (accessed 7 July 2010).

39 Equality Commission for Northern Ireland, *Statement on Key Inequalities in Northern Ireland* (Belfast, 2007), 21, http://www.equalityni.org/archive/pdf/Keyinequalities(F)1107.pdf (accessed 31 January 2011). The most recent statistics for housing available are those from the 2001 Census.

40 Office, *Good Relations Indicators*, Priority Outcome 5.

41 Office, *Good Relations Indicators*, Priority Outcome 4. The reasons for this are more complex than an unwillingness to educate children together and probably relate more closely to the educational aspirations of parents for their children.

42 Deloitte and Touche, *Research into the Financial Cost of the Divide in Northern Ireland* (Belfast, April 2007), 88.

43 Joanne Hughes and Paul Carmichael, 'Community Relations in Northern Ireland: Attitudes to Contact and Integration', in G. Robinson, D. Heenan, A. M. Gray and K. Thompson (eds), *Social Attitudes in Northern Ireland: The Seventh Report* (Aldershot, 1998). For an analysis of attitudes in the middle of this period see *The Guardian*, 4 January 2002.

44 Devine et al., 'An Age of Change?', 3.

45 Devine et al., 'An Age of Change?', 4.

46 These issues are dealt with in more depth by Acheson et al. and White in their contributions to this collection.

47 R. Wilson and R. Wilford, 'Northern Ireland: A Route to Stability?', policy paper commissioned by the Economic and Social Research Council (2003).

48 Community Relations Council, *Towards Sustainable Security*.

49 J. P. Lederach, *Building Peace: Sustainable Reconciliation in Divided Societies* (Washington, DC, 1997).

50 O'Flynn, 'Progressive Integration (and Accommodation Too)', 270.

51 McGarry and O'Leary, 'Power Shared'.

52 Lederach, *Building Peace*, 26.

53 D. Bloomfield, *Peacemaking Strategies in Northern Ireland: Building Complementarity in Conflict Management Theory* (Basingstoke, 1997); S. Byrne, 'Consociational and Civic Society Approaches to Peacebuilding in Northern Ireland', *Journal of Peace Research* 38.3 (2001), 327–52; F. Cochrane and S. Dunn, *People Power? The Role of the Voluntary and Community Sector in the Northern Ireland Conflict* (Cork, 2002); P. Dixon, 'Paths to Peace in Northern Ireland (I): Civil Society and Consociational Approaches', *Democratization* 4.2 (1997), 1–27; and A. Guelke, 'Civil Society and the Northern Irish Peace Process', *Voluntas* 3.1 (2003), 61–78.

54 Bloomfield, *Peacemaking Strategies in Northern Ireland*, 85.

55 F. Cochrane and S. Dunn, 'Peace and Conflict Resolution Organisations in Northern Ireland', in B. Gidron, S. N. Katz and Y. Hasenfeld (eds), *Mobilizing for Peace: Conflict Resolution in Northern Ireland, Israel/Palestine, and South Africa* (Oxford, 2005), 151–71 (170). The Northern Ireland Women's Coalition's participation in the negotiations were emblematic of this. See C. Murtagh, 'A Transient Transition: The Cultural and Institutional Obstacles Impeding the Northern Ireland Women's Coalition in Its Progression from Informal to Formal Politics', *Irish Political Studies* 23.1 (2008), 21–40.

56 R. A. Couto, 'The Third Sector and Civil Society: The Case of the "YES" Campaign in Northern Ireland', *Voluntas: International Journal of Voluntary and Nonprofit Organizations* 12.3 (2001), 221–38.

57 J. Ruane and J. Todd, 'The Belfast Agreement: Context, Content and Consequences', in J. Ruane and J. Todd (eds), *After the Good Friday Agreement: Analysing Political Change in Northern Ireland* (Dublin, 1999), 1–29 (17).

58 A. Varshney, *Ethnic Conflict and Civic Life: Hindus and Muslims in India* (New Haven, 2002). Although the focus of this study is on India, the form of sectarian division that he explores contains useful ideas regarding the importance of contact for peacebuilding.

59 Defined as 'routine interactions of life as Hindu and Muslim families visiting each other, eating together often enough, jointly participating in festivals, and allowing their children to play together' (Varshney, *Ethnic Conflict*, 3).

60 Some examples are 'Business associations, professional organisations, trade unions and cadre-based poitical parties' (Varshney, *Ethnic Conflict*, 3).

61 Varshney, *Ethnic Conflict*, 9.

62 Varshney, *Ethnic Conflict*, 4.

63 Varshney, *Ethnic Conflict*, 11.

64 I. O'Flynn and D. Russell, 'Deepening Democracy: The Role of Civil Society', in K. Cordell and S. Wolff (eds), *The Routledge Handbook of Ethnic Conflict* (Oxford, 2011), 225–35 (231), paraphrasing M. Walzer, *Politics and Passion: Towards a More Egalitarian Liberalism* (New Haven, 2004), 83.

65 O'Flynn and Russell, 'Deepening Democracy', 229.

66 O'Flynn and Russell, 'Deepening Democracy', 230.

67 Westmoreland General Meeting, *Preparing for Peace – by Asking the Experts to Analyse War* (Westmoreland, 2005), 36.

68 O'Flynn and Russell, 'Deepening Democracy', 226–27.

69 Varshney, *Ethnic Conflict*, 289.

70 F. Cochrane, 'Unsung Heroes or Muddle-Headed Peaceniks? A Profile and Assessment of NGO Conflict Resolution Activity in the Northern Ireland "Peace Process"', *Irish Studies in International Affairs* 12 (2001), 97–112 (108).

71 McGarry and O'Leary, 'Power Shared', 47–55.

72 Cochrane, 'Unsung Heroes or Muddle-Headed Peaceniks?', 109.

73 *Belfast Newsletter*, 3 November 2010.

74 *Belfast Newsletter*, 3 November 2010.

75 T. Paffenholz, 'Exploring Opportunities and Obstacles for a Constructive Role of Social Capital in Peacebuilding: A Framework for Analysis', in Cox (ed.), *Social Capital and Peacebuilding*, 186–201 (191).

76 G. W. Allport, *The Nature of Prejudice* (Cambridge, MA, 1954).

2

Understanding the Role of Non-aligned Civil Society in Peacebuilding in Northern Ireland: Towards a Fresh Approach

Nicholas Acheson, Carl Milofsky and Maurice Stringer

The last 30 years of the twentieth century saw the most intense violent conflict over national identity in Northern Ireland experienced anywhere in Europe during those years. Over 3,500 people were killed and about 48,000 injured.[1] The social and economic costs were formidable, exemplified by high levels of spatial and social segregation between Protestants and Catholics, matched by deep distrust, and significant levels of poverty and gross inequalities in wealth and income. Northern Ireland is among the most unequal regions in Europe.[2]

By the 1990s, civil society organisations saw themselves and were seen by government as a vehicle for achieving a peaceful society in Northern Ireland.[3] Beginning in the early 1990s this promise seemed to be a reality. There were a series of self-conscious attempts by government to support the development of, and then engage with, elements within civil society to help manage the conflict, address some of its social consequences, and help to build the peace.[4] Once the power-sharing government was formed in the wake of the 1998 'Good Friday' Agreement, however, the significance and influence of civil society organisations declined.[5] The decline is a puzzle since both social theory and government policy in the UK suggest that if civil society organisations are strong, they will play an important role in governance and also in furthering community integration.[6]

That this has not happened, we believe, shows a misunderstanding of the roles civil society organisations may play in national politics and of the significance of civil society organisations as primary actors shaping society. They can be important in the reduction of open hostility and are among the components of peacemaking that are necessary for a divided society to make progress, but they are less useful tools for advancing macro social changes like economic development, guarantees of political freedom, and creating institutional mechanisms that allow full inclusion in governance.

While these other factors may overshadow their impact, we believe civil society organisations continue to play an important role in reconciliation once open hostilities have ended. Our objective in this essay is to suggest an important but limited role. We also offer a theory of civil society organisations that is different from older theories that have promoted the importance of these organisations for peace. Where earlier theories emphasised the building of cross-community network structures, in order to better understand the limits of action within civil society, our approach presents these organisations as social movements, that is to say as collective citizen action around a shared understanding of a social problem or issue. As such they are closely tied to the formation and expression of identity. If the identities they support are sectarian or if they do not challenge sectarian identities, a dense system of civil society organisations may foster division rather than cross-community integration.

We also can see the intense, very local conflicts that continue to plague Northern Ireland as problems local civil society organisations might help to resolve, so long as the political context is supportive. In his analysis of the Holy Cross School conflict in the Ardoyne area of north Belfast, Gilligan[7] points out that even during the periods of active hostility in the 1990s cross-community relationships existed between Catholic and Protestant residents in this area of Belfast. It is only recently in the period since the 'Good Friday' agreement that a climate of fear and distrust has developed between the two communities. He argues that these feelings have not come from interaction but rather from the way power sharing has institutionalised sectarian identities. Politicians have gained a self-interest in making essentialist distinctions between Catholics and Protestants that have tended to provoke neighbourhood battles. But by forming counter-movements and building local identities based on cross-community trust and safety civil society organisations can play an important role in reducing tensions between opposing interface communities.[8] These initiatives are often rather fragile and readily undermined, relying heavily on the commitment of a few local community leaders. In contrast there are many thousand associations with cross-community membership organised around shared welfare problems and issues that have proved remarkably robust over the decades but which nevertheless have had only a marginal and indirect impact on the underlying conflict.[9] Our approach aims to go some way towards understanding this contrast.

Civil society organisations and government policy

To make our case that expectations about the effective role of civil society organisations should be scaled back, we review and critique arguments that civil society organisations can and should play a larger role in peacemaking. There are two parts to this analysis. The first is a simple documentation of governmental expectations that have been built into policies over the last two decades. The second is a consideration of social science theories that tell us why we should expect the presence of civil society organisations to be important for peace while their absence should create a predisposition to explosive social conflict.

Government policies

Although we argue that the zone of effectiveness for civil society organisations is specific and circumscribed, government policy in the past has suggested that they have a major role in peacebuilding. Their level of funding has been one indicator of this. During the 1990s, funding from regional government sources to voluntary and community organisations increased from just under £17m in 1988/89 to over £70m in 2001/02, an increase of over 400 per cent.[10] The commitment to the voluntary sector's role in the peace process was cemented in the two European Union Programmes for Peace and Reconciliation which ran between 1994 and 2006 and contributed €1,656m to Northern Ireland and the Border Counties of the Republic of Ireland.[11] Almost €1bn was spent on voluntary and community groups and in both programmes the money was administered by a combination of local area partnerships in which voluntary organisations played a leading role, and intermediary funding bodies within the sector itself. In addition it is estimated that over £50m went to the voluntary and community organisations between 1994 and 1999 from mainstream EU structural funds.

The investment in voluntary action was matched by a strong growth in the numbers of organisations. Over time, estimates find between 3,500 and 5,000 viable organisations or associations for a population of about 1.6m people, over half of which have been established since 1986.[12] Although the sector has contracted somewhat since 2003/2004, together they still provide employment for almost 29,000 people, 4.5% of the workforce, and have a combined asset base of £737m.

After 2000, funding for the civil society sector remained strong and government support seemed clear. Broadly speaking, a policy that saw civil society organisations as essential to building social capital and cross-community network connections guided the government's approach to the voluntary and community sector in Northern Ireland until around 2006, beginning with its earliest expression in the ground-breaking 1993 document, *Government Support for Voluntary Action and Community Development.*[13] In a distinct departure from Government policy in the rest of the United Kingdom at that time, this document recognised the value of community development as a promoter of cohesion and acknowledged a Government responsibility towards it. In the decade that followed the election of the New Labour government in 1997, however, policy developed in Northern Ireland in a way that more closely reflected government strategy towards the voluntary and community sector in the UK as a whole. In particular, policy documents both in Britain and in Northern Ireland reiterated the core assumption that the sector is or can be a source of better relations.[14] This general approach reflects a widely held consensus in the academic literature and in government policies around the world. From the mid-1990s onwards, civil society organisations have been seen as independent sources of social cohesion. Sensitive government policy frameworks could, policy-makers thought, help them realise their potential in this regard. This view informed the thinking in the Direct Rule administration's 'Shared Future' strategy of 2005[15] and was clearly influential in the first two European Union Programmes for Peace and Reconciliation that ran from 1994 to 2006.

However, in a process that began before the reinstatement of the devolved Assembly and Executive in 2007, government policy began to shift towards a greater focus on the role of voluntary organisations in delivering public services while the new Executive abandoned the 'shared future strategy' of 2005 but has failed to replace it, which has resulted in a policy vacuum in relation to any wider role for civil society in peacebuilding.

The continuing sectarian conflict

The central political dynamic in Northern Ireland remains a fundamental conflict over national identity between ethno-sectarian groups competing over territory and resources. A system of relationships was established in the seventeenth century that created antagonisms between Ireland and Britain and within Ireland, based on ethnicity, religion and culture that have proved very persistent.[16] The conflicts of interest have continued to feed a strong process of ethnic and cultural formation based on opposition to, and difference from, the other group.[17]

In the large literature on Northern Ireland, very little has been written about the relationship between the dynamics of the conflict and civil society. In particular, there have been very few studies of the broad role played by community-based organisations in relation to the dynamics of the core conflicts in Northern Ireland, although there have been a number of specific studies that have looked at the contribution of what has become known as 'track two' diplomacy to the peace process of the 1990s[18]

The present essay addresses this deficit. First, it considers the limitations in the three most cited theoretical approaches to understanding this relationship. Second, we sketch a new theoretical framework that seeks to overcome the disadvantages we identify in existing theory.

Theories about why civil society should matter for peace

We shall argue that effective civil society is anchored in social movements that shape identity. This represents a fundamental change from older theories that treat civil society as a structural phenomenon. Change the structures and problems of conflict, incivility, and injustice will disappear the theories seem to be saying. We must review the major theories to understand why they are insufficient. The theories are contact theory, social capital theory, and Lederach's three-tier model.

Contact theory

Contact theory is the oldest and simplest approach. In this view, if sectarian groups have little contact with each other, then specific, concrete conflicts are likely to become 'unrealistic' and expand. They encourage use of distorted information about and negative idealisations of the other. Conflicts broaden and intensify. When well-developed cross-community relationships exist, they can provide means of intervention by giving accurate information and conveying true concerns of the other side in a legitimate and believable way. Contact theory has been widely applied in practice in Northern Ireland and there has been a significant research agenda discussing its relevance and the effectiveness of providing opportunities for people from opposing backgrounds to meet. It provided the theoretical background to much early community relations work as far back as the 1970s.

The contact hypothesis[19] proposed that intergroup conflict can be reduced by bringing people together from opposing groups, subject to four conditions: equal status between groups, a requirement of cooperation between groups, competition between the groups should be avoided and lastly, that the context of intergroup contact should be legitimised through institutional support.[20] Others have noted that Allport's formulation has stood the test of time well, but have argued that for intergroup contact to be most effective in reducing intergroup anxiety, contact with one's social identity 'switched on' was necessary.[21] This means that in the case of Northern Ireland, intergroup anxiety will be most likely to be reduced in contact situations where Catholics and Protestants meet as such, rather than as, for example, people who share a particular social problem or interest.

This more recent work on contact theory demonstrates the inapplicability of the earlier formulations with the evidence showing clearly that contact is not enough in itself to ameliorate intergroup tensions. Firstly, there are genuine interest group conflicts between sectarian groups on many occasions. Simply knowing people from the opposite side and perhaps having forged relationships built on genuine trust does not resolve fundamental differences. If a Protestant fraternal society has traditionally marched down a road that runs through a changing neighbourhood with increasing numbers of Catholic residents, good fellowship alone will not eliminate the conflict or remove the potential for violence.

Second, as communities become increasingly segregated individuals find that there are greater social and cultural consequences should they cross community dividing lines. Not only can these costs become higher, but it can make it more difficult to make contact challenge already-formed assumptions about 'the other side', assumptions that may be central to individuals' self understanding as either Protestant or Catholic. We spoke with a Protestant individual active in the peace movement. He talked with frustration about his friend who was head of a college preparatory school where their football team was attacked when they visited a Catholic school for a match.

Despite having many cross-community friendships, our peace-movement informant would not release his partisan support for the Protestant school or his anger for Catholic thugs who had attacked the team. The likelihood that a Catholic team visiting a secondary school in a Protestant neighbourhood might also be attacked did not convince the individual that this was a youth problem rather than a Catholic sectarian problem. His investment in a Protestant identity and lifelong relationships with people in his community who were angry and offended maintained a sectarian sense of anger and separation for our informant. Rich, complex, self-aware, cross-community contacts were not sufficient to extinguish the sense of conflict and embitterment felt by this person. Contact theories do not explain how it is that cross-community contact is managed in such a way that people's assumptions and identities remain intact.

Social capital theory

Social capital theory offers a process understanding of cross-community partnerships. The approach emphasises how crosscutting affiliations deaden the intensity of conflict. Dense social networks existing within communities yield a strong sense of internal solidarity that may produce hostility towards other groups. When relationships bridge across community lines, however, this can allow opposed communities to reach accommodating agreements. Furthermore, linking local communities to regional and national networks allows resources to be mobilised and directed at problem solving. These also allow for building trust so that people can form effective partnerships and demonstrate accountability.[22]

The benefits of social capital have become an important theme in government policy. When rich social capital is present it encourages a bottom-up process based on interactions among people meeting in voluntary associations and linking upwards to regional and national levels. Skocpol[23] argues that effective pluralist democracy requires this sort of linkage. This is an international phenomenon and has been associated with government strategies in many developed welfare states to adjust policies in the face of globalisation and post-industrial forms of economic production.[24]

The basic idea is simply stated. First elaborated by Robert Putnam in his book on Italy,[25] social capital is related to three dimensions, namely networks, social norms of reciprocity, and generalised trust. Social capital thus encompasses social relationships, the rules governing those relationships and attitudinal factors contributing to generalised trust, or trust in strangers and trust in government. The first two attributes are aspects of social structures. The third is a social attribute in the sense that trust must be shared within a group or community. At the same time, it grows out of individual people's attitudes and in this sense it is not a structural characteristic of the system.

Putnam discovered a close association between a dense network of voluntary associations that encouraged horizontal ties among people from differing backgrounds and the relative economic success of northern Italy when compared to southern Italy. In contrast to the north, southern Italy revealed economic and social stagnation associated with weak associational life and public relationships were dominated by hierarchical arrangements.

Putnam draws a crucial distinction between what he terms 'bonding' and 'bridging' social capital.[26] The former refers to social capital generated amongst like-minded people and the latter to social capital that bridges other social divisions, for example, class, ethnic origin or age. Putnam argued that trust grows out of face-to-face interactions and since these comprise the life of associations there must be a density of these entities for community trust to develop.

Associations that draw people together from different backgrounds could foster trusting relationships that might be generalised to other situations. People addressing collective problems could then draw upon this trust to help integrative projects succeed. This leads to a policy proposition that investing in voluntary action to generate social capital is a key component in building and sustaining a successful society. It also tells why strengthening social capital might be a route to building and sustaining peace.

Two fundamental problems with the social capital approach are evident from the literature. First, while there is now a large body of evidence to link levels of generalised trust in societies and the density of voluntary associations,[27] this does not amount to proof that the hypothesis that the source of generalised trust lies in the face-to-face interactions that take place within these associations is right. It is equally possible that cause and effect flow in the opposite direction.

Indeed, there is evidence that higher levels of trust are to be found in more egalitarian societies compared to societies with greater levels of income inequality and greater reliance on means testing of social security benefits. Some have argued that redistributive welfare states are the main source of trust and that it is this government approach to social policy that encourages people to join associations.[28] The policy leads to the associations rather than the associations leading to the policy.

Thus, according to Tarrow the 'state plays a fundamental role in shaping civic capacity'.[29] This view is in contrast to the bottom-up hypothesis that is so much an emphasis of social capital theorists. One might argue that voluntary associations have more a conservative than a democratising influence. With their particular interests and their tendency to draw like-minded people together, they may be the last place to look as an important source of generalised trust. They may be a source of fragmentation and privilege or, at best, perhaps they should be viewed as a particular outcome of trust generated elsewhere.

Second, there has thus far been no convincing theory to explain why trust generated in small group settings should generalise to other settings. As with other social and economic resources, social capital is differentiated within a population by factors such as class status and membership in minority and excluded groups. The utility of social capital (its social worth or value) depends upon who is present in a network or association and to whom they are in turn connected. These connections, in turn, are socially structured and exclusionary. On balance, rich people make more effective political use of social capital than poor people do because they are more likely to be connected with other people able to exercise power or mobilise resources on their behalf.[30]

Furthermore, large social and political processes or changes seem to swamp whatever effects social capital might have on political stability or the content of policies. Anheier and Kendall explore the role that stable political settlements play in societies with high levels of generalised trust. They suggest that the relationship between voluntary associations and trust breaks down in those cases 'where the legitimacy of the social and political order is questioned in fundamental ways'.[31]

An important consequence is that bridging activities between different kinds of people within groups or between different kinds of groups may have few consequences for generalised trust in such societies. The extent to which bridging activities have a wider impact will depend upon the way these activities are located in wider social structures. This can only be understood by theorising that has as its starting point the way larger social and political patterns are reproduced in everyday life. Structures rather than relationships between people and groups become primary. Our argument is that insofar as they insist that improved levels of inter-communal trust automatically as it were arise from cross-community activity, social capital theories attempt to explain too much. What is needed is an approach that links relationships among people in voluntary associations to the structures in which those relationships are embedded. Before we develop our arguments, it is necessary to discuss one other influential approach to understanding the relationship between voluntary action and peacemaking.

Lederach's three-tier model

Contact and social capital theories are descriptive, focusing on characteristics of societies where conflict is limited and the intensity of disagreements is muted. Lederach argues for a more programmatic approach where interventions simultaneously happen at the three levels recognised in social capital theory. At the national, regional and community level self-conscious efforts must be launched to reduce sectarian conflict and increase linkage. Linkages must not only be horizontal at each level of aggregation but they must also move vertically between levels.

Lederach[32] proposed a three-tier model of peacemaking. At the top of his pyramid stands the elite leadership of the protagonists to the conflict that focuses on high-level negotiations and where the emphasis is on visible leadership from identifiable individuals. At the second tier are middle-range leaders representing leading NGOs, academics and ethnic/religious leaders.

They focus on workshops, training in conflict resolution and peace commissions. At the third level are the grassroots leaders from community-based organisations, and locally based government officials. At this level action focuses on local commissions, grassroots training, prejudice reduction and interventions to address post-war trauma. Lederach's thesis is that progress at all three levels is necessary in successful peace processes and that each level is dependent on developments at other levels.

Lederach's model is helpful in that it draws attention to the central role of both grassroots and middle-range civic action in building peace in conflict-prone societies such as Northern Ireland. But what that role might actually be is much less clear- cut. In their comparative study of experiences in Northern Ireland, South Africa and in the Israeli/Palestinian conflict, Knox and Quirk suggest that the Northern Ireland experience indicates that civil society has the potential to transform the conflict, but the authors do not specify how it might realise that potential nor the nature of the properties that give it that potential.[33]

Cochrane and Dunn consider the implications of the 'track two' activities of peace/conflict resolution organisations (P/CROs) in Northern Ireland in the context of the process that led to the 'Good Friday' agreement in 1998. They argue that at 'track two' level the emphasis tends to be process driven rather than outcome driven in that activities at this level cannot be said to lead directly to specific political deals. Nevertheless, they argue that 'while the contribution of the P/CRO sector was not crucial to the eventual outcome of the political negotiations in 1998, it was nonetheless positive and significant'.[34]

Whilst they offer little evidence for this conclusion and the extent and meaning of any effect the sector had remains contested, they concur with other commentators who have studied this period of Northern Irish history. In particular in his analysis of the 'Yes' campaign at the time of the referendum on the Agreement, Couto[35] notes the crucial role of individuals working in networks grounded in community-based organisations to establishing and sustaining campaigning activities. But from the perspective of 2010, the question posed by Guelke[36] as to why whatever impact there might have been was not sustained remains unanswered. We can now see that whatever it is that mid-range and grassroots community organisations did that may have been helpful in the 1990s, their work has failed to transform the dynamics of the conflict in any sustainable way. The question remains begged. Cochrane and Dunn offer a number of helpful observations. First, they note that all the organisations they studied were established in the face of various symptoms of the conflict and not on the basis of an analysis of what the conflict was about. Even within those voluntary agencies specialising in the conflict, there has been no shared analysis of either the nature of the problem or the necessary solution. Second, they draw attention to the view that the actual drop off in the levels of violence in Northern Ireland since the early 1990s was the result of a change in tactics by the Provisional IRA and the corresponding ceasefires by Protestant paramilitary groups. It is difficult to establish what are causes and what are effects. They say the following:

> And although its impact on the political process has been peripheral rather than central, it would be reasonable to conclude that Northern Ireland would have been a lot worse off without its contribution to peace and conflict resolution over the past 30 years ... it was often the 'glue' that held society together during the worst days of the 'troubles'. Had this 'stretcher-bearer' role not existed over the past 30 years, the social impact of the political conflict would have been much greater.[37]

Lying behind this rather unsatisfactory conclusion lies the bigger question of how the three levels suggested by Lederach actually relate to one another.

The question reflects an unresolved difficulty in conceptualising key issues in the Northern Ireland peace process. Theories have emphasised either macro-structural approaches, or micro or bottom-up approaches with little attempt to bring the two together. Tactics have varied in their emphases and there was a shift from bottom-up to top-down in the late 1990s as the peace process matured and elected politicians gained in relative power. Thus, in the early years of the peace process (up until around the year 2000) considerable emphasis was laid on the potential role of bottom-up civil society initiatives whilst political negotiations continued, but subsequently greater emphasis came to be laid on the modernisation of the economy and public services. Policy interest in civil society shifted towards its contribution to modernisation conceived in rather narrow terms focused on economic efficiency, rather than on community-based peacebuilding activity.[38]

Towards a new theoretical framework

We here sketch the groundwork of a theoretical framework that seeks to overcome some of these difficulties in framing the issue at stake. The problem we address is the absence of connection between collective identities formed as a product of associational life and political structures in Northern Ireland that have frozen the conceptualisation of identity formation as the mutually antagonistic duality of Catholic and Protestant.

Pluralist political theory is organised around the view that open political systems permit the formation of identities and the articulation of interests that in turn can influence both the manner in which social and economic problems are interpreted and the range of solutions that are available to address them.[39]

Critics of this view have focused on disparities in power among players in the game of political influence and on the 'cooptation' argument that suggests that social movements and community-based organisations that allow themselves to get too close to government lose their capacity for independent action[40] But the problem in Northern Ireland is different in that politics is constructed around the identities of Catholic or Protestant. These are at once mutually exclusive and all encompassing. They permit little expression of interests or identities in the political sphere that cut across these divisions. What the proponents of bottom-up peacemaking have to explain is how, on one hand, the processes of identity formation and interest articulation would develop so that they cut across the sectarian divide and how this overcomes the fact that, on the other hand, dynamics are at work that continually reproduce the duality of Catholic and Protestant identities.

We start with the observation that civil society organisations are institutions embedded both in the political economies of the states in which they operate and in the underlying social structures from which they emerge.[41] Their particular institutional forms are to a large extent determined by background factors such as the historic power of organised religion and the relative power of capital and labour in particular states.[42] This explains why civil society differs in the ways that it does between, for example the United Kingdom and Sweden or Germany.

Despite these systemic differences, modern industrial societies tend to have similar social programs and similar ideological movements and pluralistic formation of interest groups within the political system. All these factors are in play in Northern Ireland in the context of being part of the United Kingdom and a constituent region of the European Union and they provide the context for the development of its civil society organisations, which tend to operate in similar fields and do similar things as their counterparts in Britain for similar reasons. This dynamic provides an underlying motor for the development of activities, interest group representation and identity formation that cut across Catholic Protestant divisions. These are defined and structured by the operation in practice of UK and European Union economic and social policies.

The development of the idea of a single voluntary and community 'sector' has its basis in this underlying reality. But, it is wrong to conclude from this that the organisations within this sector are somehow above and untouched by communal divisions. This is because they are also embedded in the social structures from which they emerge. Rather crudely put, we could say that activists and community entrepreneurs in Northern Ireland generally come to the business of mobilising with their Catholic or Protestant identities intact; although this might be bracketed or set aside, these identities are likely to have considerable influence on who becomes involved in which organisation given the degree of social segregation that we have already noted.

Social movement literature on mobilisation illustrates the importance of pre-existing networks for collective action. People need to be in networks that can sustain issue identification and opportunity spotting before any organisational activity can take place[43] Networks facilitate the circulation of information and the formation of identities and/or cognitive skills. They are a source of social pressure or are the locus for the development of emotional ties. It is possible to identify three functions of networks for individual participation in collective action. They socialise prospective participants through creating an initial disposition to participate; they put prospective activists in contact with others who are either already active or who share the initial disposition; and they shape decisions to participate by ensuring that any particular individual's decision to participate is appropriately shaped by the decisions of others.[44]

Furthermore, the settings and social sites where people meet have a core role in mobilising. Without their resources it is hard to imagine how new organisations would emerge even if the opportunity were self-evident. Such sites can constrain action as much as promote it. It is not the site that is important so much as the opportunity it affords for like-minded people to meet and create 'the shared meanings and identities that legitimate emergent collective action'.[45]

This literature frames civil society organisations as embedded in two distinct processes. At the level of what we will term the social economy of welfare they incorporate a tendency to organise around themes, identities and issues that cut across communal identity formation, driven by the construction of social problems around categories of welfare citizen that are blind to Catholic Protestant division. There are many examples in Northern Ireland, organised around a type of person – pensioners, women, young people – or a type of social problem such as homelessness, or medical conditions such as multiple sclerosis. Indeed, most organisations that constitute the voluntary sector in Northern Ireland are of this type. But at the level of micromobilisation these same organisations remain embedded in the structures of everyday life. Insofar as these are structured along lines divided by competing ethnic identities so too, we hypothesise, will organisational membership be divided.

This suggests that civil society organisations embody two competing narratives or conceptions of the fundamental problems of society in Northern Ireland but they appear not to be in a position to resolve these. Whilst they resist any attempt to interpret social problems in terms of ethnic competition, their impact on peacebuilding is limited because they do not appear to have the capacity to use this resistance as a basis for resolving wider ethnic differences. The question is why not.

Identity and social change

We can only sketch in the barest bones of an answer to that question here by focusing on the role of identity in processes of mobilisation and social change. We argue that understanding the way identities are constructed in social interaction offers a route to understanding the relationship between associational life in Northern Ireland and the political identity categories of Protestant and Catholic. Recent social movement scholarship has reasserted the importance of identity for explaining the nature of social change and the role of social movements in promoting change.[46]

The argument is that it is only when institutional change is accompanied by changes in people's self-perceptions that new dynamics are created. Social movement scholars have noted that mobilisation tends to be a function of three elements. Political opportunities must emerge. Political entrepreneurs must be working in a setting and be positioned to build movements. Then a process must be put into motion that frames the circumstances as propitious, the issues must be framed and presented as appropriate for action among people who understand themselves to be affected by the issue and those individuals must see themselves as the kind of people to take action.[47] Thus, it has been suggested that identity is interrelated with institutional and interactive aspects of mobilisation; changes in people's perceptions of who they are in relation to others seem central to the process of embedding institutional change.[48]

Identity is conceived here as the experience of a set of social relations. 'Identity [is] not an essential feature of an individual or group but a characteristic and consequence of social interaction. An identity is an actor's experience of a category, tie, role, network or group, coupled with a public representation of that experience.'[49] Insofar as individual people participate in different networks or groups they can simultaneously assert a number of different identities depending on the social situation. Actors can either be comprised of individuals or of collectives and an important aspect of mobilisation is the assertion of a collective identity or the emergence of a collective actor.[50] Without this group identity, collective action would be impossible. In order to act, a group must define itself in opposition to or different from other social actors and power structures. But collective identity is developed in a circular relationship with a system of opportunities and constraints in which the identity is confirmed or recognised by some other. There can be no identity without recognition.[51] Identity and action and identity and recognition are thus analytically linked.

Ethnic conflict

How does this apply in situations of ethnic conflict? This framework analytically links together the three levels of peace process action identified by Lederach. Identity change is required for institutional change to be embedded. At the same time, grassroots mobilisation requires the development of collective identities in relationship to institutional constraints and opportunities. But how does identity formation work as a mechanism?

The political scientist Jennifer Todd argues that whilst social structures and political opportunities are important, the framing of collective identity categories is crucial to understanding collective action. This process depends on what she calls the 'cultural substratum', 'the changing ways individuals and groups understand and interrelate categories'.[52]

The core issue at stake here is the way the processes of collective identity formation in grass-roots mobilisation interrelate with the formation and reproduction of ethnic identity categories. Drawing on the sociology of Pierre Bourdieu, particularly his conception of *habitus*, Todd argues that the cultural substratum in regions of ethnic conflict such as Northern Ireland contain unexamined and deep-rooted categories of ethnic collective identity. In stable circumstances (that is to say where the conflict is reproduced in a stable manner), other identities may be assimilated to this 'master' status.

When identities related to other personal challenges or activities become connected they often offer reaffirmation of the master status. It may even occur that someone who did not previously identify may form alliances in an identity group with others who then help convert an individual to the master status. Think of a person who joins a women's discussion group and then is recruited by another group member to join a church – perhaps a church our focal person had fallen away from over the course of her life's history.

In contrast, however, where there is ambiguity and tension between social practice and an identity category, the dynamic of change cannot operate. Abowitz points this out with respect to her study of college women. There is a gap between people who hold beliefs and values that show concern about the oppression of women and those who identify with the feminist movement. The beliefs and values represent social practice. Feminism represents a corporate presence with which these women will not identify. That being true, there can be no change to the identity category through adaptation, partial change through ritual appropriation, or total change through privatisation.[53]

Adaptation occurs where the formation of new and potentially challenging identities, perhaps through 'cross-community' contact, is kept separate from pre-existing ethnic identity categories that are simultaneously kept going through other social interactions. Ritual appropriation occurs where new practices are 'accepted and assimilated within old narrative forms and ritual structures, thus ensuring continuity in meaning despite change in practice'. Privatisation corresponds to a retreat to the private sphere of the family or to a consumerist withdrawal from other public identity categories. Todd emphasises that the partial identity shifts in assimilation and ritual appropriation do affect the salience of collective identity categories often in very radical ways.[54]

Todd's analysis focuses on the impact of the Agreement on these processes, but as Lederach's theory suggests, and social movement scholarship confirms, identity shifts are simultaneously driven from above and below. Network analysis suggests that grassroots organisations are embedded in social relations that sustain the ethnic identities of Catholic and Protestant. But they are at the same time responsive to a set of structural constraints that create sets of social relations that develop other collective identities. But the institutional recognition of these collective identities that is necessary to give them life as the basis for action is subject to systemic opportunities and constraints. These in turn bear down on ethnic identity categories either to support them or to undermine them. The evidence suggests that in practice relations within civil society organisations where there is either routine or organised cross-community contact are managed in such a way as to avoid any challenge to underlying processes of ethnic identification.[55] The final section of this essay draws out the implications of this analysis for peacebuilding.

Some implications and a conclusion

Patterns of living in Northern Ireland remain based largely on avoidance; where people shop, where they socialise and with whom they socialise are to a significant extent determined by ethnic identity. In the many cases where this is not possible, including instances where people have chosen to work together across communal boundaries, ethnic identification is preserved through selective contact and by ensuring that contact is conducted according to rules that do not permit 'political' matters being raised.[56]

Our theoretical approach suggests that this by now well-observed feature of interaction across the ethnic divide in Northern Ireland is driven by the lack of recognition given to collective identities that directly challenge communal identities which remain important to people in the context of the wider competition for political recognition. People manage their relationships and collective identities in such a way as to ensure that the integrity of these funda-mental beliefs about who they are and what the 'other' is like is preserved.

Our fieldwork revealed many situations where ostensible collective action around identities that cross-communal divisions are organised in this way. Interviews with pensioner groups in 2006 revealed how group solidarity was maintained through a self-conscious adherence to an identity of senior citizen, with other identities kept firmly in the background. Pride was expressed in keeping 'politics' at the door. The issues under discussion had to be constructed in such a way that any potential for ethnic competition was avoided. Where ethnic competition was raised it could be very destructive, but the evidence suggests that groups organised around shared identities like senior citizen are very good at ensuring that this never occurred. It was more likely in cases where single-identity area communities were seeking to engage in joint action with another area not sharing that identity.

Women's organisations have long been recognised as offering spaces for women to recognise commonalities rather than differences and we were given one example of changed perceptions that had the potential to challenge deeply felt communal identity. In this case, a group of Catholic women were astounded to meet a group of Protestant women whose life stories were as materially deprived as their own, challenging their perception that 'Protes-tant women were born with a silver spoon in their mouths', a perception fundamental to their belief that Catholics were uniquely disadvantaged in the Northern Irish state.

But even here, these women were no more likely to forge a new collective identity with any transformative power than the pensioners who never got so far as to discuss the question of ethnic difference, as up to the present the necessary recognition of such identities has not been forthcoming. In its absence, adaptation tends to be the most common outcome of such encounters, one clearly expressed thus:

> We can all have our own views, obviously – they've got their views and we have our own views – we come from a Nationalist area and they come from a Protestant area but when we get together in a room that doesn't matter because we're all the same. We all have the same problems; we all have childcare problems; we all have health problems; we all have poverty.[57]

The small scale of these associations and the practical focus of groups create prospects for cross-community projects that would fail if they aimed to challenge master identities. People from adjacent neighborhoods may work on joint projects that make a peace wall that separates them seem less necessary. Modest goals and limited scope may allow modest cooperation to develop in ways that produce big effects, like the removal of a peace wall. But these small effects are quite different from the encompassing image of social integration and political representation that comes out of pluralist political theory.

Our purpose in this essay has been to offer a critique of the view that civil society is the main source of new forms of social solidarity in divided societies and to suggest that a more realistic understanding of the role of civil society in the case of Northern Ireland has been as a helpmeet to addressing what is essentially a political problem. We have proposed a theoretical approach that builds on previous approaches and which has sought in particular to suggest a mechanism that ties together the levels of intervention suggested as needed by Lederach in a single framework. The formation of new collective identities and forms of solidarity in civil society may be a necessary but can never be a sufficient condition for larger-scale change.

Notes

1 B. Hayes and I. McAllister, 'Who Backs the Bombers?', *Fortnight* (2004), 11–12.
2 G. Horgan, 'Devolution, Direct Rule and the Neoliberal Reconstruction in Northern Ireland', *Critical Social Policy* 26.3 (2006), 656–68.
3 N. Acheson, 'Welfare State Reform, Compacts and Restructuring Relations between the State and the Voluntary Sector: Reflections on Northern Ireland's Experience', *Voluntary Sector Review: An International Journal of Third Sector Research, Policy and Practice* 1.2 (2010), 175–92.
4 J. R. Kearney and A. P. Williamson, 'Northern Ireland the Delayed Devolution: The Voluntary and Community Sector in Northern Ireland: Developments since 1995/96', in *Next Steps in Voluntary Action: An Analysis of Five Years of*

Development in the Voluntary Sector in England, Scotland, Wales and Northern Ireland (London, 2001).

5 N. Acheson and C. Milofsky, 'Peacebuilding and Participation in Northern Ireland: Local Social Movements and the Policy Process since the 'Good Friday' Agreement', *Ethnopolitics* 7.1 (2008), 63–80.

6 G. A. Almond and S. Verba, *The Civic Culture: Political Attitudes and Democracy in Five Nations* (Princeton, NJ, 1963); R. Putnam, *Making Democracy Work: Civic Traditions in Modern Italy* (Princeton, NJ, 1993).

7 C. Gilligan, 'Insecurity and Community Relations: Vulnerability and the Protests at the Holy Cross Girls Primary School in Belfast', in P. Noxolo and J. Huysmans (eds), *Community, Citizenship, and the War on Terror* (Basingstoke, 2009).

8 A telling example is the Suffolk Lenadoon Interface Group in west Belfast. Its impact has depended, however, not just on effective community leadership, but on substantial funding from a private charitable trust (http://www.slig.co.uk/, accessed 15 March 2011).

9 N. Acheson, E. Cairns, M. Stringer and A. Williamson, *Voluntary Action and Community Relations in Northern Ireland* (Coleraine, 2006).

10 N. Acheson, B. Harvey, J. Kearney and A. Williamson, *Two Paths One Purpose: Voluntary Action in Ireland, North and South* (Dublin, 2004).

11 Special European Union Programmes Body, 'Peace III: EU Programme for Peace and Reconciliation, 2007–2013 Northern Ireland and the Border Region of Ireland, Operational Programme' (Belfast and Monaghan, 2008). The Third Peace Programme is much smaller than the first two and more closely focused on conflict resolution and community relations activities. For a fuller discussion of the impact of the Peace Programmes, see N. Acheson and A. Williamson, 'Civil Society in Multi-Level Public Policy: The Case of Ireland's Two Jurisdictions', *Policy and Politics* 35.1 (2007), 25–44, and Acheson and Milofsky, 'Peacebuilding and Participation'.

12 Northern Ireland Council for Voluntary Action, *State of the Sector. V. Northern Ireland Voluntary and Community Sector Almanac* (Belfast, 2009).

13 DHSS, *Strategy for Support of the Voluntary Sector and for Community Development* (Belfast, 1993).

14 Department for Social Development, *Pathways for Change: A Report of the Task Force on Resourcing the Voluntary and Community Sector* (Belfast, 2003); HM Treasury, Cabinet Office, *The Future Role of the Third Sector in Social and Economic Regeneration: the Final Report* (London, 2007).

15 Office of First Minister and Deputy First Minister, *A Shared Future: Policy and Strategic Framework for Good Relations in Northern Ireland* (Belfast, 2005).

16 J. Ruane and J. Todd, *The Dynamics of Conflict in Northern Ireland* (Cambridge, 1996).

17 B. O'Leary and J. McGarry, *The Politics of Antagonism: Understanding Northern Ireland* (London, 1996).

18 J. P. Lederach, *Building Peace: Sustainable Reconciliation in Divided Societies* (Washington, DC, 1997); C. Knox and P. Quirk, *Peacebuilding in Northern Ireland, Israel and South Africa: Transition, Transformation and Reconciliation* (Basingstoke, 2000); F. Cochrane and S. Dunn, *People Power? The Role of the Voluntary and Community Sector in the Northern Ireland Conflict* (Cork, 2006).

19 G. W. Allport, *The Nature of Prejudice* (Cambridge, MA, 1954).

20 U. Niens, E. Cairns and M. Hewstone, 'Contact and Conflict in Northern Ireland', in D. Dickson and O. Hargie (eds), *Researching the Troubles: Social Science Perspectives on the Northern Ireland Conflict* (Edinburgh, 2003).

21 R. Brown and M. Hewstone, 'An Integrative Theory of Inter-group Contact', *Advances in Experimental Social Psychology* 37 (2005), 255–343; M. Hewstone,

and R. Brown, *Contact and Conflict in Intergroup Encounters* (Oxford, 1986); U. Niens, E. Cairns and M. Hewstone, 'Contact and Conflict in Northern Ireland', in Dickson and Hargie (eds), *Researching the Troubles.*

22 J. A. Schneider, 'Small Nonprofits and Civil Society: Civic Engagement and Social Capital', in R. Cnaan and C. Milofsky (eds), *Handbook of Community Movements and Local Organizations* (New York, 2006), 74–88.

23 T. Skocpol, *Diminished Democracy* (Norman: 2003).

24 H. Anheier, 'Third Sector – Third Way: Comparative Perspectives and Policy Reflections', in J. Lewis and R. Surender (eds), *Welfare State Change: Towards a Third Way?* (Oxford, 2004).

25 R. D. Putnam, *Making Democracy Work: Civic Traditions in Modern Italy* (Princeton, NJ, 1993).

26 R. D. Putnam, *Bowling Alone: The Collapse and Revival of American Community* (New York, London, 2000).

27 H. Anheier and J. Kendall, 'Interpersonal Trust and Voluntary Associations: Examining Three Approaches', *British Journal of Sociology* 53.3 (2002), 343–62; H. Anheier, 'Third Sector – Third Way: Comparative Perspectives and Policy Reflections', in Lewis and Surender (eds), *Welfare State Change.*

28 B. Rothstein and D. Stolle, 'Social Capital, Impartiality and the Welfare State', and D. Stolle, 'The Sources of Social Capital', both in M. Hooghe and D. Stolle (eds), *Generating Social Capital: Civil Society and Institutions in Comparative Perspective* (New York and Basingstoke, 2003).

29 S. Tarrow, 'Making Social Science Work across Time and Space: A Critical Reflection on Robert Putnam's *Making Democracy Work*', *American Political Science Review* 90 (1996), 389–97 (395).

30 P. Bourdieu, 'The Forms of Capital', in J. G. Richardson (ed.), *Handbook of Theory and Research for the Sociology of Education* (Westport, CT, 1986). See also, M. W. Foley and B. Edwards, 'Is It Time to Disinvest in Social Capital?', *Journal of Public Policy* 19.2 (1999), 141–73.

31 H. Anheier and J. Kendall, 'Interpersonal Trust and Voluntary Associations: Examining Three Approaches', *British Journal of Sociology* 53.3 (2002), 343–62 (355).

32 Lederach, *Building Peace.*

33 Knox and Quirk, *Peacebuilding in Northern Ireland, Israel and South Africa.*

34 Cochrane and Dunn, *People Power*, 5.

35 R. Couto, 'The Third Sector and Civil Society: The Case of the "Yes" Campaign in Northern Ireland', *Voluntas: International Journal of Voluntary and Nonprofit Organizations* 12.3 (2001), 221–38.

36 A. Guelke, 'Civil Society and the Northern Ireland Peace Process', *Voluntas: International Journal of Voluntary and Nonprofit Organizations* 14.1 (2003), 61–78.

37 Cochrane and Dunn, *People Power*, 173.

38 These changes are documented and discussed in greater detail in Acheson and Milofsky, 'Peacebuilding and Participation', and in Acheson, 'Welfare State Reform'.

39 Almond and Verba, *The Civic Culture*; Putnam, *Making Democracy Work*; P. Selznick, *The Moral Commonwealth: Social Theory and the Promise of Community* (Berkeley and Los Angeles, 1992); and A. Etzioni, *The New Golden Rule: Community and Morality in a Democratic Society* (New York, 1998).

40 F. Hunter, *Community Power Structure: A Study of Decision Makers* (Chapel Hill, NC, 1953); G. W. Domhoff, 'Power Structure Research and the Hope for Democracy', http://sociology.ucsc.edu/whorulesamerica/methods/power_structure_research. html (accessed March 4, 2010); S. Aronowitz, 'Against the Liberal State: ACT-UP and the Emergence of Postmodern Politics', in *The Death and Rebirth of American Radicalism* (New York, 1996), 125–44; F. F. Piven and R. A. Cloward, *Poor People's*

36   *Nicholas Acheson, Carl Milofsky and Maurice Stringer*

Movements: Why They Succeed, How They Fail (New York, 1979); F. F. Piven, *Challenging Authority: How Ordinary People Change America* (Lanham, MD, 2006); and P. Selznick, *TVA and the Grassroots: A Study in the Sociology of Formal Organization* (New York, 1996).

41 S. R. Smith and K. Gronbjerg, 'The Scope and Theory of Government Non-Profit Relations', in R. Steinberg and W.W. Powell (eds), *The Non-Profit Sector: A Research Handbook* (New Haven and London, 2006); A. Evers and J.-L. Laville, 'Defining the Third Sector in Europe', in J.-L. Laville and A. Evers (eds), *The Third Sector in Europe* (Northampton, MA, 2004); and M. Diani, 'Introduction: Contentious Actions and Social Networks: From Metaphor to Substance', in M. Diani and D. McAdam (eds), *Social Movements and Networks: Relational Approaches to Collective Action* (Oxford, 2003).

42 L. Salamon and H. Anheier, 'Social Origins of Civil Society', *Voluntas* 9.3 (1998), 213–48.

43 A. Melucci, *Nomads of the Present: Social Movements and Individual Needs in Contemporary Society* (Philadelphia, 1989) and A. Melucci, *Challenging Codes: Collective Action in the Information Age* (Cambridge, 1996).

44 Diani, 'Introduction', and F. Passey, 'Social Networks Matter: But How?', in Diani and McAdam (eds), *Social Movements and Networks*.

45 D. McAdam, 'Beyond Structural Analysis: Towards a More Dynamic Understanding of Social Movements', in Diani and McAdam (eds), *Social Movements and Networks*, 290.

46 D. McAdam, S. Tarrow and C. Tilly, *Dynamics of Contention* (Cambridge, 2001).

47 C. Milofsky, *Smallville: Institutionalizing Community in Twenty-First Century America* (Hanover, NH, 2008); A. Oberschall, *Social Conflicts and Social Movements* (Engelwood Cliffs, NJ, 1973); N. J. Smelser, *Theory of Collective Behavior* (New York, 1963).

48 McAdam et al., *Dynamics of Contention*.

49 C. Tilly, *Stories, Identities and Political Change* (Lanham, MD, 2002), 75.

50 J. S. Coleman, *Foundations of Social Theory* (Cambridge, MA, 1990).

51 A. Melucci, *Challenging Codes: Collective Action in the Information Age* (Cambridge, 1996); Tilly, *Stories, Identities and Political Change*.

52 J. Todd, 'Social Transformation, Collective Categories and Identity Change', *Theory and Society* 34 (2005), 429–63 (431).

53 D. Abowitz, 'The Campus "F" Word: Feminist Self-Identification (And Not) Among Undergraduates', *International Journal of Sociology of the Family* 34.1 (2008), 43–54.

54 Todd, 'Social Transformation', 443–4.

55 N. Acheson, 'A Case of Avoiding "Political Mumbo Jumbo": Lessons from Northern Ireland for the Role of Voluntary Associations in Community Cohesion Policies', *Policy and Politics* 39.2 (2011).

56 J. Darby, *Intimidation and the Control of Conflict in Northern Ireland* (Dublin, 1986); and P. Shirlow and B. Murtagh, *Belfast: Segregation, Violence and the City* (Basingstoke, 2006).

57 Acheson et al., *Voluntary Action and Community Relations in Northern Ireland*, 53.

3

The Role of Civil Society in Promoting Peace in Northern Ireland[1]

Timothy J. White

The Good Friday or Belfast Agreement of 1998 endeavoured to create a political framework for governing Northern Ireland. Because the Agreement attempted to manage the conflict through consociationalism, or as some see it, power sharing among elites, it did not focus on mass-level politics and hence was not designed to overcome the sectarian division in Northern Ireland. The institutions of the new governing system were based on sectarian self-identification of elites and provided little incentive for politicians to transcend historic communal differences. Prosperity and peace were meant to improve both communities but not force them to live together. Many organisations have been created over the past few decades to encourage peace and societal transformation at the grassroots level. However, their effectiveness has been questioned, and many have criticised the community-relations industry. Most of the domestic as well as international efforts at fostering cross-community linkages have failed to do so.[2] One exception to this general pattern has been the faith-based Church Fora that emerged around the time of the Agreement that strove to help develop civil society in Northern Ireland.

This chapter builds upon recent scholarship that has developed theoretical frameworks to explain the resolution of ethnic conflict.[3] The assumption of this research is that one cannot just deny or manipulate identities to reduce or eliminate conflict.[4] Cochrane has demonstrated the difficulty of ending Civil Wars like the conflict in Northern Ireland due to the fact that civilians are both perpetrators and victims.[5] For peace to occur one must go beyond separating armies or paramilitaries. Instead, peace requires a redress of the fundamental conflict that exists among groups in society. While reconceptualising sovereignty and creating innovative means of incorporating minorities have helped to promote solutions in ethno-national conflicts,[6] the solution for peace must include efforts at reconciliation between the divided communities. This may be aided by external economic assistance, but ultimately the ethnic or communal groups in the conflict-torn society must come to their own internal settlement.[7] While the Agreement envisioned a Northern Ireland that belonged to no single state but to the two communities, such power sharing must not only occur among elites but also among the mass public.[8] Achieving a just and lasting peace requires not just pacts or secret agreements by political elites but a true reconciliation between the communities. This would empower citizens to demand effective governance which includes bargaining and compromise from their elected officials. One can best explain the frustration with the Agreement in terms of the difficulty in institution-alising means of reconciliation at the mass level and the resultant lack of a vibrant civil society that minimises or overcomes historic sectarian divisions.[9] This explanation is at odds with those who believe the difficulties in imple-menting the institutional processes of governing Northern Ireland according to the Agreement are due to the lack of leadership, vision and skills of polit-ical elites.[10] This chapter stresses the importance of civil society as critical in fulfilling the peace promised by the Agreement.

The Good Friday Agreement as an elite bargain

Political elites negotiated the Agreement on behalf of the communities they represented, built not on grassroots organisations but on the principles of consociationalism. While the meaning of this term is often debated or confused, its purpose is to guarantee access to power and a share in governance for minority groups.[11] It is an inclusive means of providing a governing system that brings all parties into the political process.[12] The assumption of conso-ciationalism is that by gaining representation for minorities the likelihood of ethnic-based violence will be reduced.[13] Consociationalism also assumes that the conflicting identities of the different groups in society are permanent and does not provide a mechanism to reduce existing social cleavages. No one should be surprised that surveys indicate that the sectarian divide continues and perhaps became even more polarised in the aftermath of the Agreement.[14] Consociationalism does not encourage bargaining and compromise between political actors but instead allows and incentivises political elites to represent their constituency with little or no reference to the needs of the 'other' in society. In fact, because the differences between groups is perceived to be so severe, critics of consociationalism argue that it encourages and entrenches differences between groups because elites are likely to gain electoral support only by serving (or as some see it pandering to) their own constituency.[15]

The difficulty of creating functional governmental arrangements when elites have little incentive to operate in a responsible way in terms of compro-mising and bargaining with the other parties or elites led to purposeful and constructive ambiguity in the crafting of the Agreement. The most critical issue of contention in the negotiations was the constitutional status of Northern Ireland. By allowing the future status of Northern Ireland to be changed only if a majority in the Irish Republic and Northern Ireland agreed, and by focusing on the institutional relationships across borders, the Agreement deferred if not removed the thorny issue of sovereignty from the negotiations. Thus, the Agreement, like many others, delayed to the end of the negotiations (and some would argue afterward) the most difficult issues so that the momentum of the negotiating process put pressure on the parties to secure a final agreement even if there was no clear and transparent compromise made. This has led to an ambiguity in terms of how each community has come to interpret the Agreement and seek its implementation.[16]

The momentum of the peace process that developed in the 1990s, especially after the ceasefires, put pressure on political elites to make a deal. One could argue that the Mayhew Talks in 1992 created the atmosphere and trust for continuing negotiations throughout the decade.[17] In this process of negotiations, political leaders of different governments and political parties learned to take into account how far they could push the other side in making concessions. Thus, the Unionist elites were willing to tolerate a two-year process of IRA decommissioning. They calculated that that this delay was the only way Sinn Féin could sell the Agreement to Republicans. They also recognised that the North-South bodies were essential ingredients for a peace deal for nationalists, so they were willing to concede to these new bodies if they achieved the assembly they sought as well as a British-Irish Council created in the Third Strand of the Agreement.[18] Unionists recognised that to achieve the long-term goal of creating a parliament they would have to incorporate Nationalists in the political process of this self-governing assembly and agree to a commission to review policing in Northern Ireland.[19]

Republicans came to the bargaining table recognising that they could not defeat the British army in a military contest and thus were willing to accept power sharing.[20] Nationalists were willing to concede to the principle of majority consent as part of a longer and larger strategy that they believed would help to realise their long-term goal of gradual reunification.[21] Throughout the negotiations and the subsequent effort to ratify the Agreement and operationalise its institutional framework, nationalist politicians in Northern Ireland recognised the precarious position of David Trimble. Northern nationalists as well as Irish government leaders clearly tried to 'save Dave' because they believed that if he was defeated within the UUP leadership struggle that this might mean the end of Unionist support for operating within the framework of the GFA.[22]

Because the Agreement strove to be inclusive so that all members of the community would feel that the government represented their interests, the new democratic political framework has successfully marginalised those who utilise or advocate violence.[23] Despite criticism that the Agreement did not ameliorate all of Northern Ireland's problems and replaced sectarian violence with neoliberal economic policies that marginalise those who fail to thrive in the new competitive economy, the Agreement has fundamentally changed the way violence is perceived by the public and politicians in Northern Ireland.[24] The condemnation of the killings conducted by dissident Republicans of police and soldiers in Northern Ireland testifies to the success of the Agreement of marginalising those who use deadly violence to advance their political agenda. The unanimity of all the major political parties, leaders, church and communal groups in Northern Ireland stands in stark contrast to the period of the Troubles where rationalisations or justifications for political killings were often offered.

Despite this progress, because the institutions of the new governing system remain based on self-identification of elites, they provide little if any incentive for politicians to seek to transcend the sectarian divide. Moreover, the political parties remain elite-dominated so that parties take positions based on the calculations of their leaders more than pressure from mass membership.[25] Even if political elites form good personal relations with leaders from the other community, they have little motivation to work together in the context of governing Northern Ireland.[26] Some have criticised the institutional framework created in Strand One of the GFA because it creates irresolvable tension between the parties that makes governing nearly impossible.[27] The first and second minister must come from the largest Protestant and Catholic Parties. This reality was clarified and reinforced by the St Andrews Agreement which removed the cross-community vote for the top two positions. Compelling the leaders of the Democratic Unionist Party (DUP) and Sinn Féin, the parties with the largest support and most extreme positions in their communities, makes even the prospect of sharing power under this system extremely difficult.

Other critics contend that the Agreement was not even consociational in that it did not assume that segregating the communities was the key to the peace process. Paul Dixon argues that the peace process is driven by an integrationist philosophy that assumes power sharing will be the mechanism that yields peace in Northern Ireland.[28] He also contends that politicians, especially Tony Blair, engaged in 'honourable' deceptions in order to convince the Northern Ireland public, especially the Unionists, to ratify the Agreement.[29] The loss of support among Unionists after the referendum spawned the subsequent difficulties of keeping the Northern Ireland Assembly operational and highlighted the problems with institutionalising the Agreement.[30] Perhaps there are traditions within local communities that provide mechanisms for overcoming historic sectarianism,[31] but the difficulties of keeping the Northern Ireland Assembly operational have highlighted the problem with self-government in Northern Ireland. The Agreement provides a framework for governing based on power sharing without providing the incentive for political elites to make the concessions associated with democratic bargaining and compromise that are part of the legislative and governing process. In this way, the Agreement lacked a focus on the need for transcending the sectarian divide among the masses that would have effectively not only supported peacebuilding in local communities but placed increased pressure on political leaders and the major political parties to make the institutions created by the Agreement more effective and operational once the Agreement was signed and ratified.

The importance of trust in creating social capital for civil society and peace

Many, especially Protestants, remain skeptical that the institutional arrangements for self-government envisioned in the Agreement provide a framework for effective government in Northern Ireland.[32] There have been major problems implementing the Agreement, including multiple suspensions of the Assembly. Moreover, the Agreement has not fundamentally undermined the different self-conceptions Protestants and Catholics hold.[33] Indeed, some contend that the Agreement has institutionalised new forms of sectarianism and not led to a post-sectarian Northern Ireland that the Agreement appeared to promise.[34] This lack of trust undermines the process of democratic consolidation because democracy assumes a certain level of trust among the different groups in society and the political leaders they elect. Trust has long been seen as a defining characteristic of democracy's arrival and sustenance.[35] In divided societies like Northern Ireland, trust means that individuals are not only willing to interact with members of the other community but that they are willing to allow the other community to share in governance.[36] Trust assumes that those who are perceived not to be in one's self-identified group or community seek the well-being of everyone, or at least will refrain from harmful or detrimental acts. Individuals develop trust based on their predispositions as well as experience based on interacting with members of other groups.[37] Trust is thus an expectation based on at least a partially rational evaluation of others' behaviour. The development and strengthening of trust requires a mutual process of interaction that strengthens each party's perception that the other side is committed to a continuing process of cooperation.[38] In the Northern Ireland context, this means an end to the acquiescence often given to paramilitary groups and the violence they perpetrated during the Troubles as well as increased interaction that fosters a sense of common purpose and interest among Catholics and Protestants.

When interpersonal trust is present in society, politics is no longer thought of as a zero-sum game but one of bargaining and compromise where mutual gains are possible. While governments cannot compel members of differing groups in society to trust members of other groups, they can develop policies that make trust between groups more likely. Government policies that ensure equality and fairness of treatment among the differing groups are especially important.[39] The long history of sectarianism and the Troubles in Northern Ireland makes the development of trust very difficult. When historic expectations are fear, suspicion, revenge and recrimination, it is difficult to create trust between groups. However, the Agreement was built on the expectation that enough cooperation across communities could develop that trust would gradually emerge. It was hoped that this cooperation would create what Uslaner identifies as 'moralistic trust', which allows people from different backgrounds to work toward compromise and a common good.[40]

In the near term there has been no effective crosscutting cleavage that has emerged to undermine the existing sectarian divide in Northern Ireland. Some individuals may develop particularised trust with those with whom they interact from the other community, but this does not translate into a generalised trust. This generalised trust is necessary for the creation of social capital, creating obligations of reciprocity that are derived from trust and social networks that bridge the sectarian divide. Both within cities and towns as well as within Northern Ireland as a whole, geographic differences of housing and where Catholics and Protestants live are consolidating to reinforce the existing differences. O'Reilly has identified a process whereby cultural differences and identities are being highlighted in an effort to strengthen each community's claim to heritage and traditional legitimacy in Northern Ireland.[41] As a result, contestation between communities since the Agreement can be seen as part of a continuing narrative of the competing claims of those who see a pre- or perhaps better-understood postcolonial understanding of Irish identity and those who seek to maintain their Unionist traditions.[42]

What has become apparent as the years have passed since the signing of the Agreement is that while the Agreement was creative in providing political institutions that would allow elites to share power, this is not enough to promote peace. Peace processes need to create a political dynamic that fosters a workable democracy as a way of implementing the peace because this is the only way that the new political environment can create the democratic validation for new political institutions to be seen as legitimate for all parties.[43] Thus, the political process needs to focus on the grassroots effort to achieve what scholars call a civil society. A civil society is based on the organisations and relationships that exist among individuals and groups that allow people of different backgrounds and identities to engage each other peacefully and democratically outside of the formal framework of government.[44] A civil society is necessary for the creation of social capital.[45] Social capital is built on social networks that promote norms of cooperation among groups who otherwise might be unlikely to do so by building trust, reciprocity and a fair distribution of resources in society.[46] Once social capital exists in society, it allows for the accumulated trust developed in society to overcome historic suspicion and animosity. Creating sanctions or rewards is important to ensure that cooperative behaviour continues and extant social capital is not squandered.[47]

When one examines the state of civil society in Northern Ireland, one finds that to the extent that associations exist in Northern Ireland they tend to reinforce existing community identities. Thus, these organisations and relationships serve as bonding social capital rather than linking individuals with members of diverse communities which would serve as bridging social capital.[48] A strong and vibrant civil society can multiply inequalities and tension in society and thereby cement or exacerbate differences among social groups. This problem is exacerbated by the fact that communities are physically as well as socially divided. Where communities are highly polarised, civil society may increase conflict and undermine prospects for stable democracy.[49] Dryzek has posited that an inclusive model of democracy only works when the group historically excluded from power, in the case of Northern Ireland nationalists, can buy into the existing or emerging state imperative.[50] Thus, the challenge for the emergence of an effective democratic system in Northern Ireland would require an agreement between the historic dominant group and those historically excluded from power to share power. Catholics need to believe that they have access to power and resources in order to become vested in the new Northern Ireland while Protestants have to accept power sharing with Catholics. In order to achieve this goal, Northern Ireland needs more bridges in terms of social capital to transcend sectarian differences rather than associations and organisations that reinforce existing identities and thus strengthen the existing divide between the communities.

When memberships in social groups cut across cleavages in society, social capital provides continuing goodwill even when discord might be present.[51] Social capital thus may not end communal tensions but facilitates trust among contentious groups. Thus, social capital has come to be seen as essential for the functioning of a liberal democracy.[52] The problem for creating and maintaining civil society is that it is not created by voluntary associations as much as it reflects what one scholar calls public culture. Changes in public culture prompt associational groups to emerge across communal lines and foster civil society.[53] Van Der Meer and Van Ingen have found that even if voluntary associations do not in and of themselves make social capital, these organisations represent pools of democracy that make democratic political life more stable.[54] If ethnic or sectarian groups demand independence and will settle for nothing short of this objective, then there is no hope for the creation or fostering of a civil society and peace becomes impossible.[55] The challenge for Northern Ireland is to foster an associational life that allows individuals to cross extant community barriers and develop relationships with members of the other community that both humanise and empower the other.

What do recent opinion polls tell us of the state of civil society in Northern Ireland? The results of the Northern Ireland Life and Times survey suggest that while the communal divide exists in Northern Ireland, there is some evidence that relations between Catholics and Protestants have improved. Looking back on the Agreement, nearly two-thirds of the Northern Irish population with nearly three-fourths of Catholics and almost sixty per cent of Protestants believe that the Good Friday Agreement was a good thing.[56] Sixty-Five per cent of respondents report improved relations in the last five years, thirty per cent believe relations have remained about the same, and only two per cent assert that relations have worsened.[57] The majority of Catholics and Protestants express approval of more mixing across the communal divide when it comes to marriage, work, neighborhood living and primary education.[58] It is clear that people in Northern Ireland recognise that the mixing of the two communities will create better relations, but they do not generally believe that Northern Ireland is a normal civic society in which all individuals are equal, where differences are resolved through dialogue, and where all people are treated equally.[59] While the majority of the Northern Ireland population reports a respect for the other community's culture and traditions, they admit that they do not have a great deal of understanding of the other community.[60] There remain different levels of trust reported by those who identify with different religious traditions and the parties that have different levels of sectarian support. Protestants are more likely to have greater distrust for Sinn Féin and the Social Democratic and Labour Party (SDLP) while Catholics have greater distrust for the Democratic Unionist Party (DUP) and the Ulster Unionist Party (UUP).[61]

If a civil society were to emerge in Northern Ireland, politicians would have far greater incentive to take into account the needs and interests of all in society, not just feel they are meant to represent 'their' community. Previous research has demonstrated that civil society tends to have an emancipative effect on the role of the citizen in the political process. Liberal theorists suggest that voters and members of the public come to see their role as challenging existing elites rather than following their lead.[62] This means in the Northern Irish context that politicians would have an incentive to bargain and compromise with leaders from the other community rather than refuse to concede and fear being seen as selling out to the other side. Because members of the voting public tend to perceive politics in zero-sum terms, they seek to elect representatives that are the virulent defenders of their community's interests. Sinn Féin and the DUP replaced the SDLP and the UUP as the two largest parties in Northern Ireland because the former parties had the reputation for being the strongest advocates of each community's political position. In a sense, the electoral defeat of SDLP and UUP within their own communities demonstrated the political cost associated with being the most supportive of the peace process.[63]

While many organisations have been created over the past few decades to encourage peace and societal transformation at the grassroots level, their level of effectiveness has been considered negligible given the scale of hostility and conflict between the Catholic and Protestant communities. The absence of these groups, however, may have made the period of the Troubles even worse and provided less fertile ground for the emergence of the peace process. Chapman contends that underlying individual attitudes toward politics and violence account for both associational life and support for violence in a society.[64] My argument, however, is not that a simple negative linear relationship exists between associational life and political violence. I contend that increased cross-communal association would put democratic pressure on political elites to bargain and compromise. This would consolidate the fledgling democratic framework and institutions created by the Agreement. At least, the fact that the peace process and the Agreement have reduced the level of violence in Northern Ireland has created an opening for civil society to develop.[65] Nevertheless, we have seen precious few groups or organisations that have effectively bridged the sectarian divide to help foster a civil society in Northern Ireland.

For example, the religious organisations in Northern Ireland have tended to reflect the sectarian attitudes in the community rather than help to transcend them.[66] Crotty has emphasised the churches, specifically the Roman Catholic Church, can best be understood as an interest group that operates in the realm of civil society in a democracy such as Ireland.[67] One major exception has been religious efforts such as the Church Fora that build hope for the emergence of a civil society in Northern Ireland.[68] The Church Fora foster civil society in that church members at the local level engage members of other religious traditions on matters of community concern while maintaining their religious identity. As such, they are built on a realism that recognises the existing community divide. These kinds of organisational efforts that occur outside of the framework of the Agreement or any formal governmental arrangement offer the hope that slowly, over a period of time, a sense of trust can emerge than can help build a civil society in Northern Ireland.[69]

Conclusion

Defenders of the Agreement have argued that time is needed to implement it fully and allow its institutions to gain acceptance among the people of Northern Ireland. There is some evidence that states or political institutions like those at Stormont may build trust over time and ultimately social capital by acting as enforcers of agreements between the communities and by facilitating power sharing.[70] Until now, external actors, primarily the British government and to a lesser extent the Irish government, have been seen as the enforcers of the deals or agreements between the parties. Over time, if the Northern Ireland executive and legislative functions as hoped, they may help to bring confidence in the governing institutions' capacity to ensure that all sides live up to their commitments. There is an additional argument that the longer a polity functions as a democracy, the more trust that develops among members of society. Established democracies tend to breed civil relations among contending groups in society.[71] Thus, the longer cross-communal violence is avoided and the institutional framework of Stormont functions, the more likely civil society supporting a democratic peace for Northern Ireland can take hold. Moreover, those who have identified the positive short-term effects of international development aid argue that for civil society to emerge and the long-term benefits of international aid be realised in Northern Ireland, one must wait for generational change to occur.[72] Hence, there is room for hope in that the peace process as it has evolved thus far may be able to bring the changes necessary for a deepening of peace in the future, but this would appear to be a long-term process. The peace process needs more immediate and intermediate guarantees of success so that it is not derailed.

This chapter has argued that the development of civil society in Northern Ireland is necessary in the short-term to bridge communal differences and pressure political elites to act as effective bargaining agents in a political framework of conflict and cooperation.[73] Patience is required in the process of building civil society in Northern Ireland, and no one should expect a quick and easy transformation of a highly divided society. After all, the history of the Troubles and its analysis served to sustain conflict in Northern Ireland,[74] and we should appreciate how the Good Friday Agreement has developed a new and alternative narrative for Northern Ireland. Nevertheless, we need to recognise that if civil society changes, this would have significant implications for political elites. Their desire to represent the interest of their community at the expense of the other will gradually dissipate as they see that their own constituents do not perceive politics in such polarised terms. Ultimately, the Irish peace process must operate at the mass level if democratically elected political representatives are to take the risks for peace associated with the successful implementation of the Agreement.

Notes

1 An earlier version of this chapter was presented at an Irish Model for Peace? A Conference of the Specialist Group on Peace and Conflict of the Political Studies Association of Ireland, 22 May 2009, at Trinity College, Dublin. I would like to thank Maria Power, Paul Dixon, Landon Hancock, Martin Mansergh, William Hazleton, Margaret Keiley-Listermann, Wendy Wiedenhoft and Robert Snyder for comments on earlier drafts of this essay.

2 F. Cochrane and S. Dunn, *People Power? The Role of the Voluntary and Community Sector in the Northern Ireland Conflict* (Cork, 2002), 153–55 and 166 and Landon E. Hancock, 'The Northern Irish Peace Process: From Top to Bottom', *International Studies Review* 10.2 (2008), 225. Some have also criticised international efforts at promoting reconciliation between the communities in Northern Ireland. See Sean Byrne and Cynthia Irwin, 'A Shared Common Sense: Perceptions of the Material Effects and Impacts of Economic Growth in Northern Ireland', *Civil Wars* 5.1 (2002), 79.

3 See J. Darby and R. MacGinty, *Contemporary Peacemaking: Conflict, Peace Processes and Post-War Reconstruction* (New York, 2008); C. A. Hartzell and M. Hoddie, *Crafting Peace: Power-Sharing Institutions and the Negotiated Settlement of Civil Wars* (University Park, PA, 2007); R. MacGinty, *No War, No Peace: The Rejuvenation of Stalled Peace Processes and Peace Accords* (New York, 2006); A. Oberschall, *Conflict and Peacebuilding in Divided Societies: Responses to Ethnic Violence* (London, 2007); R. Paris, *At War's End: Building Peace After Civil Conflict* (Cambridge, 2004); M. H. Ross, *Cultural Contestation in Ethnic Conflict* (New York, 2007); B. F. Walter, *Committing to Peace: The Successful Settlement of Civil Wars* (Princeton, 2001); and S. Wolff, *Ethnic Conflict: A Global Perspective* (New York, 2006).

4 For a perspective that emphasises government manipulation of identities as the key to keeping peace in ethnically divided societies, see D. L. Byman, *Keeping the Peace: Lasting Solutions to Ethnic Conflicts* (Baltimore, 2002).

5 F. Cochrane, *Ending Wars* (Cambridge, 2008), 6–7.

6 R. Wilson, 'The Politics of Contemporary Ethno-Nationalist Conflicts', *Nations and Nationalism* 7.3 (2001), 365–84.

7 For the role of external economic assistance on promoting the peace process at the grassroots in Northern Ireland, see S. Byrne, *Economic Assistance and the Northern Ireland Conflict: Building the Peace Dividend* (Madison, NJ, 2009).

8 F. O'Toole, 'The Peace Process', in Andrew Higgins Wyndham (ed.), *Re-Imagining Ireland* (Charlottesville: University of Virginia Press, 2006), 207, contends that the agreement assumes two communities jointly rule Northern Ireland. This is traditionally depicted as consociational rule by elites, but Sean Byrne contends that peace also requires efforts to create a civil society in 'Consociational and Civic Society Approaches to Peacebuilding in Northern Ireland', *Journal of Peace Research* 38.3 (2001), 327–52.

9 For various approaches to civil society relevant to Northern Ireland, see C. Farrington, 'Models of Civil Society and Their Implications for the Northern Ireland Peace Process', in C. Farrington (ed.), *Global Change, Civil Society and the Northern Ireland Peace Process: Implementing the Political Settlement* (New York, 2008), 113–41, and Paul Dixon, 'Paths to Peace in Northern Ireland (I): Civil Society and Consociational Approaches', *Democratization* 4.2 (1997), 1–27. This argument is similar to those who argue for participative democracy and decentralisation in Northern Ireland. See S. Buchanan, 'Transforming Conflict in Northern Ireland and the Border Counties: Some Lessons from the Peace Programmes on Valuing Participative Democracy', *Irish Political Studies* 23.3 (2008), 387–409.

10 For example, see S. Wolff, 'Between Stability and Collapse: Internal and External Dynamics of Post-agreement Institution Building in Northern Ireland', in S. Noel (ed.), *From Power Sharing to Democracy: Post-conflict Institutions in Ethnically Divided Societies* (Montreal, 2005), 44–66. This point of view was emphasised by Gerry Adams in a speech given at Xavier University in Cincinnati, Ohio on 3 October 2008.

11 A. Lijphart, *Democracy in Plural Societies: A Comparative Perspective* (New Haven, 1977). For how the Agreement fits this model, see B. O' Leary, 'The Belfast Agreement and the British-Irish Agreement: Consociation, Confederal Institutions, a Federacy, and a Peace Process', in A. Reynolds (ed.), *The Architecture of Democracy: Constitutional Design, Conflict Management, and Democracy* (Oxford, 2002), 293–356.

12 This sense of inclusiveness was at the heart of how the Irish government under Albert Reynolds saw the peace process and was subsequently critical to the success of the negotiations leading to the Agreement. See A. Reynolds, *Albert Reynolds: My Autobiography* (London, 2009), 198, and M. Mansergh, 'Mountain-Climbing Irish-Style: The Hidden Challenge of the Peace Process', in M. Elliott (ed.), *The Long Road to Peace in Northern Ireland* (Liverpool, 2002), 114.

13 The importance of inclusion of armed groups in these negotiations that lead to political settlements is emphasised in C. Lekha Sriram, *Peace as Governance: Power-Sharing, Armed Groups and Contemporary Peace Negotiations* (New York, 2008). The assumption that consociational systems provide better representation for minorities and thereby minimises conflict is challenged in Pippa Norris, 'Ballots Not Bullets: Testing Consociational Theories and Ethnic Conflict, Electoral Systems, and Democratization', in Reynolds (ed.), *The Architecture of Democracy*, 206–47.

14 A good review of the sectarian political divide in Ireland is provided in C. Mitchell's *Religion, Identity and Politics in Northern Ireland: Boundaries of Belonging and Belief* (Aldershot, 2006). For the survey evidence, see T. Fahey, B. C. Hayes and R. Sinnott, *Conflict and Consensus: A Study of Values and Attitudes in the Republic*

of Ireland and Northern Ireland (London, 2006), 60–66, and R. Wilford, R. Wilson and K. Clausen, *Power to the People? Assessing Democracy in Northern Ireland* (Dublin, 2006), 28–29. For an analysis of how the labour market remains spatially polarised and sectarian, see B. Murtagh and P. Shirlow, 'Spatial Segregation and Labour Market Processes in Belfast', *Policy and Politics* 35.3 (2007), 361–75.

15 Wilford, Wilson and Clausen, *Power to the People?*, 22. For further analysis on the limits of consociationalism based on the Good Friday Agreement, see R. Taylor, 'The Belfast Agreement and the Limits of Consociationalism', in Farrington (ed.), *Global Change*, 183–98.

16 D. Mitchell, 'Cooking the Fudge: Constructive Ambiguity and the Implementation of the Northern Ireland Agreement, 1998–2007', *Irish Political Studies* 24.3 (2009), 321–26; A. Aughey, *The Politics of Northern Ireland: Beyond the Good Friday Agreement* (London, 2005); J. Coakley, 'Has the Northern Ireland Problem Been Solved?', *Journal of Democracy* 19.3 (2008), 107; and E. O'Kane, *Britain, Ireland and Northern Ireland since 1980: The Totality of the Relationships* (London, 2007), 160–61.

17 D. Bloomfield, *Developing Dialogue in Northern Ireland: The Mayhew Talks, 1992* (New York, 2001).

18 T. Hennessey, 'Negotiating the Belfast Agreement', in B. Barton and P. J. Roche (eds), *The Northern Ireland Question: The Peace Process and the Belfast Agreement* (New York, 2009), 39.

19 D. Godson, *Himself Alone: David Trimble and the Ordeal of Unionism* (London, 2004), 333 and 806. For a discussion of how Trimble and the Unionists interpreted the policing issue, see F. Millar, *David Trimble: The Price of Peace* (Dublin, 2004), 86–105.

20 R. Alonso, *The IRA and Armed Struggle* (London, 2007); B. Mukherjee, 'Why Political Power-Sharing Agreements Lead to Enduring Peaceful Resolution in Some Civil Wars, But Not Others?', *International Studies Quarterly* 50.2 (2006), 479–504, demonstrates that when a decisive military victory for the government (in this case the British) is achieved it results in more effective power-sharing arrangements. Michaela Mattes and Burcu Savun agree that power sharing is critical to the success of agreements that attempt to bring an end to civil wars in 'Fostering Peace after Civil War: Commitment Problems and Agreement Design', *International Studies Quarterly* 53.3 (2009), 737–59.

21 Cillian McGrattan, 'Northern Nationalism and the Belfast Agreement', in Brian Barton and Patrick J. Roche (eds), *The Northern Ireland Question: The Peace Process and the Belfast Agreement* (New York: Palgrave Macmillan, 2009), 148.

22 This conceptualisation of 'Saving Dave' comes from P. Dixon, *Northern Ireland: The Politics of War and Peace* (2nd edn, Houndmills, 2008), 286. Martin McGuinness argues that Trimble's problem was that while looking over his shoulder at Ian Paisley he failed to lead his constituency (speech at Xavier University, Cincinnati, Ohio, 29 July 2007).

23 These conditions are emphasised in J. Darby, *The Effects of Violence on Peace Processes* (Washington, DC, 2001), 118–20.

24 This critique is offered by A. Kelly in 'Introduction: The Troubles with the Peace Process: Contemporary Northern Irish Culture', *The Irish Review* 40–41 (2009), 1–17.

25 Wilford, Wilson, and Claussen, *Power to the People?*, 129.

26 This point is emphasised in Dixon, *Northern Ireland*, 34, and A. Oberschall and L. K. Palmer, 'The Failure of Moderate Politics: The Case of Northern Ireland', in I. O'Flynn and D. Russell (eds), *Power Sharing: New Challenges for Divided Societies* (London, 2005), 77.

27 For example, see A. J. Ward, 'The Northern Ireland Constitution and Problems of Governance', paper prepared for the Political Studies Association of Ireland Annual Meeting, Galway, 2001.

28 P. Dixon, 'Why the Good Friday Agreement in Northern Ireland is Not Consociational', *Political Quarterly* 76.3 (2005), 357–67.

29 P. Dixon, 'Honourable Deceptions? The Role of Political Lying in the Northern Ireland Peace Process', lecture given on 17 April 2009 at Xavier University in Cincinnati, Ohio.

30 J. Bew, M. Frampton and I. Gurruchaga, *Talking to Terrorists: Making Peace in Northern Ireland and the Basque Country* (New York, 2009), 149–54.

31 R. Cashman in *Storytelling on the Northern Irish Border: Characters and Community* (Bloomington, 2008), 9, emphasises how local identities complicate and potentially transcend reductive binary thinking associated with sectarian politics in Northern Ireland.

32 See S. Elliott, 'The Electoral Dynamics of the Belfast Agreement', in B. Barton and P. J. Roche (eds), *The Northern Ireland Question: The Peace Process and the Belfast Agreement* (New York, 2009), 123–24.

33 This ethnic or sectarian divide is stressed in P. Geoghegan, 'Beyond Orange and Green? The Awkwardness of Negotiating Difference in Northern Ireland', *Irish Studies Review* 16.1 (2008), 173–94, and R. Whitaker, 'Where the Difference Lies: Democracy and the Ethnographic Imagination in Northern Ireland', in A. Findlay (ed.), *Nationalism and Multiculturalsim: Irish Identity, Citizenship and the Peace Process* (New Brunswick, NJ, 2004), 157–82.

34 See R. McVeigh and B. Rolston, 'From Good Friday to Good Relations: Sectarianism, Racism and the Northern Ireland State', *Race and Class* 48.4 (2007), 1–23.

35 See R. Inglehart, *Culture Shift in Advanced Industrial Society* (Princeton, 1990), 37–40; O. O'Neill, *A Question of Trust* (Cambridge, 2002), 27; C. Tilly, *Trust and Rule* (New York, 2005); D. Stolle, S. Soroka and R. Johnston, 'When Does Diversity Erode Trust? Neighborhood Diversity, Interpersonal Trust and the Mediating Effect of Social Interactions', *Political Studies* 56.1 (2008), 57–75; and Patti Tamara Lenard, 'Trust Your Compatriots, but Count Your Change: The Roles of Trust, Mistrust, and Distrust in Democracy', *Political Studies* 56.1 (2008), 1–21.

36 This has been the fundamental challenge to implementing the Agreement since its signing. See W. A. Hazleton, 'Devolution and the Diffusion of Power: The Internal and Transnational Dimensions of the Belfast Agreement', *Irish Political Studies* 15 (2000), 25–38.

37 This definition comes from M. Freitag and R. Traunmüller, 'Spheres of Trust: An Empirical Analysis of the Foundations of Particularized and Generalized Trust', *European Journal of Political Research* 48.6 (2009), 782–803.

38 This analysis of trust comes from F. Herreros, *The Problem of Forming Social Capital: Why Trust?* (New York, 2004), 8–9, and M. Freitag and R. Traunmüller, 'Spheres of Trust: An Empirical Analysis of the Foundations of Particularized and Generalized Trust', *European Journal of Political Research* 48.6 (2009), 782–803.

39 For a further elaboration of this argument, see E. M. Uslaner, 'Trust, Democracy and Governance: Can Government Policies Influence Generalized Trust?', in M. Hooghe and D. Stolle (eds), *Generating Social Capital: Civil Society and Institutions in Comparative Perspective* (New York, 2003), 171–90. For the realisation that trust needed to be developed after the Agreement, see J. Powell, *Great Hatred, Little Room: Making Peace in Northern Ireland* (London, 2008), 312.

40 E. M. Uslaner, 'Producing and Consuming Trust', *Political Science Quarterly* 115.4 (2000–2001), 572.

41 C. O'Reilly, 'The Politics of Culture in Northern Ireland', in J. Neuheiser and S.

Wolff (eds), *Peace at Last? The Impact of the Good Friday Agreement on Northern Ireland* (New York, 2002), 168–87.

42 For this perspective, see Andrew Finlay, 'Introduction', in Andrew Finlay (ed.), *Nationalism and Multiculturalism: Irish Identity, Citizenship and the Peace Process* (New Brunswick, NJ, 2004), 1–32.

43 Ben Reilly, 'Democratic Validation', in John Darby and Roger MacGinty (eds), *Contemporary Peacemaking: Conflict, Peace Processes and Post-War Reconstruction* (New York, 2008), 230–41.

44 For similar definitions, see Helmut K. Anheier, *Civil Society: Measurement, Evaluation, Policy* (London, 2004), 22; John Ehrenberg, *Civil Society: The Critical History of an Idea* (New York, 1999), 235; and Mark E. Warren, *Democracy and Association* (Princeton, 2001), 56–58. For the nexus between civil society and peacebuilding, see Mathijs van Leeuwen, *Partners in Peace: Discourses and Practices of Civil-Society Peacebuilding* (Farnham, 2009).

45 For theory of how civil society creates social capital, see Robert Putnam, *Making Democracy Work: Civic Traditions in Modern Italy* (Princeton, 1993), and Putnam, *Bowling Alone: The Collapse and Revival of American Community* (New York, 2000).

46 J. L. Glanville and E. J. Bienenstock, 'A Typology for Understanding the Connections among Different Forms of Social Capital', *American Behavioral Scientist* 52.11 (2009), 1507–30, and Putnam, *Making Democracy Work*, 167.

47 D. Halpern, *Social Capital* (Cambridge, 2005), 10–11. The need to focus on social capital in groups and communities is also stressed by K. Anderson, 'Community Social Capital', in G. King, K. Lehman Schlozman and N. H. Nie (eds), *The Future of Political Science: 100 Perspectives* (New York, 2009), 42–43.

48 I would like to thank Wendy Wiedenhoft for bringing this distinction to my attention. For this differentiation, see Putnam, *Bowling Alone*, 22–23 and Halpern, *Social Capital*, 19–22. For the Northern Ireland context, see R. Belloni, 'Northern Ireland: Civil Society and the Slow Building of Peace', in T. Paffenholz (ed.), *Civil Society and Peacebuilding: A Critical Assessment* (Boulder, 2010), 105. Wilford, Wilson and Claussen, *Power to the People?*, 197, claim that a significant amount of voluntary activity does cross the sectarian divide and thus helps to build social capital in Northern Ireland.

49 A. Little, *Democracy and Northern Ireland: Beyond the Liberal Paradigm* (New York, 2004), 4, and A. C. Armony, *The Dubious Link: Civic Engagement and Democratization* (Stanford, 2004).

50 J. S. Dryzek, *Deliberative Democracy and beyond: Liberals, Critics, Contestations* (Oxford, 2000), 88.

51 For the importance in civil society of building peace, see P. van Tangeren, M. Brenk, M. Hellema and Juliette Verhoeven (eds), *People Building Peace. II. Successful Stories of Civil Society* (Boulder, 2005). In the Irish context, see A. Edwards and S. Bloomer, 'Transforming the Peace Process from Terrorism to Democratic Politics?', in A. Edwards and S. Bloomer (eds), *Transforming the Peace Process in Northern Ireland: From Terrorism to Democratic Peace* (Dublin, 2008), 6–8.

52 C. Rile Hayward, 'Binding Problems, Boundary Problems: The Trouble with "Democratic Citizenship"', in S. Benhabib, I. Shapiro and D. Petranović (eds), *Identities, Affiliations, and Allegiances* (Cambridge, 2007), 181, and William A. Moloney, Jan W. van Deth and Sigrid Roßteutscher, 'Civic Orientations: Does Associational Type Matter?', *Political Studies* 56.2 (2008), 261–87.

53 S. Roßteutscher, 'Advocate or Reflection? Associations and Political Culture', *Political Studies* 50.3 (2002), 514–28.

54 T. W. G. Van Der Meer and E. J. Van Ingen, 'Schools of Democracy? Disentangling

the Relationship between Civic Participation and Political Action in 17 European Countries', *European Journal of Political Research* 48.2 (2009), 281–308.

55 Wolff, *Ethnic Conflict*, 186–87. For an excellent analysis of the problems of ethnic conflict in this context, see M. Duffy Toft, *The Geography of Ethnic Violence: Identity, Interests, and the Indivisibility of Territory* (Princeton, 2003).

56 Northern Ireland Life and Times Survey 2007, www.ark.ac.uk/nilt/2007/Political_Attitudes/GFAORNI.html (accessed 3 November 2009). Surveys do indicate that more think the GFA has benefited nationalists more than unionists. See Dixon, *Northern Ireland*, 289.

57 Northern Ireland Life and Times Survey 2007, www.ark.ac.uk/nilt/2007/Community_Relations/RLREGO.html (accessed 3 November 2009).

58 Northern Ireland Life and Times Survey 2007, www.ark.ac.uk/nilt/2007/Community_Relations/MIXDMARR.html; www.ark.ac.uk/nilt/2007/Community_Relations/ MIXCWORK.html; www.ark.ac.uk/nilt/2007/Community_Relations/MIXDLIV.html; www.ark.ac.uk/nilt/2007/Community_Relations/MIXDPRIM.html (all accessed 3 November 2009).

59 Catholics (88%) and Protestants (84%) agree with the assertion that mixing will improve relations according to the Northern Ireland Life and Times Survey 2007, www.ark.ac.uk/nilt/2007/Community_Relations/PROTRCMX.html (accessed 3 November 2009). However, when asked to evaluate how far along Northern Ireland is toward realising a civic society (as measured on a seven point scale where 1=definitely not been achieved and 10=the achievement of a civic society), only 3% said conditions justified a 10 and 64% indicated that Northern Ireland deserved a 5 or below. See Northern Ireland Life and Times Survey 2007, www.ark.ac.uk/nilt/2007/Community_Relations/TARGET1.html (accessed 3 November 2009).

60 Northern Ireland Life and Times Survey 2007, www.ark.ac.uk/nilt/2007/Community_Relations/RESPPROT.html; www.ark.ac.uk/nilt/2007/Community_Relations/ RESPCATH.html; www.ark.ac.uk/nilt/2007/Community_Relations/PROTCULT.html; www.ark.ac.uk/nilt/2007/Community_Relations/CATHCULT.html (all accessed 3 November 2009).

61 *Irish Political Studies, Data Yearbook 2010* 25 (2010), 261–62.

62 M. Glasius, D. Lewis and H. Seckinelgin, 'Exploring Civil Society Internationally', in M. Glasius, D. Lewis and H. Seckinelgin (eds), *Exploring Civil Society: Political and Cultural Contexts* (New York, 2004), 6, and C. Welzel, R. Inglehart and F. Deutsch, 'Social Capital, Voluntary Associations and Collective Action: Which Aspects of Social Capital Have the Greatest "Civic" Payoff', *Journal of Civil Society* 2 (2005), 121–46.

63 See P. Mitchell, G. Evans and B. O'Leary, 'Extremist Outbidding in Ethnic Party Systems Is Not Inevitable: Tribune Parties in Northern Ireland', *Political Studies* 57.2 (2009), 397–401. Jonathan Tonge argues that there has been a nationalist convergence among the SDLP and Sinn Féin in 'Nationalist Convergence? The Evolution of Sinn Féin and SDLP Politics', in Edwards and Bloomer (eds), *Transforming the Peace Process in Northern Ireland*, 59–76.

64 T. L. Chapman, 'Unraveling the Ties Between Civic Institutions and Attitudes toward Political Violence', *International Studies Quarterly* 52.3 (2008), 515–32.

65 Cochrane and Dunn, *People Power?*, 173. J. Keane argues that violence is the great antagonist to civil society in *Civil Society: Old Images, New Visions* (Stanford, 1998), 141.

66 C. A. Reilly, *Peacebuilding in Guatemala and Northern Ireland* (New York, 2009), 99 and N. Southern, 'After Conflict: Religion and Peacebuilding in West Belfast', *Irish Studies in International Affairs* 20 (2009), 83–101.

67 W. Crotty, 'The Catholic Church in Ireland and Northern Ireland: Nationalism, Identity, and Opposition', in P. C. Manuel, L. C. Reardon and C. Wilcox (eds), *The*

Catholic Church and the Nation-State: Comparative Perspectives (Washington, DC, 2006), 118.

68 For a further analysis of the role of the Civic Fora, see Cochrane and Dunn, *People Power?*, 180–81.

69 For the role of the churches in promoting civil society and peace in Northern Ireland, see D. Bacon, *Communities, Churches and Social Capital in Northern Ireland* (Coleraine, 2003); G. Ganiel and P. Dixon, 'Religion, Pragmatic Fundamentalism and the Transformation of the Northern Ireland Conflict', *Journal of Peace Research* 45.3 (2008), 419–36; M. Power, *From Ecumenism to Community Relations: Inter-Church Relationships in Northern Ireland 1980–2005* (Dublin, 2007); and R. Wells, *People Behind the Peace: Community and Reconciliation in Northern Ireland* (Grand Rapids, MI, 1999).

70 This argument is made in F. Herreros and H. Criado, 'The State and the Development of Trust', *International Political Science Review* 29.1 (2008), 53–71, and M. Freitag and M. Bühlman, 'Crafting Trust: The Role of Political Institutions in a Comparative Perspective', *Comparative Political Studies* 42.12 (2009), 1537–66.

71 R. Inglehart, 'The Renaissance of Political Culture', *American Political Science Review* 82.4 (1988), 1211–15, and P. Sztompka, 'Trust, Distrust and Two Paradoxes of Democracy', *European Journal of Social Theory* 1.1 (1998), 19–32.

72 S. Byrne, C. Thiessen, E. Fissuh, C. Irwin and M. Hawranik, 'Economic Assistance, Development and Peacebuilding: The Role of IFI and EU Peace II Fund in Northern Ireland', *Civil Wars* 10.2 (2008), 120.

73 This formulation of linking the public and elites differs from earlier efforts at explaining the peace process in Northern Ireland. See Hancock, 'The Northern Irish Peace Process', 225–31.

74 M. O'Callaghan, 'Genealogies of Partition: History, History-Writing and the "Troubles" in Ireland', *Critical Review of International Social and Political Philosophy* 9.4 (2006), 619–34.

4

The Contribution of Integrated Schools to Peacebuilding in Northern Ireland[1]

Claire McGlynn

This essay will explore the contribution of integrated (mixed Catholic and Protestant) schools to peacebuilding in Northern Ireland and it will highlight some of the challenges ahead in an increasingly diverse society with a legacy of conflict. It draws on and is illustrated by exemplars from the extensive data that I have gathered over more than ten years. The essay will focus on three particular areas – the long-term impact of attending an integrated school, variation in leadership approaches to integration within the schools and emergent models of good practice in response to the cultural diversity of students. A number of theoretical perspectives will be brought to bear upon the data, including social identity theory and political science perspectives on multiculturalism. I will argue that integrated education provides a unique opportunity, in a still segregated society, for children and young people to learn from each other, enjoy sustained engagement and interaction with other perspectives, develop empathy and build long-term friendships across the divide. At the same time, I will question whether the current approaches to integrated education hold equal possibilities for peacebuilding.

The context for peacebuilding through education

In divided societies like Northern Ireland, emerging from a period of intense community violence, the role of education in peacebuilding is complex and needs to be carefully contextualised not least historically, politically and socially. Looking first at history we see that prior to partition in 1922, the six counties of Northern Ireland shared a general Irish education system based on the National School system. The Irish government had attempted to provide free elementary education for Protestant and Catholic pupils in jointly managed schools, but by the end of the nineteenth century a struggle for control of education by the main churches resulted in predominantly denominational schools.[2] The newly emergent Northern Irish State inherited this denominational system of schooling. The situation was further exacerbated when many Catholic schools refused to recognise the authority of the Minister of Education, resulting in lack of Catholic representation on the Lynn educational policy committees. Ministry-run schools received 100 per cent grants for capital costs and maintenance, but catered exclusively for Protestants. Schools choosing to remain independent received only limited financial assistance and were called 'voluntary' schools.[3] In the 1920s and 1930s, bitter controversies raged over education and resulted not only in perpetuating separate schooling, but in giving the churches a more powerful voice in their representation in school management. The 1947 Education Act (Northern Ireland)[4] and the 1967 Amendment Act (Northern Ireland)[5] affected many aspects of funding, curriculum and resource provision. When voluntary Catholic schools were offered 85 per cent (raised to 100 per cent in 1991) capital costs and 100 per cent maintenance costs in the 1977 Education Act (Northern Ireland),[6] many took on 'maintained' status. Although the funding issue has been largely resolved, the religious divide remains.[7] Education continues to be separate with most children either attending Catholic maintained schools or *de facto* Protestant-controlled schools.

Political progress towards a more peaceful and democratic society in Northern Ireland has been slow and at times extremely fragile. Indeed, some commentators such as Gallagher[8] have observed that the Good Friday Agreement of 1998, the settlement that heralded the end of the recent thirty-year conflict, may have actually served to institutionalise sectarianism, resulting in greater political and social segregation due to its very careful attention to acknowledging the differences and demands of the conflicting groups. The 'peace process' has been painstaking, with political partiality characterising decision making on many key social issues, including education particularly with regards to the abolition of academic selection, with Republicans largely supportive and Unionists opposed. The last part of the Good Friday Agreement, the devolution of policing and justice powers to the Northern Ireland Assembly through the Hillsborough Agreement, finally took place in the spring of 2010, rescuing power sharing from a potential collapse.

Identification as 'Catholic' or 'Protestant', understood as a complex amalgam of national (Irish or British), religious, political (Nationalist or Unionist) and cultural aspects, remains the basis of the ongoing divide in Northern Ireland. This is most clearly seen in community interface areas, where it has been claimed that experiences of conflict and marginalisation persist for many children and young people, who know all too well the often violent consequences of straying out of their community area and whose sectarian reality is less than peaceful.[9] Even for those living elsewhere there remain many challenges at a social level to break down boundaries between members of the Catholic and Protestant communities who continue for the main part to live, work and play separately. Whilst for the majority of the population violence has receded, it is not clear whether long-term peace can be sustained through a largely parallel existence between the two identity groups.

In addition, the arrival of minority group members, particularly from newly acceded eastern European countries, brings a new national, cultural and linguistic diversity to many classrooms. It is only in the last few years that children with first languages other than English have arrived in Northern Irish schools. As the most recent population census was conducted in 2001,[10] these new arrivals do not feature in the statistics but they have certainly made an impression in schools which previously only had English-speaking pupils. In most schools, English-language learners represent approximately 2–3% of the school population, although in some areas the number may be higher due to greater availability of jobs for migrant workers. According to the 2001 census, 40.26% of the Northern Ireland population was Catholic, 45.57% was Protestant, 0.3% other religions and 13.88% of no religion. By contrast, minority ethnic groups constitute only 0.85% of Northern Ireland's 2001 population, one of the smallest ethnic minority populations in the European Union. Whilst many see this diversity as enriching, others feel threatened and there has been a proportionate growth in societal race hate crime. The total number of racial incidents,[11] for example, increased from 226 in 2002/3 to 990 in 2008/9. After a particularly odious series of race hate attacks in June 2009, more than one hundred members of the Romanian Roma community left Belfast.

This, then, is the Northern Ireland context, a society still divided by religion, sectarianism and needing to respond to the legacy of conflict, but also a society facing the challenges of incoming populations and new forms of racism. One hopeful development for peacebuilding is the emergence of integrated education which, on a daily basis, brings together in the classroom children who are more usually educated separately in Catholic and de facto Protestant schools. In such a way it has been hoped that children and young people not only learn to respect the unknown 'other' but also make and sustain friendships across the divide.

Integrated education in Northern Ireland

Integrated education was established in Northern Ireland with the opening of the first planned integrated post-primary school by parents in 1981. A further 59 primary and post-primary schools have since been established either by parent groups or by parental ballot.[12] Integrated education is defined as the education together, in equal numbers, of Catholic and Protestant children, who are more usually educated separately, providing an opportunity for them to develop respect and understanding for alternative cultures and perspectives. Under the 1989 Education Reform (Northern Ireland) Order[13] the government has a duty to meet the needs of parents requesting integrated education, but only 20,000 children (six per cent of all pupils) attend integrated schools (either planned-integrated or controlled-Protestant schools that have transformed to integrated status).

What, then, is the contribution of integrated education to peacebuilding in Northern Ireland? Research evidence to date suggests that integrated

education may impact positively on identity, outgroup attitudes and forgiveness, with potential to heal division[14] and promote a less sectarian outlook,[15]
suggesting that integrated education may provide a valuable middle ground
where Catholic and Protestant children can get to know each other and
challenge the prevalent stereotypes. However, it would also appear that the
issues of religion and politics important to such a process are avoided in
some integrated schools.[16] I now focus on my three main areas of research
into integrated education – the long-term impact, leadership approaches and
emergent models of good practice and consider their implications for peacebuilding.

Long-term impact

I used a retrospective approach, including quantitative and qualitative
methodologies, with a sample of 159 former pupils of the first two integrated
post-primary schools to explore the long-term impact of integrated education
on respect for diversity, friendships and social identity.[17] This project was my
doctoral research and was also part of a large-scale review of integrated education undertaken by Queen's University, Belfast and the University of Ulster,
funded by the Nuffield Foundation. Whilst integrated education was seen as
important with regards to socialisation, maturation and family were considered to be more significant factors, in line with theories of political socialisation.[18] The former pupils most impacted by integrated education appeared,
not surprisingly, to be those who had least contact with the 'other' group prior
to integrated schooling.

The impact of this contact has important implications for peacebuilding. Of
the 159 past pupils sampled, 93% felt that integrated education had impacted
positively on their lives by increasing their respect for diversity, that is, for
the Catholic or Protestant 'other'. Also, by enabling them to feel more secure
in mixed educational and/or working environments, integrated education
endowed former students with the skills to feel comfortable with difference
which potentially has economic benefits with regards to productivity, as well
as for improving the inter-community relations necessary for peacebuilding.
Indeed, for some the transition to the workplace was difficult when colleagues
failed to be as open-minded as their friends at integrated school had been.

Education for peace was delivered in two ways, through the planned
formal curriculum, which offered the opportunity to express opinions
and discuss traumatic events and also through the informal daily encounters which combined to promote effective integration. This is in contrast to
a common culture of avoidance of divisive issues relating to religion and
identity in Northern Ireland. At the time the past pupils attended integrated
school, schools were largely seen as 'oases' where the Troubles were left at the
school gates. By contrast, in the two schools studied former students reported

that teachers facilitated debates and discussions around the violent events that were occurring, rather than teach in a social vacuum. This resulted in a challenge to stereotypes and sectarianism that developed the skills of multiple perspectivity so crucial to peacebuilding. This was indicated by student comments such as, 'You listen to others' and '[You are] taught to see both sides of the argument'.

For the former pupils in the study, inter-community connectivity was significantly enhanced. They reported that attending an integrated school increased their friendships with the 'other' group, from 41% prior to attending integrated school to 67% afterwards. This is impressive when you consider the difficulties of continuing mixed friendships in a segregated society. Previous research on short-term cross-community projects has indicated that friend-ships often are not maintained because of the difficulties encountered when participants return to their segregated communities.[19] My study clearly indicated that in many cases integration not only encourages the mainte-nance of these friendships in the long term but also extends to the choice of partners, as more than half of the past pupils with a partner had one from a different background to themselves. In comparison, data from the Northern Ireland Life and Times Survey (NILT)[20] at the time indicated that only eight per cent of marriages in Northern Ireland were inter-community. The choice of life partners and the sustainability of inter-community friendships indicates an important way in which integrated education may lead to breaking down the persistent barriers between Catholics and Protestants that endanger peacebuilding.

In a divided society where identity as Catholic or Protestant is a defining characteristic, opponents of integrated education have claimed that it 'dilutes' social identity and creates individuals who lose their group identity. I was thus particularly interested to see what the past pupils could tell me about the impact of integrated education on self-perceptions of identity. Of the survey respondents, 63 per cent reported no change in their social identity as Catholic or Protestant, but considered themselves to have become more tolerant as a result of attending an integrated school. Of respondents, 33 per cent reported that their identity had changed and they considered this to be for the better, as they had more respect for others. While there was evidence that self-perceptions of identity had been challenged, some suggested that their sense of social identity had been strengthened, others that it had been diminished and for others again that it had been transformed. A number of past pupils suggested that rather than affirming or disaffirming identity, integrated education encouraged exploration and allowed for the emergence of a sense of self. For example, past pupils reported:

> I am less Roman Catholic than previously ... unless the opportunity to think rationally had been presented I would not have been able to classify myself accurately.

[I am] more a Protestant – able to stand up to people.

I think some people think I'm less Catholic because I went to an integrated school but I'm not – I'm the same as them …

School A is not set up to make you less Catholic or Protestant but to be yourself.

I would like to see a box 'None of your damn business!'

These divergent outcomes may be significant with regards to peace-building – could it be that students who attend Catholic or de facto Protestant schools are ascribed a social identity, whereas those who attend an integrated school have more autonomy to explore their identity and the opportunity to define themselves? Further investigation by both longitudinal and compara-tive research is needed to see if this hypothesis holds true.

Former pupils were also asked about the impact of integrated education on religious and political identity. Religious identity appeared unaffected, as many did not have strong beliefs prior to attending integrated schools. There was also little evident impact on political identity for the majority of respond-ents who were disinterested in, and disaffected from, local politics. Both of these findings indicate that the former students may have been growing up in homes that may be less polarised and more liberal than others with regards to the divide. However, in the context of Northern Ireland, where membership of social groups is generally non-transferable, it was significant to note the emergence of a new identity form among past-integrated pupils – what they called an 'integrated identity', which may be significant for peacebuilding as it constitutes a possible social bond between opposing groups. The majority of former students reported they had acquired an integrated identity in addition to their religious social identity. They defined integrated identity in terms of the shared attributes of broadmindedness, understanding and tolerance:

Integrated means to be broadminded and understanding.

More tolerant people, better listeners.

Integrated schools churn out people with a particular identity: better informed, more rounded, probably more positive.

Better … for mixing in the real working world.

[I am] proud of [my] integrated identity.

As such, integrated education appears to offer these former pupils the opportunity to explore a wider choice of identities than those usually claimed in Northern Ireland. It may encourage young people to take an active and reflective part in discovering aspects of their own ethnic and personal identi-fication, and help to shift the emphasis away from traditional group aspects towards more individual components of identity.

Implications of long-term impact for peacebuilding

Social Identity Theory (SIT)[21] and Self-Categorisation Theory (SCT)[22] have been used to explore the relationship between identity and conflict. SIT maintains that aspects of self are derived from the social categories to which one perceives oneself to belong. Indeed, there is research evidence to indicate that the conflict in Northern Ireland has been both perpetuated and inflamed by social identification[23] and personal investment in group membership. However, SIT has been criticised for neglecting the emotional dimension of conflict, an aspect recognised by Weinreich[24] who describes the 'emotionally charged' combination of national and religious identity in Northern Ireland. SCT recognises the importance of social group membership and provides an understanding of how social identity extends into the private self, which is a strong characteristic of Northern Ireland where people tend to perceive themselves as group members rather than as possessing individual identity components.

The data I collected from the former pupils of the two integrated schools indicates that integrated schooling can impact on social identity in a variety of ways, but for all pupils it appears to allow for exploration and adaptation of self-perceptions of identity. As students are exposed to multiple perspectives and narratives that they would not otherwise encounter, their sense of group membership is challenged. In this way we see identity construction as a more fluid process, constantly in flux and open to modification as a result of the human interaction that occurs in the integrated school. We also see evidence of the former students making choices about how they portray themselves, with some refusing to be classified by the salient categories. Whilst the majority of past pupils continue to ascribe to the traditional memberships of the Catholic and Protestant groups, these affiliations have also been modified to a more tolerant position that allows for other points of view.

In addition, the former students have adopted an additional form of social identification, their 'integrated identity' which embraces the two main conflicting groups in a broader identity category. Gaertner, Dovidio, Anastasio, Bachevan and Rust[25] have identified a superordinate recategorisation as the main strategy for effective intergroup contact. This is an interesting finding with relation to the two integrated schools in the study, not least as both schools appeared to make significant efforts to reflect both Catholic and Protestant as important group categories. Nonetheless, all former students referred to this overarching identity category and generally spoke of it with considerable pride. Thus, whilst the schools did not deliberately set out to generate a new identity form, for the past pupils this identity form emerged from their experiences at an integrated school and, possibly more importantly, was sustained despite experiences in the segregated 'real' world outside of school.

The past-pupil study indicates a number of important findings with regards to the potential of integrated education for peacebuilding. First, it appears to increase respect for diverse others. Second, it helps increase and sustain over time the number of inter-community friendships and it may impact positively on choosing a partner from across the divide. Third, it seems to offer the chance to determine rather than to merely inherit social identification and, connected with this, it allows students to see themselves as connected via an 'integrated' identity form that can incorporate both Catholic and Protestant identities. Taking these three findings into account, the study would appear to support the proposition that integrated education can provide an important middle ground in a divided society.

Leadership approaches

Having gained some insight into the long-term impact of integrated education on former pupils, I became interested in the approaches that principals in integrated schools take to integration and hence the impact that different approaches might have on peacebuilding opportunities. A passive approach to integration had been observed in a review of integrated education practice,[26] although reactive and pro-active models of integration were also noted. The difference here is between passive approaches that allow integration to occur 'naturally', reactive approaches that respond to events only when and if they occur (such as sectarian bullying) and pro-active approaches that include planned curriculum activities to address issues of religion, politics and identity in a bid to increase understanding. In a pilot study of leadership in several integrated schools[27] I noted that some principals adopt liberal approaches to multicultural education, that is, they tend to emphasise similarity rather than difference between Catholic and Protestant pupils.

To explore this further I undertook a qualitative study, funded by the International Fund for Ireland (IFI), of 52 integrated school principals. Semi-structured interviews were conducted with 33 principals of planned- and 19 principals of transformed-integrated schools. Interviews sought to determine what principals understand by integration and to explore their leadership visions. Data were analysed using qualitative methods, whereby units of relevant meanings were clustered and common themes were determined before themes general and unique to all interviews were identified.[28] There are two provisos to the findings from this data. First, it should be noted that the breadth and depth of response to questions regarding vision and practice of integration varied greatly between principals, indicating a variation in the degree of importance allocated to this aspect of school function. Second, it was apparent that some principals were not satisfied with their current approach to integration and wished to develop it further. However, distinctive categories of approach to integration, identified by the emphasis placed on cultural difference or similarity and/or willingness to tackle inequalities, emerged from the data. Principals' approaches to integration constituted five main categories, namely liberal, plural, critical, liberal/plural and liberal/

critical, of which two categories were further self-divided. Each of these will be considered in turn and illustrated by quotations from the principals.

Liberal integration

Eighteen principals described approaches to integration that can be categorised as liberal, that is, where the emphasis is placed on cultural commonality rather than difference, reflecting the liberal position that individuals from diverse groups share a natural equality and common humanity and endorsing the joint ideals of liberty and equality. However, the approaches reported can be further divided into *liberal pro-active* where the emphasis on commonality is deliberate (nine principals) and *liberal passive* where it is coincidental (nine principals).

The *liberal pro-active* approach is typified by the following comments: 'Integration is everyone working together, all classes and all creeds. It should be all one family under the one sky. Respect is the core value.' In this principal's school there was active work on developing conflict-resolution skills, including a peer-mediation programme. An intentional focus on similarity was reflected by other pro-active liberal principals, for example: 'Integration here is not too much in your face. It is about more than the things that divide us. A balanced celebration of events is difficult ... Integration features through all levels in the school.' Such comments reflected a conscious effort to find common ground ('we are all human first and foremost') but also indicated a reluctance to focus on difference. Instead, there was a desire to build a united school community: 'We see integration as being welcoming, friendly and serving the wider community. It is about breaking down suspicions ... we are seeking to encourage the sense of community within the school.'

By contrast, the *liberal passive* approach was characterised by a belief that integration can happen 'naturally'. Whilst integration was perceived as a child-friendly and welcoming concept there was some evidence of the avoidance of divisive issues ('Do we look at symbols and emblems? No!') and there was an acknowledgement that it is a challenge to keep integration to the fore. A typical comment illustrates that integration is not the primary purpose: 'Our core business is the education of children. We would love to have more time on the integrated ethos but it is a bit of a luxury being able to do that.' For this principal, integration is about the day-to-day contact with Catholics and Protestants that happens organically in the school. No particular further leadership or curricular emphasis is required.

Plural integration

A pluralist approach to integration that embraces the celebration of diversity, history and cultural heritage was described by 16 principals. However, these principals do not stress any challenge to bias to discrimination, that is, a critical perspective is absent. The plural approach noted can be further sub-divided into *plural inclusive*, where the focus was on celebrating all aspects of difference (13 principals) and *plural limited*, where although world religions and ethnic minority groups were recognised, references to Catholic/Protestant differences were actively avoided (3 principals).

Principals reflecting a *plural inclusive* approach articulated a clear focus on all forms of cultural and religious difference: 'We recognize differences and encourage children to celebrate these differences. Everything should be out in the open – for discussion. We celebrate all religions.' This approach to integration is clearly an intrinsic part of school development planning and was reflected in the formal and informal curricula. The celebration of cultural tradition and the expression of cultural identity is a priority: 'We celebrate cultural diversity ... you should be proud of who you are and what you believe in but have respect for others' cultures.'

By contrast, three principals described an approach to integration that was *plural limited* in that overt references to Catholic/Protestant differences were avoided although recognition was given to other diverse groups. These principals reported a range of curricular and other activities that celebrate 'world religions and culture, for example, Ramadan'. Whilst attempts were made to celebrate some traditions, these principals did not focus on denominational, cultural or political differences between Catholic and Protestant pupils. Thus, the 'exotic' is worthy of celebration but that which is at the root of the conflict is largely ignored.

Critical integration

A small number (four) of principals exhibited a *critical* approach to integration. This was characterised not only by a policy of recognising and celebrating all differences, both denominational and other, but also by a desire to tackle social injustice:

> While we recognize and celebrate difference, we appreciate that school is not a neutral haven. Issues of prejudice must be addressed. We are inclusive in all respects ... we address the needs of all faiths and we are challenged by supporting the needs of our ethnic minority pupils.

These principals described a range of initiatives that promoted the celebration of difference, including the existence of integration committees and integration development plans; whole-school celebration of the Catholic sacraments of confession, communion and confirmation; the teaching of world faiths; visits to Christian and non-Christian places of worship and displays of cultural symbols and emblems. What distinguishes this approach from the *plural inclusive* one, however, is an accompanying emphasis on challenging inequality, bias and discrimination: 'School should be different. We are tackling controversial issues and conflict resolution. You need to be comfortable with difference. This is the challenge of an increasingly multicultural society. We have to confront racist attacks.' Principals also reported human rights and anti-bullying initiatives as central to their *critical* practice of integrated education. This approach recognises that diversity must be considered alongside issues of social justice.

Liberal/plural integration

An approach that incorporates aspects of both *liberal* and *plural* models of integration was reported by six principals. Whilst cultural difference was acknowledged, commonality and equality were also stressed: 'Integration is primarily about equal opportunity, all are welcome. School is safe and child-centred. All children are special and unique – we value and celebrate difference and promote tolerance and respect.'

While offering pupils 'the freedom to be different', the *liberal/plural* approach attempts to construct an inclusive school community where '*children and staff feel valued*'. The inclusion of diverse groups pivots on the liberal principle of equality: 'Children come first. Everyone is welcome and all are treated with respect ... all children are educated together. Children are treated equally. Our school tries to instill an attitude of respect.' As such, the *liberal/plural* approach promotes a model of integration that reconciles cultural difference within the concept of a common school community, an attempt at 'unity through diversity'.

Liberal/critical integration

The *liberal/critical* approach to integration reported by eight principals also seeks common ground between diverse groups. Whilst overtly acknowledging commonality, this approach also commits to challenging injustice such as sectarianism and racism head on:

> Integration is about a shared community open to everyone. An all inclusive school should be at the heart of a shared community. Integration should drive all areas and the teaching should reflect this. Children will be looking at contentious issues ... we have a constant awareness of anti-bias, anti-bullying and conflict resolution.

Another principal, whilst clearly in favour of seeking commonality, views initiatives on difference and injustice as a route to promoting equality:

> The ideal is no awareness of Protestant or Catholic. We have a firm discipline policy on sectarianism ... we tackle sectarian abuse. Integration is promoted through assemblies – we take a compassionate view of those in need, for example, tsunami victims and children in need.

The data indicates that this *liberal/critical* group of principals actively reflected on how they might draw together an eclectic school community comprised of Catholics, Protestants, those of other faiths and no faith, boys, girls, all abilities, social classes and ethnic backgrounds. Pro-active anti-bias and anti-prejudice work was seen as vital. This model demonstrates an attempt to balance unity and diversity, whilst clearly also challenging injustice and discrimination.

Implications of approaches for peacebuilding

Thus, within even a small education sector of sixty schools deliberately established to educate Catholic and Protestant children together, we see that there are a number of quite different approaches to dealing with cultural diversity. Whilst such a typology of approaches may provide us with a tool for categorising approaches to educational efforts, we need also to consider the potential implications of this variation for peacebuilding. To do so I will draw on the theoretical literature around multiculturalism and multicultural education.

A central issue is the necessity to strike a balance between respecting group and individual rights, what Reich[29] calls navigating between the 'pluribus' and the 'unum'. Kincheloe and Steinberg[30] warn that *liberal* approaches may promote cultural invisibility and fail to challenge prejudice and injustice towards minority groups. However, *liberal pro-active* endorsement of commonality, liberty and equality might also help to construct the common ground that is sorely needed to build peace between conflicting communities. The weaker *liberal passive* model, also reported in this study, may, at best, leave the building of such common ground to chance. More *plural* approaches that purely advocate the celebration of diversity also have their imitations. It is difficult to defend a *plural limited* model that, whilst willing to recognise more 'exotic' minorities, appears to deny recognition to the two majority groups, Catholics and Protestants. Avoidance of the major divide is not helpful to peacebuilding. Although the *plural inclusive* approach may be more easily supported due to its willingness to acknowledge and celebrate all forms of diversity, without a critical edge it appears to promise equality it cannot deliver. *Plural* approaches also risk the reification of difference by presenting group identities as homogeneous and fixed. This is also a difficulty for *critical* approaches, which, whilst challenging hegemonic culture, may also unintentionally reinforce group boundaries. To build peace one is primarily looking to break down, rather than to reinforce, the barriers between groups and the strategies for so doing must be carefully thought through.

Sen[31] resists over-simplistic categorisation of people purely on the basis of their religion or culture. He argues for the autonomy of the individual in celebrating whichever aspects of their culture that they choose. Only 2 of the 52 principals interviewed reported that the development of pupil autonomy was a central aspect of their approach to integration. This does not imply that they believe that education cannot contribute to this, but rather that they tend to prioritise the bringing together of groups of children, that is, the group aspects. Niens and Cairns[32] suggest that the contact hypothesis[33] has been an unspoken guiding principle behind integrated education. However, developments of the contact hypothesis[34] indicate the importance of group salience in the process of prejudice reduction. This risks reifying difference. Whereas contact theory foregrounds difference, Sen's approach challenges our tendency to reduce difference to the lowest common denominator. Indeed, to promote a culture of peace he advocates the development of understanding of the pluralities of human identity.[35] Davies[36] warns of the vulnerability of singular identities that can be mobilised for conflict, proposing that 'Efforts to "preserve" or "celebrate" distinct cultures ... may be counterproductive: it would be better to acknowledge hybridity as a positive identity.'

Identity may be a more helpful construct to us than the much-contested 'culture', not least because in Northern Ireland identity as a 'Catholic' or 'Protestant' can be understood as a complex amalgam of religious, political, social and ethnic aspects. We must also recognise that identities are complex and continually in flux. It is difficult, however, to imagine how a recognition of identity hybridity might be reflected in classroom practice whilst also effectively tackling bias, when the latter requires a recognition of group distinctiveness. Whereas Reich[37] outlines a theory of liberal multicultural education that promotes the development of self-reflective individuals who are empowered to make autonomous decisions about shaping their own lives, his model lacks the critical edge needed to counteract sectarianism and racism. The *liberal/critical* approach reported here represents an attempt to unify, whilst also proactively challenging prejudice and injustice. An extension of this *liberal/critical* model that acknowledges hybridity as a positive identity and that promotes the development of more autonomous individuals may be a more useful policy direction for peacebuilding. In conflicted societies like Northern Ireland, education needs to affirm and protect minority group members, but also to tackle the legacy of conflict by challenging stereotypes, engaging with other perspectives and reducing prejudice.

We see here that multiculturalism and multicultural education can provide a useful frame for analysis of integrated education policy and practice. One thing must be remembered: the socialising role of schools is limited and it remains to be seen whether educational initiatives such as integrated education can overcome the 'socializing tyranny of categorization'.[38] The motto 'Ut sint unum' (together we are one) of the first integrated school in Northern Ireland, Lagan College, is a powerful rallying call to integration and cultural interaction: its translation into practice is an ongoing challenge when the needs of individuals and groups must be negotiated, discrimination must be tackled and peace must be built. What I am suggesting is that to maximise the possibilities for developing positive community relations and peacebuilding, those involved in integrated education need to think carefully about the approach that they take, lest they inadvertently reinforce the divisions they seek to challenge. Rather than to present identity – Catholic, Protestant or other – as a 'reality', education should encourage children and young people to understand identity as a complex social construct that evolves rather than is inherited, that can be distinctive as well as hybrid and to see how it can be manipulated for conflict. Integrated education also offers great opportunity to challenge injustice, whether sectarian, racist or other. A thoughtful leadership approach that bridges liberal/critical models may provide the best possibilities for supporting peacebuilding through education.

Emergent models of good practice

Whilst further research into the approaches outlined above is currently in progress, my attention has also been drawn to classroom practice with regards to response to integration. How can what goes on at the classroom level, with regards to responding to cultural diversity, support peacebuilding? I identified eight case-study schools from a total of sixty-two schools, not all formally integrated, that were participating in the 'Integrating Education' development project (led by the Northern Ireland Council for Integration[39] and funded by the International Fund for Ireland). Data was collected by the author in eight of the project schools, of which four were primary (one Catholic, one planned integrated and two transformed integrated) and four were post-primary (one Protestant, one Catholic, one planned integrated and one transformed integrated).

Semi-structured interviews were conducted in each school with principals, classroom teachers, support staff, including classroom assistants and focus groups of children. Those interviewed were selected by school principals on the basis that they had been involved in integration initiatives. Themes explored include identifying responses to cultural diversity, how cultural integration is promoted, strengths and challenges of current initiatives, teacher development, addressing cultural difference and evaluation. The limitations of this research relate mainly to the selection of the case-study schools, that is, they were not selected on the basis of empirical evidence that they are more effective, rather the schools were identified as developing good practice. It was my intention to illuminate and explore practice by considering the multiple perspectives of those individuals involved and from this to draw out some characteristics of good practice. The context of each case-study school is described more fully, as are the findings, in a journal article.[40] Here I present a brief summary of the two main themes to emerge from the data, namely attitudes to diversity and integration strategies.

Attitudes to diversity

Openness to diversity (both in terms of personal qualities, relationships and school policy) was evident in the discourses of both staff and students in the case-study schools, which appear keen to embrace all children without assimilation ('I don't want to airbrush their culture' [principal]). There is a strong sense that Northern Ireland is moving on ('5 or 10 years ago it would have orange [Protestant] and green [Catholic]. Now it is orange, green, Portuguese, Lithuanian, Polish, the whole gambit of what is out there' [teacher]) and that these developments should be reflected in school life.

The advent of English language learners has been a marked feature of Northern Irish schools in recent years. Responses such as translation provision, first-language clubs, EAL resources, after school activities and English language courses characterise their openness to diversity. Learning how best to respond to need is acknowledged as an ongoing process. The case-study schools, however, report being unafraid to challenge a xenophobic 'they are coming over here and taking our jobs' attitude by directly expressing their welcome for new migrants. Openness to diversity is enhanced by the conviction that interaction with children from diverse cultural backgrounds provides a valuable opportunity to learn from each other, both for the pupils and for the adults involved.

To be open to learning from cultural difference requires a willingness both to mix and to challenge previous assumptions. Some adults report surprise at the ease with which students mix. As a result of their experiences, the study school teachers exhort other teachers to embrace diversity. For those involved, exposure to cultural diversity is a welcome learning curve. However, the extent to which schools draw attention to cultural difference varies. Children appear largely unconcerned about the identity categories (Catholic/Protestant) that concern adults.[41] The latter often seek ways to balance cultural difference and similarity, for example: 'We aim to enable each child to develop a positive self identity and then a positive view of his/her own culture as well as being tolerant and respectful towards others from a different belief. So it would be difference and similarities' (principal).

Integration strategies

Openness to diversity and a willingness to learn from other perspectives has lead to a range of strategies (evident at the levels of policy, curriculum and relationships) in each of the case-study schools, all designed to maximise the opportunities available for engagement with cultural diversity. Teachers reported the need to work with adults before contentious issues such as culture and identity can be addressed in the classroom ('if adults haven't actually learnt how to resolve their difficulties then they can't act as role models for children'). Diversity training with families is also considered important, particularly by the integrated schools.

A very wide range of teaching and learning strategies to promote cultural integration was reported. Strategies include circle time ('It is where people are appreciated for their opinions and their beliefs'), assemblies, worry-box questions and the celebration of diverse festivals such as Chinese New Year. The importance of allowing children to pursue their interests by asking questions about other cultures is recognised by the teachers. At the level of the taught curriculum, the study schools are discovering the confidence to learn from diverse students and teachers describe opportunities for mutual enrichment and understanding that have arisen in curriculum activities, such as citizenship:

> [The Costa Rican pupil] was able ... to talk about racism and attitudes to
> people coming in from other countries as some of the girls can be quite
> verbose about 'people coming in, taking work' that type of thing ... and
> then she went on to explain to the girls even though it wasn't about

Catholic/Protestant they do not like the people from the neighbouring country. (teacher)

Elsewhere the content of the curriculum is seen as crucial to developing cultural integration, including the balancing of perspectives. Equal importance is accorded to the mode of delivery of the curriculum with the widespread use of active learning strategies and teaching and assessment strategies that raise pupil self-esteem, promote collaboration and improve achievement.

Implications of practice for peacebuilding

The case-study schools are involved in maximising the opportunities for Catholics, Protestants and others to mix. However, they go beyond this and actively encourage critical engagement with diversity on the parts of both adults and children. This requires movement outside of comfort zones in order to allow cultural exchange to take place and for alternative perspectives to be explored, both valuable and necessary steps for peacebuilding. To help us evaluate the data further we will now consider Parekh,[42] who has re-conceptualised the policy doctrine of multiculturalism as a broader perspective on human life. He provides us with three central insights, first that human beings are culturally embedded, second that whilst cultural diversity is both desirable and a reality, dialogue between cultures is mutually beneficial and third that cultures are internally plural. In a divided society like Northern Ireland, these insights can help us to evaluate classroom activities designed to lead to inter-community understanding and peacebuilding.

The embracement of cultural diversity by the study schools implies an acknowledgement that human beings are culturally embedded, at least in as much as these schools actively recognise distinct groups and their needs, for example in preparation for the Catholic sacraments. There is evidence also of care taken to affirm children's identity by celebrating first languages, cultural symbols, traditions and festivals. This indicates that the study schools recognise the importance that affiliation to group identity and practices signifies for people in Northern Ireland. However, the schools go beyond this by actively promoting intercultural interaction that can promote better relations between Catholics and Protestants. A willingness to explore other cultures is evident, demonstrating a desire for embracing the cultural interrogation and widening of horizons recommended by Parekh. The schools appear to construct, both at a whole-school and at an individual classroom level, environments that allow intercultural encounters to flourish, with reported benefits for both children and adults. To actively encounter the 'other' and explore his/her perspective in the safety of the classroom is an important way of challenging the stereotypes that can perpetuate division and conflict. Whilst the teachers view facilitating intercultural encounters as sometimes requiring personal discomfort, once they have begun they are keen to encourage other teachers to do likewise.

Although the study schools clearly value and acknowledge cultural diversity and allow for the expansion of horizons of thought, some teachers are uncomfortable with bringing attention to difference and this is potentially problematic, revealing a tension between the competing pressures of cultural recognition and assimilation. Interestingly, the children pay little attention to identity categories – although they can recognise these categories they appear to apply others, such as personal attributes, more readily. There are concerns expressed by the adults that they might expose or make a fetish of difference but also an acknowledgment that different cultural backgrounds can be a rich educational resource. It is clear that teachers need further training and support to enable them fully to engage with these issues in the classroom.

However, there is little reflection in the case-study school data of Parekh's third aspect, that is, that a wide variety of hybrid and hyphenated identities and lifestyles need also to be accommodated. Whilst there is evidence of recognition of distinct cultural identities, there is little to suggest that these schools are encouraging understandings of identity as heterogeneous. This study illuminates some characteristics of perceived good practice with regard to response to cultural diversity. Whilst the practices emerging appear to fit well with Parekh's view of multiculturalism, both in terms of embracement of diversity and promotion of intercultural dialogue, there is a clear need to explore how schools in Northern Ireland might also challenge the presentation of identity as fixed and homogeneous, an understanding that can perpetuate conflict. To build peace, educators must seek ways of challenging the salient social categories of Catholic and Protestant and lead their pupils to reflect on the multiplicity of identity forms in an increasingly multicultural society.

Some conclusions about integrated education

Inevitably, any review of research reveals more about what we do not know than about that which we do and this essay does not fare any differently in that respect. However, we do find a picture emerging of a form of education that provides a daily opportunity for children and young people, growing up in a divided society, to become friends and to learn about other perspectives. We have also seen that it can also allow young people to explore their identity, gain an understanding of other identities and to develop a shared identity. For the past pupils studied, integrated education enabled them to feel comfortable with difference in further education and/or the workplace. A range of classroom practices have been developed that appear to embrace diversity and to promote intercultural dialogue, incorporating the challenges of integrating minorities as well as Catholics and Protestants. Thus, integrated education provides an important middle ground for peacebuilding where children can learn together and from each other and which can provide them with the skills and confidence to live in a shared society. It challenges the dominant social model of co-existence, demonstrating that integration is not only possible but desirable. In addition it holds the potential to develop social capital by increasing inter-community friendships, by breaking down suspicion and by developing new identity forms.

However, it is also clear that not all of the current approaches to integrated education may be equally conducive to peacebuilding and that some opportunities for this may be lost. A key concern is how identity is presented – as a homogeneous, fixed notion that needs to be preserved, or as a heterogeneous, fluid and multi-faceted concept that benefits from interaction with others? Considerable attention must now be given to exploring which approaches to dealing with social identity in integrated education might make the best contribution to peacebuilding. I suggest that a combination of liberal/critical strategies that attempt to balance unity and diversity, whilst also challenging discrimination, may be the most hopeful direction.

The reality for children and young people in Northern Ireland remains that most attend separate Catholic and de facto Protestant schools and thus do not experience any kind of integration approach on a daily basis. Whilst there is parental demand for integrated education, evidenced by polls that indicate that parents want more integrated education for their children,[43] there seems to be little political will to encourage the development of new integrated schools. Rather the preference seems to be to work with the existing system, trying where possible to increase contact between children through curriculum initiatives such as the entitlement framework[44] which are arguably more motivated by saving costs than by promoting positive community relations. Recent comments by the First Minister of Northern Ireland Peter Robinson[45] calling for more integration in the school system have been fiercely resisted by Sinn Féin and other members of the Catholic community as a thinly veiled attack on Catholic education. Thus, an opportunity to debate this important issue immediately becomes polarised along political lines, demonstrating the challenges of trying to bring about significant changes to the educational status quo in a jurisdiction whose political administration is constructed on the principle of equal but separate, not integration.

Notes

1   This research has been made possible by funding from the Nuffield Foundation, the International Fund for Ireland and The Esmee Fairbairn Foundation. The support of Stranmillis University College, Belfast, the School of Education at Queen's University, Belfast and Professor Alan Smith of the UNESCO Centre at the University of Ulster is gratefully acknowledged. Most of all I would like to thank all of those involved in the integrated schools who have given their time so willingly to my research.

2   V. Morgan, S. Dunn, E. Cairns and G. Fraser, *Breaking the Mould: The Roles of Parents and Teachers in the Integrated Schools in Northern Ireland* (Coleraine, 1992).

3   C. McClenahan, 'The Impact and Nature of Intergroup Contact in Planned Integrated and Desegregated Schools in Northern Ireland' (University of Ulster at Coleraine,

unpublished PhD thesis, 1995).

4 Education Act (Northern Ireland) (Belfast, 1947).

5 Education Act (Northern Ireland) (Belfast, 1967).

6 Education Act (Northern Ireland) (Belfast, 1977)

7 Morgan et al., *Breaking the Mould*, and McClenahan, 'The Impact and Nature of Intergroup Contact'.

8 T. Gallagher, 'Balancing Difference and the Common Good: Lessons from a Post-conflict Society', *Compare* 35.4 (2005), 429–42.

9 S. McAlister, P. Scraton and D. Haydon, *Childhood in Transition: Experiencing Marginalisation and Conflict in Northern Ireland* (Save the Children, 2009).

10 Northern Ireland Statistics and Research Agency (NISRA), www.nicensus2001.gov. uk/nica/public/index.html (accessed 16 March 2011).

11 Police Service of Northern Ireland (PSNI), www.psni.police.uk/index/updates/ updates_statistics (accessed 16 March 2011).

12 Northern Ireland Council for Integrated Education (NICIE), www.nicie.org (accessed 16 March 2011).

13 Education Reform (Northern Ireland) Order. S.I 1989, no. 2406 (NI20) (Belfast, 1989).

14 C. McGlynn, U. Niens, E. Cairns and M. Hewstone, 'Moving Out of Conflict: The Contribution of Integrated Schools in Northern Ireland to Identity, Attitudes, Forgiveness and Reconciliation', *Journal of Peace Education* 1.2 (2004), 147–63.

15 B. C. Hayes, I. McAllister and L. Dowds, 'In Search of the Middle Ground: Integrated Education and Northern Ireland Politics', *Research Update* 42.

16 J. Hughes and C. Donnelly, 'Is the Policy Sufficient? An Exploration of Integrated Education in Northern Ireland and Bi-lingual/bi-national Education in Israel', in Z. Bekerman and C. McGlynn (eds), *Addressing Ethnic Conflict through Peace Education: International Perspectives* (New York, 2007), 121–33.

17 C. W. McGlynn, 'The Impact of Post Primary Integrated Education in Northern Ireland on Past Pupils: a Study' (University of Ulster at Jordanstown, unpublished EdD dissertation, 2001).

18 C. K. Atkin, 'Communication and Political Socialization', in D.Nimmo and K. Saunders (eds), *Handbook of Political Communication* (Beverly Hills, 1981), 299–328; M. K. Jennings and R. G. Niemi, *Generations and Politics: A Panel Study of Young Adults and Their Parents* (Princeton, NJ, 1981); S. Verba, K. L. Schlozman and H. E. Brady, *Voice and Equality: Civic Voluntarism in American Politics* (Cambridge, 1995), 416–61.

19 K. Trew, 'Catholic-Protestant Contact in Northern Ireland', in M. Hewstone and R. Brown (eds), *Contact and Conflict in Intergroup Encounters* (Oxford, 1986), 93–106.

20 Northern Ireland Life and Times Survey 2000, www.ark.ac.uk/nilt/datasets/ (accessed 16 March 2011).

21 H. Tajfel, *Differentiation between Social Groups: Studies in the Social Psychology of Intergroup Relations* (London, 1978).

22 J. Turner, *Social Influence* (Milton Keynes, 1991).

23 J. Harbinson (ed.), *A Society under Stress* (Somerset, 1980).

24 P. Weinreich, 'Variations in Ethnic Identity: Identity Structure Analysis', in K. Liebkind (ed.), *New Identities in Europe: Immigrant Ancestry and the Ethnic Identity of You* (Aldershot, 1989), 65.

25 S. Gaertner, J. F. Dovidio, P. A. Anastasio, B. A. Bachevan and M. C. Rust, 'The Common Ingroup Identity Model: Recategorization and the Reduction of Intergroup Bias', in W. Stroewe and M. Hewstone (eds), *European Review of Social Psychology* (Chichester, 1993), 1–26.

26 A. Montgomery, G. Fraser, C. McGlynn, A. Smith and T. Gallagher, *Integrated Educa-tion in Northern Ireland: Integration in Practice* (UNESCO Centre, University of Ulster at Coleraine, 2003).

27 C. McGlynn, 'Leading Integrated Schools: A Study of the Multicultural Perspectives of Northern Irish Principals', *Journal of Peace Education* 5.1 (2008), 3–16.

28 Freebody, *Qualitative Research in Education: Interaction and Practice* (London, 2003); J. Mason, *Qualitative Researching* (London, 1996); K. F. Punch, *Introduction to Social Research: Quantitative and Qualitative Approaches* (London, 1998).

29 R. Reich, *Bridging Liberalism and Multiculturalism in American Education* (Chicago, 2002), 116.

30 J. Kincheloe and S. R. Steinberg, *Changing Multiculturalism* (Buckingham, Phila-delphia, 1997).

31 A. Sen, *Identity and Violence* (New York, 2006).

32 U. Niens and E. Cairns, *Integrated Education in Northern Ireland: A Review* (forth-coming).

33 G. W. Allport, *The Nature of Prejudice* (London, 1954); T. F. Pettigrew and L. R. Tropp, 'Does Intergroup Contact Reduce Prejudice? Recent Metanalytic Findings', in S. Oskamp (ed.), *Reducing Prejudice and Discrimination* (Mahwah, NJ, 2000), 93–114.

34 M. Hewstone, 'Contact and Categorisation: Social Psychological Interventions to Change Intergroup Relations', in C. N. Macrae and C. Stangor and M. Hewstone (eds), *Foundations of Stereotypes and Stereotyping* (New York, 1996), 323–68.

35 Sen, *Identity and Violence.*

36 L. Davies, *Education and Conflict: Complexity and Chaos* (London, 2004), 87.

37 Reich, *Bridging Liberalism*, 116.

38 R. Jenkins, *Social identity* (London, 2004), 183.

39 Northern Ireland Council for Integrated Education, http://www.nicie.org (accessed 16 March 2011).

40 C. McGlynn, 'Integrating Education: Parekhian Multiculturalism and Good Practice', *Intercultural Education* 20.4 (2009), 299–310.

41 See also Z. Bekerman, M. Zembylas and C. McGlynn, 'Working towards the De-essentialization of Identity Categories in Conflict and Post-conflict Societies: Israel, Cyprus, and Northern Ireland', *Comparative Education Review* 53.2 (2009), 213–34.

42 B. Parekh, *Rethinking Multiculturalism: Cultural Diversity and Political Theory* (Hampshire, New York, 2006).

43 Northern Ireland Council for Integrated Education, https://www.nicie.org (accessed 16 March 2011).

44 Department of Education, Northern Ireland, 'Entitlement Framework', http://www.deni.gov.uk/index/80-curriculum-and-assessment/108-entitlement-frame-work.htm (accessed 16 March 2011).

45 *Belfast Telegraph*, 10 October 2010.

5

Providing a Prophetic Voice? Churches and Peacebuilding, 1968–2005[1]

Maria Power

When the Troubles began, the Protestant[2] and Catholic Churches, long seen as 'tribal chaplains' to the two main cultural traditions in Northern Ireland, came under close scrutiny and questions were asked regarding their role in perpetuating the conflict as well as the efforts they were making towards peace and reconciliation. For example, in an article published in the *Guardian* in 1973, a former Church of Ireland Bishop, Richard Hanson, reflected upon these issues:

> the innocent English inquirer asks 'What are the Churches doing about this situation? Surely this is precisely a situation in which applied Christianity can heal?' Innocent simpleton. The Churches are part of the situation. They have very largely contributed to produce it and it could indeed be argued that they benefit from it: All the major denominations in Northern Ireland: Roman Catholics, Presbyterians, Church of Ireland and Methodists ... are captive Churches. They have long ago sold their integrity and spiritual and intellectual independence to political ideologies in return for the massive support of the people of Northern Ireland.[3]

The article concludes with a suggestion that 'much more could be done to encourage the mixing together for religious purposes of Catholics and Protestants'.[4] Such assessments have been repeated through various media over the past 40 years.[5] As the conflict has worn on, these 'pleas for peace' have matured, moving away from a culture of blame, towards one in which practical suggestions were made for progression:

> Disputes between believers are a scandal. There is an urgent need for the Churches throughout Ireland to encourage their members to address in a constructive fashion the issues and traditions which divide believers. This requires internal debate and self-examination as well as dialogue and meetings between Churches at every level.[6]

But were such questions justified? The work of local churches and faith-based organisations for peace in Northern Ireland is well known.[7] Within communities, religion has attempted to act as a mechanism for challenging the conflict. Since the 1960s, the institutional churches and other faith-based organisations[8] have identified opportunities to promote peace and have worked towards achieving the goal of peace and reconciliation in Northern Ireland. A variety of methods were employed including single-identity work, internal denominational debate and reflection, ecumenical dialogue between the leaderships of the churches, local prayer groups, community develop-ment work and public statements intended to inform political debates. Whilst such techniques were vastly different, they were all informed by the premise that in a conflict based upon identity 'other cultures are not a threat to the pristine purity of our cultural identity, but a potential source of its enrich-ment. Inhabited by people who are courageous enough simply not to belong, intersecting and overlapping cultures can mutually contribute to the dynamic vitality of each.'[9]

However, it was not local inter-church groups that were the focus of Hanson and others' criticism but the leaders of the Protestant and Catholic Churches who, it was argued in the early 1970s, could not 'any longer afford to live as though the others did not exist' and needed officially to take 'imagi-native action'.[10] This essay will elucidate the hitherto neglected historical role of the leaders of the Protestant and Catholic Churches in building peace in Northern Ireland. The leaderships were far from silent on the question of peace throughout the period in question. Individual denominations published official statements and pastoral letters, well-known clergy, such as Robin Eames, Cahal Daly and Eric Gallagher, produced considerations on matters relating to the conflict and peacebuilding and the Protestant and Catholic leaderships engaged in joint displays of solidarity as well as making regular statements together. These methods enabled them 'to use their moral authority and influence to encourage mutual understanding within their communities'[11] thereby promoting more peaceful relationships. However, before an exploration of the peacebuilding efforts of the church leaderships is undertaken, the arguments for their involvement in peacebuilding will be briefly considered.

Religious involvement in peacebuilding: the Northern Irish case

The relationship of religion to peacebuilding has been established by, amongst others, Gopin and Powers.[12] Internationally, there are many examples of churches and faith-based organisations working towards the goals of peace and reconciliation at a number of different levels. For example, the efforts of churches in challenging apartheid in South Africa,[13] the Community of Sant' Egidio's work in persuading warring parties to negotiate with one another[14] and the involvement of religious leaders in reconciliation in Bosnia-Herzegovina,[15] all provide illustrations of the different means through which religion can act as an agent for peace. In addition, there are a number of other reasons which would justify the church leaders becoming involved in peace and reconciliation in Northern Ireland. First, religion has played a role in the conflict there through its role in Northern Irish civil society and second, the peacebuilding tradition within Christianity.

The role of religion in the perpetuation of the conflict in Northern Ireland has sparked controversy: some see it as a substantial factor and others do not.[16] Although 'the Churches are not sending their faithful out to shoot and bomb in the name of the Lord',[17] religion has played some part. This has happened on a number of levels ranging from the use of religious language to make political points to the integral role played by religion in the formation of the identity of the Nationalist, Republican, Unionist and Loyalist communities. Religious and political leaders such as Ian Paisley have employed religious rhetoric to further their political causes, for example the aftermath of the 1985 Anglo-Irish Agreement[18] whilst Sinn Féin employed a version of Aquinas's Just War theory to justify their actions.[19] Furthermore, in a clash that was essentially based upon two differing socio-political identities, religion has contributed to their formation:

> in modern Ireland political identity has often taken a sectarian and negative route and sectarianism always has a religious element. Sectarianism was there before modern nationalism developed, and the political division of Ireland was the consequence of such sectarianism, rather than the cause of it. If sectarianism had not been so deep-rooted, the Northern Ireland Troubles would not have happened. They happened because both sides acted as the stereotypes said they would.[20]

This argument is further strengthened by the role of the churches within communities, most notably in the areas of affiliation and civil society. Despite a slow trend towards secularisation since 1968, Northern Ireland has some of the highest levels of religious identification, affiliation and practice in Western Europe.[21] For example, by 2008, approximately 33% of the adult population were attending church once a week and 'the figures also suggest that frequent church attendance has been replaced by less frequent church attendance, rather than by complete non-attendance' indicating that the 'secularization that is taking place should be understood as more a matter of the privatization of religion rather than a complete shift to irreligion ... the vast majority of individuals still claim a religious affiliation, but a significant majority continue to espouse some of the main tenets of the Christian faith, most notably a general belief in God'.[22] Furthermore, Mitchell has concluded that 'association with religious community, rather than theological position, continues to form the strongest basis for political preferences':[23] thus, 'for the majority of people in Northern Ireland their political identity and their religious affiliation are almost coterminous'.[24] This coalescence of religious adherence and political identity, when combined with the fact that religion has the ability to affect people's attitudes,[25] indicates that churches have the potential to provide direction to the communities in the areas of politics, peace and reconciliation.

Such an argument is augmented by the 'record of the churches' during the conflict. In a society with two separate civil societies, in which the churches played no small part, separation rather than integration was the norm. Or to use the parlance of Putnam,²⁶ the churches have historically contributed to the creation of bonding rather than bridging social capital. As Morrow observed, 'our structures have still continued to be the cultural cement of divided communities and we have been unable to transcend and break down the sectarianism which is endemic to our society'.²⁷ There were many instances of the churches actively discouraging the development of integration and relationships between the communities. One of the most famous examples of these was the churches' reaction to the integrated education movement. The segregated nature of education in Northern Ireland means children generally do not encounter anyone from the 'other' community until entering University or the workplace.²⁸ When attempts were made from the 1970s onwards to establish integrated schools, the Catholic Church in particular stood in the way of its development by, for example, refusing to provide these schools with chaplains and narrowly defining Canon law on this issue. Additionally, the official links between the Protestant Churches and the loyal orders have also created bonding rather than bridging social capital, an aspect of the church's history which was brought into sharp relief by the events surrounding Drumcree in the 1990s.²⁹ Finally, the lack of leadership at a national level on ecumenical matters also signalled that the Protestant and Catholic Churches were more interested in maintaining clear boundaries between the two communities than in creating peaceful relationships. Thus, the churches, whether wittingly or not, have played some role in the conflict in Northern Ireland. They therefore had a responsibility to become involved in (and support efforts towards) peacebuilding by attempting to utilise what authority they had within their communities.³⁰

This responsibility was underscored by clear instructions for peacebuilding given to Christians in the gospel. This was acknowledged by church leaders who stated in June 2010, 'As Christian leaders, we believe that reconciliation is at the very heart of the Christian message.'³¹ Although the Irish Council of Churches argued that 'biblical teaching may not, indeed does not, set down detailed guidelines about how precisely to achieve a reconciled community',³² the message of the New Testament is one of peace rather than conflict and separation.³³ The leaderships of the Protestant and Catholic Churches in Northern Ireland therefore found themselves with a common mandate to become engaged in peace and reconciliation work by using the universal elements of their spiritually to overcome their historical alignments to the mutually hostile communities. Such a fiat is enhanced by the fact that 'religions ... represent considerable potential for peacebuilding. All religions offer ethical visions that support social justice and facilitate empathy with the suffering of those on the other side, which can motivate people to act in support of reconciliation.'³⁴ The peacebuilding process is built upon essentially religious values with concepts such as truth, justice, forgiveness and reconciliation dominating the discourse, not only within Northern Ireland but internationally. Therefore, 'if one accepts that there are fundamental theological values embedded within the concept, most notably forgiveness, it thereby ensues that religious actors have an important part to play in the reconciliation processes.'[35] The Protestant and Catholic Churches in Northern Ireland therefore had a foundation upon which to build. Thus, as leaders (disputed or otherwise) within their communities, they had a platform from which to demonstrate that communication with the 'other' was acceptable and that peacebuilding was part of the Christian faith.

Providing a prophetic voice: speaking out for peace

Peace and reconciliation were for churches and faith-based organisations 'the most urgent problem'.[36] From the outset of the troubles, the leaderships of the institutional churches undertook schemes, such as the Four Leaders Group and the Irish Inter-Church Meeting, which were to become a crucial part of the peacebuilding efforts of the institutional churches. These initiatives provided a sign to the clergy and laity that peacebuilding should be a priority in their ministry as well as documents designed to provoke thought on the matter.[37] In addition, initiatives instituted by groups of individual clergy such as the Feakle talks[38] also demonstrated a strong commitment to these issues. However, one of the most important contributions made by churches and faith-based organisations to peacebuilding was the provision of a 'prophetic voice of integrity, courage and truth'.[39] No one denomination or faith-based organisation took the lead in this, with its forms being as diverse as calls for an end to violence and reflections upon the situation in Northern Ireland and practical schemes aimed at its solution. Although this work was done by both leaderships and individual members of various denominations,[40] it was a method also employed by other groups such as the Inter-Church Group on Faith and Politics[41] and ECONI.[42] All of this work was based upon the need to promote understanding within Northern Ireland. It was argued that

> removal of fear must be the key to dismantling religious sectarianism. Fear of the unknown, of what people will say or do, of how they will react, of what goes to make up the institutional life of another religious denomination or Church is born out of ignorance. Knowledge must take the place of ignorance.[43]

Such work provided a platform upon which the mandate for peacebuilding given in the gospel could be publicly declared. The church leaders demonstrated an innate sensitivity to the needs of the Northern Irish situation by providing a starting point from which people from the different communities could begin to understand one another's religious beliefs and the impact these had upon their political ideologies. This section will examine the work of the Four Leaders Group and the 'pleas for peace' made by the Catholic Church before concluding with a consideration of the projects established by the Presbyterian Church and the Church of Ireland.

On the second World Day of Peace, 1 January 1968, the leaders of the main Protestant and Catholic Churches in Northern Ireland made the first of many joint pleas for peace. This statement, issued before Northern Ireland descended into conflict, called on people to remember 'that prayer and action are demanded continually if peace is to be built and if it is to endure, let us seek to bring the hope of peace to those who have no hope and strive for the healing of those ills and evils which destroy peace between man and man'.[44] In the wake of growing civil unrest which saw each of the four main churches individually 'call for calm',[45] this ad hoc contact became more formal, although never official. In autumn 1968, the Protestant Churches (through the Irish Council of Churches) wrote to the Catholic hierarchy suggesting that joint action be undertaken:

> We write as persons holding positions of major responsibility in our Churches … We have long been concerned for the establishment of justice and mutual respect in Northern Ireland [but] recent events have under-lined the need for urgent action … We believe that the achievement of [justice and respect] may be advanced by a better understanding of each other's position and concerns and, where possible, joint action … there may be advantage from some sort of joint consultative body … We believe that in normal circumstances such a suggestion has much to commend it, but at this present time we are particularly anxious for bridges to be built and kept open.[46]

Understanding was seen to be the solution to the crisis facing Northern Ireland and any form of relationship which could be used to inform not only religious but political perspectives was something to be encouraged. Contact between the churches could therefore only serve to benefit the two communities by demonstrating that cross-community dialogue was possible. This desire was practically expressed through prayer vigils[47] and the visit by the Four Leaders to Derry in the aftermath of the rioting there.[48]

These ideas and actions were to set the tone of the Four Leaders' work: members of congregations were asked to pray for reconciliation, strive to understand the perspective and identity of the 'other' community and accept difference. The statements and work of this group evolved overtime. The frequent joint statements begun in 1968 were joined in Christmas 1974 by a campaign to 'reverse the trend of the community towards violence'.[49] Methods employed included 'advertisements and articles in newspapers, programmes on radio and television, sermons and prayers'[50] – all of which encouraged people to pray for peace. The underlying premise was the long-term promo-tion of understanding between the two main communities:

Neither the Church leaders nor those supporting them believe for one moment that this campaign means an end to political and theological differences. They do believe that through THOUGHT, PRAYER and TALK these differences can be understood and that their respective people will be able to come to terms with them.[51]

This campaign was followed by joint statements in the aftermath of atrocities[52] as well as support for peace initiatives taking place within local communities and calls for political dialogue between nationalists and unionists to begin.[53]

In 1975, the four leaders stated that 'As Christians we must not allow the situation to weaken our faith or take away our hope from God. This is why so many prayed and still must go on praying ... that every effort may be made to deal with out differences in peace and mutual understanding.'[54] Here, the message is summarised: prayer and dialogue equals understanding between hostile communities resulting in peace. However, the effectiveness and contribution to peace and reconciliation of this initiative within Northern Ireland is somewhat harder to discern or indeed quantify. Their work was dependent upon the relationships between the leaders (who in the case of the Presbyterian and Methodist Churches changed frequently) and once the 1974 campaign was launched, did not evolve much further, although their areas of interest did, as their calls for political dialogue demonstrate.[55] For many, the statements and acts of witness provided by the Four Leaders Group were mere gestures; a means through which churches could be seen to do something whilst remaining rooted in their own communities. During the conflict, the contents of their statements never went beyond exhortations to prayer and reconciliation. Such ideas demonstrate a misunderstanding of the role of churches within their communities and the nature of cultural denomination-alism whereby the churches did not have as much power to shape and control the politics and actions of their members as is sometimes assumed.[56] Further-more, given the nature of the conflict in Northern Ireland could much more have been expected? As it has frequently been noted, peace and reconciliation in Northern Ireland is a long-term goal, expected to take decades rather than years. Instead, the contribution of the Four Leaders Group lay in the symbolic power of their gestures which provided a spearhead for the promotion of peace and understanding. As a group, they could not really do much more than promote a message of understanding and the gospel to those engaged both in conflict and in cross-community work.

Individual denominations also did much to provide a public face and voice to peace and reconciliation work as well as emphasising the fact that violence was not religiously justifiable. Statements of this nature which spoke out against violence and political unrest and those which encouraged members of the churches to engage with one another were common throughout the conflict. Those written by the Catholic Church provide the best example of their form and development.

The 1970s witnessed some of the worst violence in Northern Ireland's history. This prompted the Catholic Church publicly to consider the issues of peace and conflict, both through official statements and the writings of bishops, such as Cahal Daly. The result was a discourse attacking the use of violence by paramilitary organisations and statements encouraging Catholics to become involved in peace and reconciliation work which continued throughout the period in question.[57] The Catholic Church's main concern at the beginning of the conflict was the association in some people's minds of Republican paramilitary violence with the entire Catholic community:

> Such evil initiatives are contrary to the law of Christ and must bring harm to thousands of innocent people. Moreover if such acts can be pointed to as the beginning of serious trouble it is not the handful of self-appointed activists who will be blamed but the whole Catholic community. Already people are not above suggesting that what has happened in recent days convicts the Catholic community for what happened last August.[58]

Such ideas were developed further by Pope John Paul II during his visit to Ireland in 1979.[59] In his sermon at Drogheda, he emphasised the commandment 'thou shalt not kill' by begging paramilitaries to 'turn away from the paths of violence and to return to the ways of peace'.[60] The primary goal of the Catholic Church was to support the creation of a peace process in Northern Ireland by attempting to use what little moral authority it had with Republican paramilitaries. Such pleas were, however, rejected. Speaking in response to Pope John Paul II's plea for an end to violence in Northern Ireland, Provisional Sinn Féin stated, 'With all the opportunities for political action denied to them [the Nationalist community] the people organised their own physical resistance to British terror. This action was totally in keeping with the traditional Christian teaching on the right to resist oppression.'[61] Despite this, these condemnations of violence continued in the 1980s and 1990s with both Tomas O'Fiaich (Primate from 1978–1990) and Cahal Daly (Primate from 1990–1996) speaking out against paramilitary violence and appealing for victims to forgive their perpetrators.[62] However, the tone of these changed slightly. The Catholic Church began focusing more upon the ambiguity towards violence present within sections of the nationalist community and the damage that this was doing to the chances of reconciliation between the Protestant and Catholic communities. For example, in 1987 the Irish Bishops stated,

> There is no room for ambivalence. In the face of the present campaigns of republican violence the choice for all Catholics is clear. It is a choice between good and evil.
> It is sinful to join organisations committed to violence or to remain in them. It is sinful to support such organisations or to call on others to support them ... People must choose. There is no longer any room for romantic illusion. There is no excuse for thinking that the present violence in Ireland can be morally justified.[63]

In 1991 Daly stated that 'violence makes reconciliation between our two communities inordinately difficult. Violence serves – and one must indeed wonder whether it is intended to serve – to drive our two communities further apart.'[64] In so publicly chastising the Republicans and their supporters, the church leadership was providing a strong illustration of the Catholic Church's position on the matter, thereby speaking out for peace at a time when the entire Catholic community was associated with violence.[65] In doing so, it presented a more nuanced picture of the Catholic community as a whole and improved prospects for peacebuilding by enabling Protestants to understand that some sort of a 'holy war' was not being waged against them.

This period also saw the churches give encouragement and support to those engaged in peacebuilding activities within local communities and praise was given to their efforts and in particular their 'spirit of Christian forgiveness'.[66] For the Catholic Church, this took the form of statements and once more, understanding between the two communities was seen as central to progress as people were told 'never think you are betraying your own community by seeking to understand and respect and accept those of a different tradition'.[67] The means through which this understanding, and therefore peace and recon-ciliation, could be achieved were given much thought, particularly by Cahal Daly. He argued that the 'moderate middle ground' needed to continue to assert itself through ecumenical or cross-community contact to overcome the 'wide chasm of mutual suspicion, fear and prejudice separating the two Northern communities'.[68] Prayer was the central means through which it was believed such contact could be strengthened as the 'greatest force for peace is our prayer'.[69] People were advised to engage in ecumenical contact whilst honouring and respecting the rights of the Protestant community. The idea of acknowledging the plurality of Northern Irish society was significant as it was argued to be the only way to create a peace: 'We do not forget today that the future Ireland is one in which we must and will find a place, in equal enjoy-ment of human rights and freedom, for a million Northern Protestants.'[70] This pastoral letter sums up the tone of the Catholic Church's thinking on the matter of peacebuilding:

> We therefore ask our people to make their voices heard in repudiation of individuals or groups who may appear to be interested in a continuation of violence. We ask them to cooperate with those groups who genuinely reflect the peaceful intentions of the people as a whole and who are working hard to restrain militant elements.[71]

Through such statements, pastoral letters and sermons, the Catholic Church were attempting to redefine the Catholic community in Northern Ireland which was seen at this point purely through the lens of Republican violence. It emphasised the teachings of the Catholic faith on issues such as violence and peacebuilding, thereby trying to promote an understanding of the Catholic Church's perspective on these matters. This was crucial to the development of relationships not only between the Protestant and Catholic Churches but between the two communities as well.

The Protestant Churches were by no means silent regarding cross-community peacebuilding and spoke out frequently against violence with, for example, the Methodist Church 'condemning terrorists'[72] and urging people to 'vote for peace'.[73] They emphasised the need to support and encourage members of the Church's congregations to engage in such work and this was generally expressed in practical terms. From the mid-1980s onwards, the leaderships of the Protestant churches did much to create peacebuilding infrastructures within their churches and the Presbyterian Church and the Church of Ireland were at the forefront of this.[74]

> However, it has taken a long time for the main Churches to consider formally how their congregations might best contribute to building a more normal society. So, in the early days Churches did not receive funding centrally for peacebuilding. This has now changed and it has been recognised that if Churches have been part of the problem they must also be encouraged to be part of any successful solution.[75]

This work built upon the statements and dialogue that had been occurring within and between the main churches since the outset of the conflict. The churches had come to understand that contact between the main communities needed to be supported in a structured manner.

The Presbyterian Church sought to achieve this through its Peacemaking Programme established at the 1986 General Assembly. Its remit was 'to examine issues concerning peace and peacemaking locally and internationally in order to educate our own denomination on them and to call the church to constructive action where possible'. The programme sought to empower local communities to engage in this work themselves:

> From the outset it was not so much the task of this committee to do peacemaking on behalf of PCI but to encourage, challenge, equip, support and resource the congregations, Presbyteries, boards, agencies and members of the Church to do so. In June 2004, the Committee was renamed the 'Peacemaking Panel' operating under the Global Concerns Committee of the General Board. Reporting to the General Board provided the Panel with a connection to all other boards and to all Presbyteries.[76]

In 1996, it adopted the Peace Vocation statement to further encourage ownership of this work within communities.[77] The intention was to integrate peacebuilding into every aspect of church life and to encourage congregations to make it their central concern. Its aims demonstrate this clearly:

- to increase acceptance within PCI that peacebuilding and reconciliation are a priority in the ministry of the whole of the Church;
- to deepen understanding of the measures required for a stable peace and good relations by leaders and activists within PCI;

- to strengthen the capacity and infrastructure in the Church to sustain long-term peacemaking activities;
- to increase the number of PCI congregations developing on-going initiatives that will contribute to peace in society;
- to encourage boards, committees and agencies within PCI to explore and make a commitment to their own contribution to community relations in this society.[78]

Structures were therefore put in place to facilitate this: two full-time peacemaking officers were employed, Presbytery Peacemaking Agents (who themselves set up structures within their Presbyteries) and Congregational Peacemaking Agents were appointed who were supported by peacemaking groups. This structure was supported by a training programme and an annual conference[79] and suggestions were provided which included 'building friendship and exploring areas of common concern' with local Catholics.[80] Similar structures were also put in place to support young people. The execution of this programme illustrated perfectly the Presbyterian Church's attitude to peacebuilding. In 1992, it had argued that

> Genuine religion, while undoubtedly exercising the role of a strengthening bond among a particular faith community, ought to promote a spirituality in which people are set free from limited goals, transcend their fears and animosities of the past and seek the larger human unity in justice, reconciliation and peace towards which the vision of the Kingdom of God points.[81]

Thus, peacebuilding was more than just being friendly with local Catholics, and focused closely on enabling those involved to realise what they had in common as well as understand their differences. Furthermore, the centrality of this project demonstrated the seriousness with which peace and reconciliation was approached within Presbyterianism. It was evident that the leadership of the church wanted to try and unite a fractious organisation, large sections of which were traditionally opposed to contact with Catholics, and convince it of the importance of such activity.

The Church of Ireland had also long given a voice to its desire to engage in peacebuilding and reconciliation. For example, in 1984 it was stated at its General Synod that

> The Church of Ireland has a vocation to work at reconciling the different cultural traditions for three main reasons: Historically because of our major role in Irish history both as the established Church and in the years since. Secondly because as Anglicans we can reconcile different theological traditions within one communion of faith and thirdly because our Church includes within its membership people of different political commitments, aspirations and a diversity of cultural interests.

Such issues did not begin to come to prominence until Drumcree, the aftermath of which forced the leadership of the Church of Ireland 'to address the issues that lay behind it'[82] and in 1997, the General Synod adopted a motion stating that it opposed sectarianism. It thus began a series of projects aimed at dealing with sectarianism and assisting 'parishes to increase their capacity to deal positively with difference issues'.[83] This 'started a process of self-examination with the intention of determining how "to promote, at all levels of Church life tolerance, dialogue, co-operation and mutual respect between the Churches and in society"'.[84] A report aimed at exploring the ways in which the Church of Ireland could begin to deal with sectarianism and diversity was commissioned and as a consequence the Hard Gospel project and the Diocese of Down and Dromore's Think Again scheme began. The work of the Think Again Initiative[85] is emblematic of the Church of Ireland's approach to the issue of peace and reconciliation and demonstrates clearly how the leadership of the Church of Ireland was attempting to develop its approach to these issues.

The Think Again initiative began life as the 'Community Bridge-Building Working Group' in 1997,[86] £500,000 was invested by the Diocese and a dedicated Reconciliation Development Officer was appointed in 1999.[87] It aimed to make peacebuilding, and in particular an improvement of relationships with Catholics,[88] the focus of the work of the Diocese and to have it 'embedded into the life of the parish within five years (2000–2005)'.[89] A Diocesan commitment to community bridge building[90] was put into place in 1998 and this was followed by a series of 'guiding principles' which included the renewal of parishes in the Diocese and finding ways to help congregations become more involved in the work of the church.

> Reconciliation is the central theme which transcends the various aspects of the Think Again initiative. The Diocese of Down and Dromore has clearly identified the need to improve relationships between members of the main religious/cultural traditions in Northern Ireland, relationships which have suffered through the experiences of the last 30 year period. The Diocese of Down and Dromore, through Think Again and other initiatives, is striving to create a new and more positive series of relationships between the Church of Ireland and other religious denominations within Northern Ireland.[91]

Like its counterpart in the Presbyterian Church, 'the project has mainstreamed peacebuilding and reconciliation work within the management structure of the Church of Ireland and within individual churches and those involved have reported that the project has enabled them to have new relationships and added a new dynamic to reconciliation'.[92] The practical focus of this project was, therefore, to put structures in place to allow peacebuilding activities to take place. Such a method was chosen because, as the Reconciliation Officer put it, 'parishes tend to do one off ad hoc things, so there is no strategy or forward thinking, so we are introducing them to strategic thinking and to give them models for reconciliation and peacemaking'.[93] The Church Reconciliation Officers supported dedicated teams of 'Bridge-Builders' which were created within each parish. These Bridge-Builders were expected to 'show leadership in helping their parish to find ways to building bridges in the wider community' and to 'encourage Bible study, discussion and learning about peacebuilding'.[94] Parish projects to arise from this initiative included participation on Habitat for Humanity's Bridging the Gap course,[95] a year of reconciliation (2003–2004), cross-community prayer and Bible study groups, activities aimed specifically at young people, community development work and Alpha courses.[96]

A position paper written on the Think Again Initiative sums up the Church of Ireland's assessment of its significance:

> from the perspective of the wider society within Northern Ireland the Think Again initiative has clearly demonstrated the enhanced role which the Church can play in relation to issues like reconciliation ... The profile of the Church, the leadership which is provided by the Church, the resources which the Church has at its disposal and the ways which the Church is connected into every community/parish within Northern Ireland would indicate that the Church is uniquely positioned to play a more active and assertive role around issues which are of relevance/concern within society as a whole and, in the context of the Diocese of Down and Dromore, issues relating to spiritual renewal, reconciliation and young people. The Diocese of Down and Dromore has played a positive and constructive role in exploring ways in which the Church might most effectively progress God's mission.[97]

However, the reality proved to be more problematic than this as the Reconciliation Officer found it difficult to encourage people to become involved:

> in some places they have just not got off the ground, in other places they are working very quietly, almost clandestinely without the parish knowing but in other parishes they are working quite openly. So it varies, urban parishes tend to find it easier, rural parishes it's difficult, some parishes find it difficult where there's a strong Orange Order influence.[98]

The Church of Ireland needed to give prominence to the issue of combating sectarianism and building peace and reconciliation in the aftermath of Drumcree, and this initiative, along with the Hard Gospel project, did just that. However, the significance of this programme, along with its counterpart in the Presbyterian Church, can be seen in its sheer existence and the move towards making peacebuilding central to church activities that it signals. Such programmes would have been unimaginable in the late 1960s. They demonstrate the maturation of the church leaderships' approach to these issues: communicating through statements and high-level meetings and merely encouraging people to become involved was no longer enough and the structures needed to move beyond this mode of peacebuilding were implemented through these initiatives.

Conclusion

Historically, the church leaderships in Northern Ireland have been stuck between a rock and a hard place when it comes to peacebuilding and reconciliation: criticised for not doing enough on the one hand and accused of betraying their communities on the other if they speak out against violence or encourage their congregations to become involved in cross-community activities. Robin Eames, Church of Ireland Archbishop of Armagh, pointed out that 'for those involved, a special sort of vision of what is possible and desirable, a degree of moral and at times physical courage, and confidence in what one says or does are primary requirements'.[99] The tone of commentary coming from those involved was that *any* action that might build peace was enough and indeed anyone that spoke for peace ought to be congratulated for their bravery. But what did the church leaders achieve in the realm of peacebuilding between 1968 and 2005? Their main aim was to promote understanding between the Protestant and Catholic communities and in this aim they showed leadership to the Northern Irish people in their comprehension of the fundamental nature of the problem in Northern Ireland. This they achieved to a certain extent, more often than not through the individual church statements rather than the work of the joint leaders. However, these statements became emblematic of the fundamental problem in Northern Irish peacebuilding as the Protestant and Catholic churches had a tendency to talk past rather than to one another when explaining their perspectives. Even the joint statements of the Four Leaders Group, which had the potential to promote a united message by highlighting commonalities between the communities, displayed this inclination, never moving beyond 'pleas for peace'. In the 1980s, the leaderships began to recognise this problem, leading to the second and possibly more important achievement: the structures implemented to support congregations in their peacebuilding work. These initiatives indicated to people how seriously the churches were taking the issue. These structures enabled the leaderships to promote the message of the gospel without the confrontation and antagonism inherent in the condemnations of terrorism and the pleas for peace. However, the success or failure of these has yet to be seen. The churches are confronted with a choice to which they have yet to find a solution: move at a slower pace which will satisfy the critics of peacebuilding or act swiftly to meet the demands of some that they provide leadership by example.

Writing in 2002, in a book reflecting upon the contribution religion has to make to peace in the twenty-first century, the UK's Chief Rabbi, Jonathan Sacks, commented,

> The pursuit of peace can come to seem to be a kind of betrayal. It involves compromise. It means settling for less than one would like. It has none of the purity and clarity of war, in which the issues – self-defence, national

honour, patriotism, pride – are unambiguous and compelling. War speaks to our most fundamental sense of identity: there is an 'us' and a 'them' and no possibility of confusing the two. When, though, enemies shake hands, who is now the 'us' and who is the 'them'? Peace involves a profound crisis of identity. The boundaries of self and other, friend and foe, must be redrawn.[100]

The church leaderships in Northern Ireland have discovered this and to some extent have confronted it. They have capitalised on their positions as community leaders. They have spoken out against the terrorists within their own communities and promoted the message of peace in the gospel to their congregations by a variety of means. However, peacebuilding is a long-term process and the church leaderships, like the rest of Northern Irish society, have only taken the first step on what could be a long journey.

Notes

1 The author would like to thank Lucy Xavier for her research assistance in the preparation of this piece and Marianne Elliott and Diane Urquhart for their comments on earlier versions of this chapter.
2 Generally, the term 'Protestant churches' in this discourse was taken to mean the Presbyterian Church in Ireland, the Church of Ireland and the Methodist Church, membership of which in 1968 made up 55% of the entire Northern Irish population.
3 *The Guardian*, 14 September 1973. Hannon was not alone in his criticisms. For example, see *Irish Times*, 24 October 1975 and *Irish Independent*, 8 November 1974, 27 February 1977 and 23 April 1984.
4 *The Guardian*, 14 September 1973.
5 See, for example: A. Pollak (ed.), *A Citizen's Enquiry: The Opsahl Report on Northern Ireland* (Dublin, 1993), 100–104 and G. Smyth, 'In the Middle Ground and Meantime: A Call to the Churches in Northern Ireland to Find Themselves on the Edge', in J. Mackey and E. McDonagh (eds), *Religion and Politics in Ireland at the Turn of the Millennium* (Dublin, 2003), 84–106 (96–97).
6 C. Kenny (ed.), *Imprisoned within Structures? The Role of Believing Communities in Building Peace in Northern Ireland (the Believers Inquiry 1997/8)* (Glencree, 1998), 200.
7 See, for example, M. Power, *From Ecumenism to Community Relations: Inter-Church Relationships in Northern Ireland 1980–2005* (Dublin, 2007), and G. Ganiel, *Evangelicalism and Conflict in Northern Ireland* (Basingstoke, 2008).
8 For the purposes of this essay, faith-based organisations are those not affiliated to a particular denomination.
9 M. Volf, *Exclusion and Embrace: A Theological Exploration of Identity, Otherness, and Reconciliation* (Nashville, 1996), 52.
10 E. Gallagher, *A Better Way for Irish Protestants and Roman Catholics: Advice from John Wesley* (Belfast, c. 1973), 15–16.
11 D. Johnston, 'Introduction Chapter: The Religious Dimension of Peacebuilding', European Centre for Conflict Prevention, *People Building Peace* (n.d.), http://www.peoplebuildingpeace.org/thestories/article.php?id=91&typ=theme&pid=21 (accessed 11 June 2010).

12 M. Gopin, *Between Eden and Armageddon: The Future of World Religions, Violence and Peacemaking* (Oxford, 2000), and F. Powers, 'Religion and Peacebuilding', in Daniel Philpott and G. F. Powers (eds), *Strategies of Peace: Transforming Conflict in a Violent World* (Oxford, 2010), 317–52.

13 T. A. Borer, *Challenging the State: Churches as Political Actors in South Africa, 1980–1994* (Notre Dame, 1998).

14 The most recent example of this being in Guinea. Community Sant' Egidio, 'Making Peace: Peace and reconciliation in Guinea Pass from Sant' Egidio. Signing of the Sant' Egidio Declaration and of the General Political Agreement', 28 May 2010, http://www.santegidio.org/index.php?idLng=1064&pageID=1692 (accessed 16 June 2010).

15 G. F. Powers, 'Religion, Conflict and Prospects for Peace in Bosnia, Croatia and Yugoslavia', *Journal of International Affairs* 50.1 (1996), 221–53. However, this has recently been disputed by J. N. Clark, 'Religion and Reconciliation in Bosnia and Herzegovina: Are Religious Actors Doing Enough?', *Europe-Asia Studies* 64.2 (2010), 671–94.

16 For a discussion of this literature, see B. Walker, 'Religion and Politics: The Case of Northern Ireland', *Peace and Conflict Studies* 14.2 (2007), 4–92.

17 Gallagher, *A Better Way for Irish Protestants and Roman Catholics*, 3.

18 See, for example, *Irish Times*, 17 April 1999, which explores the relationship between religious rhetoric and Unionism, and P. Bew, *Ireland The Politics of Enmity, 1789–2006* (Oxford, 2007), 532, for a demonstration of the religious language used by some Unionist leaders in their opposition to the Anglo-Irish Agreement.

19 Thomas Aquinas, *Summa Theologiae*, IIa IIae, q.40, in R. W. Dyson (ed.), *Aquinas: Political Writings* (Cambridge, 2002), 239–47. *Irish Times*, 3 October 1979. For a discussion of whether Just War theory can be applied to the Republican campaign in Northern Ireland, see P. Simpson, 'Just War Theory and the IRA', in *Journal of Applied Philosophy* 3.1 (1986), 73–88.

20 M. Elliott, *When God Took Sides: Religion and Identity in Ireland – Unfinished History* (Oxford, 2009), 4.

21 C. Mitchell, *Religion, Identity and Politics in Northern Ireland: Boundaries of Belonging and Belief* (Aldershot, 2006), 22.

22 B. C. Hayes and L. Dowds, 'Vacant Seats and Empty Pews', *Ark Research Update* 65, February 2010, http://www.ark.ac.uk/publications/updates/update65.pdf (accessed 18 March 2010). This report provides the most up-to-date analysis of the changes in religious identification and practice in Northern Ireland.

23 Mitchell, *Religion, Identity and Politics in Northern Ireland*, 29.

24 Mitchell, *Religion, Identity and Politics in Northern Ireland*, 28.

25 A. S. Miller, 'The Influence of Religious Affiliation on the Clustering of Social Attitudes', *Review of Religious Research* 37.3 (1996), 219–32 (233).

26 R. Putnam, *Bowling Alone: The Collapse and Revival of American Community* (New York, 2001).

27 J. Morrow, *My Ecumenical Vision* (Dublin, 1993), 14.

28 A. Smith, 'Religious Segregation and the Emergence of Integrated Schools in Northern Ireland', *Oxford Review of Education* 27.4 (2001), 559–75.

29 *Irish Times*, 24 April 1999. See also E. Storey, *Traditional Roots: An Appropriate Relationship between the Church of Ireland and the Orange Order* (Dublin, 2002).

30 This notion of authority, moral or otherwise, is not a simple one within the Northern Irish arena. Some Protestants argue that religion has nothing to do with Protestantism: as one Presbyterian Minister commented, 'At a recent loyalist funeral, over half of the young men refused to enter the Church because of their hostility towards the Church: for them Protestantism doesn't have anything to do with religion and in fact they resent you putting a religious emphasis on Protestantism.

They say "what has Protestantism got to do with God?"' (author's interview with a Presbyterian minister, Belfast, October 2000). Furthermore, the IRA rejects the Catholic Church's authority in matters relating to its conflict with the British state.

31 BBC News, 'Protestant Leaders Meet with Bloody Sunday Families', http://news. bbc.co.uk/1/hi/northern_ireland/10325241.stm (accessed 17 June 2010).

32 Irish Council of Churches, *What the Bible Says about Reconciliation* (Belfast, 1988), 18. However, this could be said of most issues in the gospel in particular. Furthermore, whilst no clear instructions were provided, the example set by Jesus was one of dialogue without preconditions. See, for example, his willingness to speak to tax collectors (Luke 19:1–10).

33 Ephesians 6:15 and Matthew 5:9.

34 B. Sterland and J. Beauclerk, 'Faith Communities as Potential Agents for Peace Building in the Balkans: An analysis of Faith-based Interventions towards Conflict Transformation and Lasting Reconciliation in Post-conflict Countries of Former Yugoslavia' (2008), http://www.kirkensnodhjelp.no/Documents/Kirkens%20 Nødhjelp/Publikasjoner/Temahefter/Faith%20Communities%20Balkans.pdf (accessed 15 May 2010), 2.

35 Clark, 'Religion and Reconciliation in Bosnia and Herzegovina', 676.

36 Pope John Paul II, 'Address at Drogheda 29 September 1979', in *The Pope in Ireland: Addresses and Homilies* (2nd edn, Dublin, 2004), 15.

37 Power, *From Ecumenism to Community Relations*, 27–71.

38 E. Gallagher and S. Worrall, *Christians in Ulster 1968–1980* (Oxford, 1982), 99–102, and *Irish Times*, 8 December 1989.

39 R. Eames, *Chains to be Broken* (Belfast, 1992), 93.

40 C. Daly, *Peace: The Work of Justice – Addresses on the Northern Tragedy, 1973–79* (Dublin, 1979); idem, *Communities without Consensus: The Northern Tragedy* (Dublin, 1985); J. Dunlop, *A Precarious Belonging: Presbyterians and the Conflict in Ireland* (Belfast, 1995); and Eames, *Chains to be Broken*.

41 This group 'formulated questions and proposed answers to some of the deepest issues of political life'; An InterChurch Group on Faith and Politics, *Breaking Down the Enmity: Faith and Politics in the Northern Ireland Conflict* (Belfast, 1993), 6.

42 ECONI reflected upon and explained the positions of the evangelical community. See M. Power, 'Preparing Protestants for Peace: The Work of the Evangelical Contribution on Northern Ireland', *Journal of Contemporary Religion* 26.1 (2011), 57–72.

43 Eames, *Chains to be Broken*, 91.

44 *Irish Times*, 1 January 1968. Issued by William Conway (Roman Catholic), James McCann (Church of Ireland), William Boyd (Presbyterian) and Eric Gallagher (Methodist).

45 Gallagher and Worrall, *Christians in Ulster*, 41–42.

46 Cited in N. Taggart, *Controversy, Conflict and Co-operation: The Irish Council of Churches and the Troubles 1968–1972* (Dublin, 2004), 94. This invitation led to the creation of the Ad Hoc Committee in 1969 which acted as an advisory board to the Four Leaders. See Power, *From Ecumenism to Community Relations*, 18.

47 Gallagher and Worrall, *Christians in Ulster*, 42.

48 Power, *From Ecumenism to Community Relations*, 18.

49 *Irish Independent*, 12 December 1974. Another newspaper report is at pains to emphasise the fact that this is not just a statement: *Leitrim Observer*, 14 December 1974.

50 *Irish Independent*, 12 December 1974. This publication also carried one of these advertisements which said, 'For God's sake let peace begin in our land this Christmastime.'

51 *Leitrim Observer*, 14 December 1974.

52 See, for example, *Irish Independent*, 4 June 1993.

53 *Fortnight*, February 1988.

54 *Irish Times*, 1 February 1975.

55 The most recent of these was in January 2010: Irish Methodist Church, 'Four
    Church Leaders Urge Parties to Reach a Settlement', http://www.irishmethodist
    org/news/2010/01/four_Church_leaders_urge_parties_to_reach_a_settlement.php
    (accessed 16 June 2010). The church leaders have also publicly criticised the
    banking system, *Belfast Telegraph*, 17 June 2010 and met with the PSNI's Chief
    Constable to discuss policing reform, PSNI, 'Four Church Leaders met PSNI Chief
    Constable Matt Baggott', http://www.psni.police.uk/021109_four_Church_leaders_
    meet_psni_chief_constable_matt_baggott (accessed 16 June 2010). This demon-
    strates an evolution of their work which is not discussed here as it does not fall
    within the timeframe of the essay.

56 F. Burton, *The Politics of Legitimacy: Struggles in a Belfast Community* (London,
    1978).

57 The Catholic Church also began to speak out about human rights and social justice
    issues, the violations of which it believed were blocking any chance of a peaceful
    political settlement. See, for example, *Irish Times*, 17 March 1980, *Andersonstown
    News*, 8 June 1974 and 10 October 1974, and *Guardian*, 31 December 1971 and 11
    December 1975, as well as C. Daly, *The Price of Peace* (Belfast, 1991).

58 *Justice, Love and Peace: Pastoral Letters of the Irish Bishops 1969–1979* (Dublin,
    1979), 21 May 1970, 37–38.

59 This did not include a visit to Northern Ireland due to security concerns (*Sunday
    Business Post*, 3 January 2010).

60 *The Pope in Ireland*, 19. This sermon was written by Cahal Daly.

61 *Irish Times*, 3 October 1979.

62 *Irish Times*, 4 December 1989.

63 'Statement of the Standing Committee of Irish Bishops', 9 November 1987, quoted
    in Daly, *The Price of Peace*, 51.

64 Daly, *The Price of Peace*, 51.

65 Catholic priests also occasionally refused to bury members of the IRA, see *Ander-
    sonstown News*, 26 January 1980.

66 *The Pope in Ireland*, 15–20.

67 *The Pope in Ireland*, 15–20.

68 Daly, *Communities without Consensus*, 22–23. See also, Cahal Daly, *Violence in
    Ireland and Christian Conscience* (Dublin, 1973), 85–86.

69 Daly, *Communities without Consensus*, 28. At this point, prayer groups were one of
    the main means of ecumenical contact in Northern Ireland (Power, *From Ecumen-
    ism to Community Relations*, 74–83).

70 Daly, *Violence in Ireland*, 16.

71 *Justice, Love and Peace*, 38. Cf. Cahal Daly, *Communities without Consensus*, 29.

72 See, for example, *Irish Times*, 11 October 1969. The Presbyterian Church was also
    vocal on this issue as was the Church of Ireland. See, for example, *Irish Independ-
    ent*, 27 August 1969, 19 February 1972, 17 August 1991, 6 January 1992, 1 March
    1992, 16 September 1994 and 8 October 1994.

73 *Irish Times*, 11 June 1987.

74 The Catholic Church was also involved in creating infrastructures for peacebuild-
    ing. For details of this, see Commission for Catholic Education, 'Reconciliation and
    Peacebuilding', http://catholiceducation-ni.com/content/view/14/28/ (accessed 16
    July 2010).

75 M. McNulty and C. Leeke, *A Time to Heal: Community Bridge Building in the
    Church of Ireland Diocese of Down and Dromore* (Belfast, 2003), 4.

76 Presbyterian Church in Ireland, 'Peacemaking Programme: History of the Panel',
    http://www.presbyterianireland.org/peacemaking/history.html (accessed 16 June
    2010).
77 Presbyterian Church in Ireland, 'The Church's Peace Vocation', 1, http://www.
    presbyterianireland.org/about/peace.htm (accessed 16 June 2010). For example,
    one part of the statement says, 'WE AFFIRM that to be Christian peacemakers
    in our own situation: We must be initiators of programmes of action which will
    contribute to peace in our community. We must therefore provide resources and
    encouragement to enable congregations to move forward at the local level in the
    field of inter-community relations.'
78 Presbyterian Church in Ireland, 'About the Peacemaking Programme', http://www.
    presbyterianireland.org/peacemaking/index.html (accessed 16 June 2010).
79 Presbyterian Church in Ireland, 'About the Peacemaking Programme'.
80 Presbyterian Church in Ireland, 'Suggestions for Implementing the Church's Peace
    Vocation in Presbyteries', http://www.presbyterianireland.org/peacemaking/
    downloads/Suggestions_for_Impementing.doc (accessed 16 June 2010).
81 Presbyterian Church in Ireland, *Presbyterian Principles and Political Witness in
    Northern Ireland* (Belfast, c. 1992), 13.
82 *Irish News*, 26 April 2007. Drumcree brought into focus the relationship of the
    Church of Ireland to the Orange Order and caused many to question the Church
    of Ireland's commitment to reconciliation. See *Irish Times*, 6 August 1996, and V.
    Griffin, 'Lecture', in *Brokenness, Forgiveness, Healing and Peace in Ireland: What
    Should the Churches Do? – Lectures at St Anne's* (Belfast, 1996), 11, which asked,
    'Isn't it about time that in the interests of reconciliation we in the Churches asked
    the Orange Order ... when parading or choosing a route to avoid any display of
    antagonism to the Roman Catholic community which not only inflames sectarian
    passions on both sides but places the police in an intolerable "no-win" situation?'
83 *Christian Today*, 7 March 2006.
84 Church of Ireland, 'The Hard Gospel in Context', http://ireland.anglican.org/
    archive/hardgospel/index.php?id=4 (accessed 16 June 2010).
85 This initiative was part of a wider programme of renewal within the Church of
    Ireland based upon the three principals of Reconciliation, Outreach and Youth and
    led by Bishop Harold Miller.
86 McNulty and Leeke, *A Time to Heal*, 1.
87 Author's interview with Rev. Charlie Leeke, Belfast, 12 February 2002.
88 Rourke, *Think Again about Investing in People*, 4 and McNulty and Leeke, *A Time
    to Heal*, 1.
89 Interview with Rev. Charlie Leeke.
90 The text of which can be found in McNulty and Leeke, *A Time to Heal*, 3. Every
    parish in the Diocese was invited to sign this commitment at an event held at St
    Anne's Cathedral, Belfast in May 1998.
91 Rourke, *Think Again about Investing in People*, 7–8.
92 D. Williamson, D. Brown and G. Irvine, *Dreams Judged upon Delivery: A Report
    on the Work of Church-Based Groups Supported by the Community Relations
    Council* (Belfast, 2001), 17.
93 Interview with Rev. Charlie Leeke.
94 McNulty and Leeke, *A Time to Heal*, 12.
95 J. McMaster and J. Kyle, *Bridging the Gap: A Programme to Discover More about
    Yourself and Those around You and a Tool for Building a Way forward Together*
    (Belfast, 2000).
96 McNulty and Leeke, *A Time to Heal*, 13–29.
97 Rourke, *Think Again about Investing in People*, 19–20.

98 Interview with Rev. Charlie Leeke.
99 Eames, *Chains to be Broken*, 120.
100 J. Sacks, *The Dignity of Difference: How to Avoid the Clash of Civilizations* (2nd edn, London, 2002), 8.

6

'Peace Women', Gender and Peacebuilding in Northern Ireland
From Reconciliation and Political Inclusion to Human Rights and Human Security[1]

Marie Hammond-Callaghan

Peacebuilding, like peace, is a highly contested arena both 'academi- cally and politically' due to its theoretical and value-laden qualities.[2] Feminist scholars have long argued that 'all scholarship has political commit- ments'; however, this is especially apparent in disciplines such as Interna- tional Relations and Peace Studies.[3] Traditional political approaches to peace processes tend to focus on state actors and reflect the status quo,[4] which in turn excludes and undermines the role of the civic arena – where women's political engagement is usually most prevalent. Feminist and peace theorists have shared much in common on the topic of peacebuilding, but perhaps most explicitly in their expressed goals of social and political transforma- tion.[5] While there has been a growing recognition of the significance of grassroots people-to-people initiatives in building peace, peace studies schol- arship has often ignored or misunderstood the critical role of gender – both in mainstream peace theories and peace processes.[6] Contemporary feminist literature on peacebuilding and conflict is distinguished not only by a 'polit- ical commitment to understanding the world from the viewpoints of margin- alized peoples and actors', but also by a complex, gender-based analysis of peace, security and conflict, attentive to 'bottom-up' processes.[7] Is it possible that a 'gender-blind' approach to peace and conflict may even contribute to the global failure to achieve sustainable peace?[8]

As the renowned historian Joan W. Scott has cogently argued, 'Gender is a constitutive element of social relationships based on perceived differences between the sexes' and 'gender is a primary way of signifying relationships of power'.[9] Feminist theorist Judith Lorber has defined gender as multi-faceted, a 'social status, a legal designation, and a personal identity ... [and] a system of power privileging some groups of people and disadvantaging others in conjunction with other systems of power'. Furthermore, gender is multiple and intersectional: 'genders' intersect 'men's and women's social statuses, personal identities, and life chances' that 'are intricately tied up with their racial, ethnic, and religious groups, their social class, their family background, and their place of residence'.[10] Thus, gender is not merely 'synonymous with sex', rather it is a 'social construct that embodies power relations' at all levels of human interaction.[11] Employing the lens of gender is imperative for a more thorough investigation of the structural, social and cultural dimensions of peacebuilding. This chapter asks not only 'where are the women' in peacebuilding projects or processes, but also 'who' are these women?[12] Furthermore, it aims to initiate new questions, such as 'where' and 'who' are the men?

Over the past few decades, gender analysis has transformed a variety of academic disciplines, yielding rich insights on war and violence and shaping new international policies on political conflict.[13] The unanimous adoption of United Nations Security Council (UNSC) Resolution 1325 on 31 October 2000 represented the culmination of almost a century of feminist peace activism and scholarship as well as signalling an unprecedented international recognition of gender issues and women's peacebuilding roles in society at large.[14] Distinct from the oft-examined male-dominated activities of peacemaking and peacekeeping, peacebuilding is a much broader, albeit less-examined concept, and perhaps not surprisingly also an area where women's peace activities usually stand out most.[15] According to some, peacebuilding encompasses a 'wide range of activities that receive less publicity' within the 'social, psychological and economic environment at the grass-roots level'; but more specifically, it emphasises 'equality and social justice, improved relationships and meeting of basic human needs'.[16] Subsequently, women's peacebuilding interests are 'culturally and contextually-based and usually located at community and regional levels'. Women's peacebuilding efforts commonly emphasise reconciliation and demilitarisation but are especially attentive to gender-specific violence.[17]

Some scholars argue that women's civic activism is not only invaluable for informal peacebuilding processes, but also provides a vital bridge for women's inclusion in formal peace processes.[18] Elisabeth Porter contends that women's official inclusion is necessary because (1) 'women are affected by conflict and thus by the consequences of a peace agreement'; (2) 'women's inclusion at all stages of peace processes is crucial for inclusive social justice'; and (3) 'the presence of women makes a difference to the sorts of issues generally brought to peace processes'. Although women are often excluded due to their lack of resources and a perceived lack of authority (usually understood to be the sole preserve of military leaders, combatants and political decision-makers), they have a 'huge stake in community stability' and bring vitally important new approaches to conflict resolution from their positions of 'family care and civil activism'.[19] As Porter rightly points out, 'A peace settlement is not merely about ending a war, but also about establishing the conditions for a new just polity.' But is women's inclusion in formal peace processes sufficient to strengthen successful outcomes of those processes?

Any study of women's peacebuilding efforts in the North of Ireland must extend beyond an examination of women's inclusion (or non-inclusion) in official peace processes. Northern Irish women's peacebuilding has taken many forms – from cross-community activities to participation in official political arenas. This chapter pays most attention to the cross-community organising of women's peace groups to encourage a more complex analysis of how operations of gender in peace activism need to be grounded in a socially, culturally and historically specific context of conflict. Exposing links between militarism, violence and unjust socio-political orders,[20] a critical gender lens transforms traditional paradigms of peace and security.

This chapter has three key goals. First, it locates Northern Irish women's peace activism of the 1970s within the broader historical framework of twentieth-century international women's peace movements, considering the extent to which contemporary Irish activists shared similar influences and problems akin to their forerunners. Second, it aims to characterise the peacebuilding efforts of Northern Irish women's peace groups (especially in relation to feminist groups such as the Northern Ireland Women's Coalition), exploring how their strategies were shaped by gender, conditions of political conflict and access to resources. To what extent did their political margin-alisation shape their sex-segregated character and conventionally feminine focus on peacebuilding at the community level? Also, how has the historical specificity of the conflict shaped both the gender order and the conservative nature of Northern Irish women's peace groups in formative ways? Finally, this chapter highlights some new directions in contemporary gender scholarship for peacebuilding literature and practitioners. While the UNSC Resolution 1325 (2000) is legally binding, and endorses women's political participation and gender analysis at all levels of international decision-making on peace issues,[21] women's presence in official peace processes has remained largely negligible, especially in Northern Ireland, Afghanistan, Iraq and the Middle East.[22] In the absence of more comprehensive gender analyses that incorporate a focus on masculinity and violence as well as firm political commitments to transforming peace processes and security policies, UNSC 1325 will likely remain more an aspiration than a reality.[23]

Peacebuilding and feminism in historical perspective

Since the late nineteenth century, European and North American women campaigned to prevent or end war, as well as radically 'redefine the nature of *realpolitik*'. Linking international peace and domestic peace, as well as social and economic justice, early twentieth-century activists made 'women's citizenship rights' as well as foreign policy an 'integral part of their platform'.[24] In protest against World War I, feminists and pacifists organised the Inter-national Congress of Women at the Hague in 1915 and established the Inter-national Committee of Women for Permanent Peace (ICWPP), which later became re-organised in 1919 as the Women's International League for Peace and Freedom (WILPF) with international headquarters in Geneva, Switzerland. Since WILPF saw militarism and male-dominance as fundamentally related to the subordination of women in society, it struggled relentlessly to increase women's official decision-making power to avert armed conflict. Emphasising 'preventative measures' to war, WILPF also promoted peace education, international disarmament and campaigned against conscription.[25]

According to feminist peace historians, the 'separate' or independent organisation of women enabled them to develop their own social networks, as well as gender-based analyses and campaigns against war, while also maintaining female autonomy over their organisations.[26] Three dominant 'discourses' of 'maternalism, materialism and feminism' distinguished twentieth-century 'women's critiques and protests' against militarism and war.[27] American historian, Sandi Cooper, has contended that 'motherist' arguments have often been at the root of twentieth-century feminist peace analysis, 'uncovering the domestic consequences of militarism', creating 'independent women's peace societies', supporting 'the creation of the welfare state' and challenging 'national security' rationales.[28] Rooted in nineteenth-century 'separate spheres' gender ideology, maternalism laid claim to a 'natural' or 'special' role for women in creating peace and preserving humanity as the 'biological life-givers' and 'socially-assigned caretakers'.[29] By the early twentieth century, maternalism was mobilised to 'legitimise women's activism outside the home, yet in the absence of feminist influences, 'women's commitment to peace work tended to be framed entirely in terms of their maternal role'.[30] Although criticised for allowing 'women to mobilise without seriously challenging' gendered power relations, maternalist discourse nonetheless embodied 'the seeds of its own transformation' and could be employed 'to embolden women'.[31]

The Irish branch of WILPF in the early twentieth century reflected both maternalist and feminist discourses which found expression in political debates around issues of nationhood and self-determination.[32] With the partition of Ireland and advent of civil war in the early 1920s, the Irish branch became increasingly divided over the issue of 'justifiable warfare'. As Rosemary Cullen Owens has highlighted, while many Irish WILPF members 'condemned militarism in its imperialistic mode', others 'accepted the need for further military action to attain national objectives'.[33] Maternalist discourse was utilised on both sides of this debate. Emphasising the principle of 'freedom', those supporting armed resistance appealed to concepts of the 'citizen mother in relation to building up a strong and independent nation'. By contrast, WILPF pacifists stressed 'non-violent' democratic means to peace, invoking the 'mother element' to encourage Irish women to 'instil in their children ideas of peace and humanity'.[34] Ultimately, irreconcilable differences within Irish WILPF brought an end to its existence in 1932, which effectively saw the end of 'women-only' peace organisations in Ireland up until the late twentieth century.[35] However, such divisions within women's organisations were not exceptional in the early twentieth century, as World War I had 'split the international women's movement in all belligerent countries between a pro-war majority and an anti-war minority'.[36] Peace historian April Carter has observed, 'Whether peace should be an absolute priority or whether at times political freedom, human rights or social justice should take precedence has always been a problem for peace activists.'[37]

From early community reconciliation efforts of the 1970s to the peace process of the 1990s, women of the North have rallied across political, social and sectarian divides protesting violence and seeking just resolutions. For decades they have faced persistent political dilemmas deeply rooted in the 'structural bind' of Northern Irish politics following partition and a much longer colonial legacy on the island of Ireland.[38] The historic structural inequalities reflected in 'asymmetrical power relations' between Protestant unionist and Catholic nationalist communities have been formative to this political conflict, shaping women's social as well as political identities.[39] In the 1970s, peace groups including Women Together for Peace and the Peace People reached across such differences in reconciliation-oriented strategies, while others such as the Derry Peace Women worked for civil rights as well as an end to both army and paramilitary violence. In the 1980s, the women's movement inspired organisations including the Women's Information Group (WIG) and the Women's Support Network, Belfast, working across community divides in an effort to address the gendered and socio-economic roots of the conflict. Yet, peace proved elusive in the absence of political solutions and ever-intensifying military strategies. For decades, a highly protracted conflict and growing polarisation undermined the possibility of a broad-based women's alliance or movement. Further conditions of political marginalisation, social isolation and conservatism also made many women's groups far less inclined to unify around political issues or confront state officials about security matters at the time. By the 1990s, the growth of feminism and the development of a women's sector supported by European Union initiatives, had facilitated a wide range of peacebuilding strategies amongst women's organisations across the North. Historical and contemporary evidence suggests that 'multi-dimensional' peacebuilding approaches, embracing social justice, political equality and human rights, are often only made possible in the presence of a strong feminist movement.[40]

'Peace women', community relations, reconciliation and demilitarisation

Contemporary Northern Irish women's peace groups represent something of an anomaly in the context of international women's movements as they not only rejected feminism but also tended to support state security policies.[41] Unlike many of their predecessors and contemporaries, Northern Irish women peace activists rejected feminist affiliation and embraced the conservative gender trope of 'peace woman'. Originating in the mainstream media, the label 'peace women' signified their social respectability, distinguishing them from groups viewed as political, subversive and divisive. It proved a convenient construct for government authorities in state counter-insurgency efforts to encourage nationalist and republican communities to expose 'the men of violence'. Who better to achieve this than wives and mothers, the 'natural peacemakers' of the domestic sphere?[42] While motherist motives and 'accidental activism'[43] illuminate the response of 'peace women' in this political conflict, their attempts to participate politically 'as women' should also be examined. The peacebuilding efforts of Northern Irish women's groups, although explicitly non-feminist (and even anti-feminist), did embrace empowerment strategies for women, most significantly at psycho-social and community levels. As feminist historian Frances Early has pointed out, 'women might clothe their actions in maternalist myths, but observation would lead to the suggestion that the women often also had strong personal motives for undertaking activism that had little to do with maternalist motives'. Indeed, women's peace groups furnished 'venues' not only for female activism and political engagement, but also for women's personal, intellectual and social needs.[44]

Throughout the 1970s political conflict, maternalist discourse dominated the peacebuilding projects of Women Together (WT) and the Derry Peace Women (DPW), but was not as significant within Peace People (PP). In spite of their vast female membership, the PP's peace strategy of 'alternative' community politics was disproportionately led by men.[45] By contrast, WT was a women-only group which grew out of the Northern Irish ecumenical movement,[46] and placed significant emphasis on the maternal role as a tool for peace. While reconciliation and community building were the primary peace strategies of WT and PP, the DPW was uniquely driven by the goals of the Northern Irish civil rights movement seeking political and social reform, demilitarisation and an end to internment policy. To this end, the DPW's 'motherist' protests challenged both paramilitary and state violence as mothers of a Catholic nationalist community in an area most dramatically affected by the conflict.[47]

The Peace People (Belfast, 1976–): reconciliation and community building

Although some sources usually regard the Peace People as the beginning of the Northern Irish women's peace movement, Women Together and the Derry Peace Women actually pre-existed this organisation by several years.[48] Originally known as the 'Women for Peace Movement' following the tragic deaths of the Maguire children in Andersonstown on 10 August 1976, many WT members and DPW activists joined their massive peace rallies and marches from the outset. Initially led by Mairead Corrigan (the children's aunt) and Betty Williams (a witness at the scene),[49] the PP was comprised of about 95 per cent women, yet men dominated the executive level as it became a mixed-sex organisation.[50] Was this disproportionate representation due to women's lack of confidence or doubts in women's leadership abilities? A number of factors including social and political conservatism may have played a role. Like other peace groups at the time, they had a reconciliation focus, and like other women's peace groups, they reflected maternal or feminine identities while rejecting feminism.[51] Although the PP ultimately failed to create a new more democratic community politics,[52] it nonetheless furnished an important space for women's cross-community networking, as well as opportunities to cultivate leadership skills.

Women Together for Peace (Belfast, 1970–): reconciliation, violence prevention and community development

Women Together for Peace was inspired by the religious dream of Ruth Agnew, an East Belfast Protestant, and founded in Belfast in November 1970 following consultations between members of Protestant and Catholic Encounter (PACE) and the newly established Community Relations Commission (CRC).[53] As hundreds of Protestant and Catholic women met under armed escort for an inaugural ceremony at the Belfast War Memorial Hall, the newly appointed Chair Monica Patterson urged women to 'join in cross-community efforts' and 'harness women's energy' to 'resist and prevent violence in their streets'.[54] WT's primary objective was 'to give women a corporate strength to resist undesirable pressures and to use their maternal influence for peace'. Charac-terised as 'largely psychological', WT's purpose was to strengthen women's self-confidence, develop their community leadership skills and provide a place for them to learn about each other.[55] Patterson asserted, 'We exist to give hope and to provide opportunities for women to fulfill themselves in practical and positive ways. Women here accept their role as second class with compla-cency – I think they are now seeing how important they are and what they can achieve.' At the same time, she defended WT's 'exclusively' female profile explaining that this merely reflected their 'feminine' rather than 'feminist' identity: 'Women are slightly less regimented than men ... [and] it is far more in women's nature to heal and reconcile than to be aggressive.' WT provided an outlet for women to employ 'their feminine traits of sympathy and under-standing, developing their very real influence on the inside of society, nursing it back to health'.[56]

While the 'maternalist' role envisioned for WT in Northern Irish society clearly paralleled the traditional role of women in the home, it also threat-ened to encroach upon the traditionally male preserve of politics. In a state-ment somewhat reminiscent of early twentieth-century WILPF activists, who argued forcefully that women's inclusion in the public sphere would facilitate 'compassion' and 'conciliation' in political and international affairs,[57] a WT editorial asserted, 'We [the women] have been silenced too long while the men shout at each other across our television screens and carry us from one disaster to another.'[58] Early WT Newsletters took a swipe at male politicians for 'not taking women seriously' and using Northern Ireland as a 'chess board' and its people as 'pawns'.[59] Believing WT to be making a vital contribution, Patterson pressured the Community Relations Commission (albeit unsuccessfully) for sustaining funding, which likely put WT in a competitive position with other male-led reconciliation organisations. WT's psycho-social goals of 'women's empowerment' may not have been shared by government officials in Belfast and London, some of whom tried to direct WT towards more traditionally gendered activities such as 'peaceful playgroups for children' and took a rather dim view of what they saw as Patterson's 'demanding' ways and 'importunate' publicity of the organisation.[60]

Although WT attempted to influence state security policies and practices, their efforts throughout the 1970s steered away from formal or structural peacebuilding processes.[61] In character with other women building peace in conflict zones, WT's initiatives were 'culture-specific and gendered', focusing largely on 'people and relationships' at the 'community level'.[62] As one WT Newsletter editorial noted, 'it is at the person to person level that understanding and tolerance begin'.[63] From the outset, WT undertook violence prevention, community development, fundraising and supporting the work of other peace and reconciliation campaigns, as well as involvement in interdenominational events and Peace People rallies. Their violence prevention activities included 'separating rival gangs by acting as human shields, stopping riots, vandalism, intimidation, theft', and more generally, encouraging community resistance against paramilitary involvement. WT's community volunteerism encompassed a wide range of work, from cleaning churches, streets and homes after bombs or riots, to creating playgroups and organising holidays for children, youth and the elderly. They also worked in collaboration with other groups including, PACE, Corrymeela, Peace Point, Society of Friends and the Women's Forum, and eventually embraced feminist projects, working with women's centres on issues of violence against women.[64] However, the activities of WT groups in some of the 'most-affected' areas of conflict, especially Andersonstown and East Belfast, had come to an end by the 1980s.[65] In spite of their non-feminist identity, WT's separatist reconciliation strategy not only gave women a role to play in community peacebuilding and cross-community dialogue, but also created spaces for women's friendships, female-centered support, informal learning networks, and nurtured women's organisational, intellectual and political skills in a number of profound ways.

The Derry Peace Women (Derry, 1972–77): demilitarisation, protest and political reform

The Derry Peace Women (DPW) was founded by five women who led a mass protest of local Catholic women at the Official IRA headquarters in Derry in May 1972 when a young British soldier from their community – Ranger William Best – was killed by the Officials as part of a larger republican campaign to target the British army in Northern Ireland following Bloody Sunday.[66] An

escalation in state and insurgency violence provoked this primarily maternalist and nationalist community response to Best's death. Indeed, their
outrage against the killing provoked the DPW to accuse the IRA of 'doing the
same' as the British Army in their community. As 'women and mothers who
have suffered the most', they demanded that the Officials 'cease their firing
and stick to their defense'. Within days of the DPW protest, the Official IRA
announced a permanent ceasefire, leading media to speculate about the role
played by their protest.[67]

Although collaborating with other peace groups, such as WT and the
PP, the DPW was distinctive from reconciliation groups. Rooted solely in
working-class Catholic nationalist areas of the Bogside and Creggan, they had
supported the Northern Ireland Civil Rights Movement which began in Derry.
Most notably perhaps, they condemned all forms of violence – both army
and paramilitary – and openly protested against the state security policy of
internment which they felt only made more recruits for the IRA. In essence,
the DPW peace strategy revealed a structural approach to peacebuilding that
embraced social and economic justice as well as equal political rights. In an
interview, a former DPW member highlighted what she saw as serious imped-
iments to peace, including discrimination against Catholics in employment
and housing, the state's brutal suppression of civil rights protests, the lack
of political reform and bitterness of 'a trampled-down community' passed
from one generation to the next.[68] Contradicting mainstream narratives of the
conflict (often held by other peace groups at the time), the DPW viewed the
IRA as a product rather than a sole cause of the violence. Subsequently, they
targeted a host of agents in the conflict – from the Provisional IRA to British
military officials and politicians – calling for 'the release of internees, the use
of diplomacy, the removal of British troops, a locally recruited police force,
and a permanent end to Stormont'. Yet, in the end, the DPW appear to have
viewed their peacebuilding role as only temporary, concluding that once these
objectives had been achieved 'then, that's us finished. We'll go back to our
children and our nappies as they are long neglected.'[69]

Unfortunately, the brevity of DPW's existence was not due to their success,
but rather may have been a consequence of British counter-insurgency
campaigns fuelling suspicion and animosity towards peace groups in nationalist and republican communities. In particular, DPW's participation in the
Peace People seems to have prompted their decline in much the same way
as the nationalist Andersonstown WT group in Belfast. Since the DPW only
survived into the late 1970s they were unable to usher in the Good Friday
Agreement alongside of Women Together and the Peace People whose overall
organisations remained intact, albeit severely diminished in number.

Maternalism, gender and women's political participation

This brief examination of Northern Irish women's peace groups raises several
theoretical questions for further exploration. First, do women's groups

'regardless of ideological or feminist orientation, employ the same strategies and tactics' towards the state 'simply because they are women?'[70] While
maternalism was an ostensible driving force for women's peace activism in
WT and the DPW, there was also often a less explicit or visible agenda: women
needed the company of other women to learn and grow on a personal level –
but also to create public spaces as a collective where they could engage with,
and shape, the political processes affecting the material conditions of their
lives within militarised societies.[71] Although WT's goals embraced somewhat
narrow, conservative peace strategies focused on 'community restoration' or
in their terms, 'a return to normal society',[72] their peacebuilding activities
often implicitly challenged both community and state authorities to broaden
official political agendas to engage women's perspectives.

How the state interacts with both feminist and non-feminist women's
movements differently, holds the potential to shape women's political
strategies as well as prevent cross-community alliances amongst women in
conflict settings.[73] Favoring Northern Irish women's peace groups, the British
government gave them access and resources, and also attempted to use them
to repress feminist, socialist and republican challenges to the state. Such state
alignment furnished political openings for Northern Irish women's peace
groups that were far less available to other women's groups at the time. In
addition, this had the effect of further dividing and alienating them from
other women's groups at the height of political conflict.[74]

Finally, we need to ask, to what extent are the politics and language of
feminism ever compatible with female politicisation within conservative
women's groups?[75] Empowerment is viewed as 'a key concept in understanding the importance of developing women-only space'.[76] However, as
Kim Nielson has succinctly pointed out, 'Empowered women do not necessarily feminists make.' Understanding how conservative non-feminist women
are gendered requires, as Nielson argues, understanding that gender is not
only 'present' in their 'bodies' but is also 'at the core of right-wing ideologies,
formulations and negotiations of power'.[77]

The Northern Ireland Women's Coalition (NIWC) and feminist peacebuilding: towards political inclusion and human rights

From Northern Irish women's peace groups in the 1970s to the Northern
Ireland Women's Coalition (NIWC) of the 1990s, maternalist and feminist
politics have shaped women's peacebuilding strategies in both culturally
specific and gender-specific ways. Cross-community feminist alliances facilitated by the Women's Support Network, and the growth of a 'women's sector'
assisted by the European Union's Special Support Programme for Peace and
Reconciliation, have made significant impacts in the wider communities of

Northern Ireland affected by political violence.[78] For many Northern Irish women, the formation of the NIWC in 1996 signalled a much-needed expansion of women's roles in the creation of civil society and promised to shape the peace process and the future of Northern Ireland in substantive ways.[79] However, for others the NIWC represented a potentially dangerous erasure of the very real political and social differences amongst Northern Irish women, and it was feared that 'a woman's party representing women as women would be obliged to adopt *neutrality* on issues that were at stake in the constitutional debate'.[80] In addition, the achievements of women in other political parties appeared to have been sidelined by overwhelming media attention on the NIWC.[81] Since the story of the NIWC has been fairly well documented elsewhere,[82] their feminist vision of peacebuilding is discussed only briefly within the limited scope of this essay.

By the mid-1990s, the recent declaration of IRA and paramilitary cease-fires and a newly elected Labor administration in Westminster created a new political climate for Peace Talks which, after much wrangling, embraced proportional representation and opened up space for politically marginalised groups. As is often the case with women's groups, the 'bold idea for a women's coalition contesting the election' had its genesis around a kitchen table. Following a dramatically swift and successful campaign in the spring of 1996, the NIWC came in ninth amongst all parties in the election, securing for them 'two seats in the Forum for Political Dialogue and the right to send two delegates to the All-Party Talks'.[83] The two NIWC delegates selected for these roles were Monica McWilliams (co-founder of NIWC), a senior lecturer at the University of Ulster, Jordanstown, and Pearl Sagar, a community worker from a unionist background.[84]

Winning a place at the official peace talks on a campaign of three core principles of 'inclusion, equality and human rights', the NIWC distinguished itself from 'cross-community groups' through their 'explicit incorporation of unionists and nationalists' and direct tackling of 'political differences' within the organisation.[85] According to Fearon and McWilliams, NIWC dialogue on the political inclusion of Sinn Féin, humanitarian-based policies on paramilitary prisoners, and constructive discussions on the Orange parade issue had been greatly facilitated by preparatory feminist work 'carried out for the Northern Ireland delegation at the NGO Forum of the UN Fourth Conference on the Status of Women in Beijing'. In addition, NIWC's ongoing open monthly meetings permitted lengthy discussions of such contentious issues amongst all women who wished to attend. Ultimately, the NIWC emphasised the importance of 'inclusive dialogue' taking place 'alongside' of a commitment to non-violence and decommissioning in order to achieve these goals. Moreover, they understood that 'if party politics was to become participatory, it will have to become more inclusive of those outside of the electoral system'.[86]

Upon the signing of the Good Friday Peace Accord on 10 April 1998, the NIWC had successfully contributed to the document its core principles of inclusion, equality and human rights in 'provisions relating to policing reform, judicial reform, equality legislation, human rights protection, a civic forum and measures related to prisoners, victims, and language rights'.[87] Indeed, NIWC's important role in helping to achieve the historic Good Friday Agreement had been acknowledged at the highest levels of peace negotiations.[88] Significantly, the NIWC was also solely responsible for a 'separate clause' in the Accord ensuring the 'right of women to full and equal political participation' under the section on equality and human rights protection.[89] Unfortunately, however, this clause was not realised. In the end, only 14 of the 110 members (or 13 per cent) of the new Northern Ireland Assembly were women. In addition, issues of women's equality have been sidelined in debates which continue to prioritise constitutional and military issues, particularly in view of obtaining both nationalist and unionist cooperation.[90] According to Margaret Ward, the NIWC's strong influence over the early phase of the peace process was not sustained, and consequently, women's equality was 'not consolidated' in later phases. Consequently, she argues, the issues of the peace process have 'narrowed to decommissioning and disbandment of paramilitary organizations', largely the purview of the 'hard men' in the Northern Irish conflict.[91]

Conclusion: United Nations Security Resolution 1325, new directions for feminist peacebuilding and human security

The lack of political commitment to women's equal participation reflected in the Northern Irish peace process signals serious global implications for the UNSC Resolution 1325 as a mechanism for promoting women's inclusion in formal peace processes. Most crucially perhaps, the Resolution ignores the relationship between gender order and militarised discourses of security as a likely source of women's absence at national peace tables. Some have argued that the 'revolutionary potential' of 1325 may in fact be 'delimited' by its discursive construction, which poses 'practical impacts for implementation' just as far-reaching as the structural barriers of UN and member states.[92] In this sense perhaps, inadequate formulations of gender may be equally as detrimental to global peace and security as the virtual absence of women and gender in the peace theories and processes themselves. As long as women are represented erroneously as the sole markers of gender, and viewed as largely peaceful, men and masculine identities 'escape serious analysis'.[93]

Contemporary feminist theorising on gender, security and militarism enables a deeper understanding of the structural, cultural and political contexts necessary for peacebuilding. According to Confortini, it is 'the gender order' that 'makes violence possible' not only because of women's structural subordination in many societies, but also due to normative cultural constructions of hegemonic masculinity and femininity.[94] Further to this point, Ward contends, 'there can be no sustainable future' or peace until 'there is a strong social and political movement against the culture of violent masculinity'.[95] In the context of Northern Ireland, the militarisation of cultural, legal, economic and security dimensions of society[96] needs to be examined in relation to the gender structures and processes that facilitate violence, especially the multiple feminine and masculine identities intersecting with a variety of contending ethnic and political allegiances.

The gendered 'manoeuvres'[97] of both state military and paramilitary regimes in Northern Ireland effectively inhibit the development of a strong civil society, thwarting peacebuilding efforts and reinforcing a gender order which prevents women's political participation. Successful peacebuilding efforts also require the inclusion and reintegration of former paramilitary actors, including female combatants.[98] Attentiveness to social inclusion as a fundamental tool of peacebuilding also evaluates women's civic work which, according to some, 'may be even more crucial in sustaining cross-community cooperation, fostering inclusive democracy, and advancing gender equity' than formal peace processes.[99] As this essay has shown, WT and the DPW's early community-building and demilitarisation efforts were a vital part of a much larger mosaic of Northern Irish women's peacebuilding contributions.

Ultimately, the intention of peacebuilding is to 'create a structure of peace that is based on justice, equity, and cooperation (i.e., positive peace), thereby addressing the underlying causes of violent conflict so that they become less likely in the future'.[100] However, without a comprehensive gender analysis of violence and conflict, attentive to 'human processes and human needs',[101] theories of peace and security remain impoverished and ungrounded. Successful implementation of UNSC 1325 requires radically new approaches to peacebuilding, shifting the lens from state actors to civil society, away from privileging state security over human rights and human security. Transnational feminist interrogation of neo-colonialist Western policies of governance and globalisation in conflict settings promise new insights and approaches here.[102] With the recent rise in 'protracted social conflicts' since 9/11[103] and the growth of both female and male suicide bombers, a more thorough gender analysis promises to enrich our vision and expand our tools for peacebuilding in the twenty-first century.

Notes

1 I would like to dedicate this article to feminist peacebuilding women who profoundly shaped my life and contributed immensely to this dialogue in Canadian society: Muriel Duckworth (1908–2009) and Kay Macpherson (1913–1999). Both were founding members of the Canadian Voice of Women for Peace (1960–).

2 M. I. Gawerc, 'Peace-building: Theoretical and Concrete Perspectives', *Peace and Change* 31.4 (2006), 435.

3 L. Sjoberg, 'Introduction to Security Studies: Feminist Contributions', *Security Studies* 18.2 (2009), 192; C. C. Confortini, 'Galtung, Violence, and Gender: The Case

for a Peace Studies/Feminism Alliance', *Peace and Change* 31.3 (2006), 333–67.

4 For example, see P. Dixon, 'Performing the Northern Ireland Peace Process on the World Stage', *Political Science Quarterly* 121 (Spring 2006), 61–91.

5 Confortini, 'Galtung, Violence, and Gender'.

6 See Johan Galtung, *Peace by Peaceful Means: Peace and Conflict, Development and Civilization* (London, 1996); and J. P. Lederach, *The Moral Imagination: The Art and Soul of Building Peace* (New York, 2005).

7 Sjoberg, 'Introduction to Security Studies: Feminist Contributions', 192–97.

8 M. Ward, 'Gender, Citizenship, and the Future of the Northern Ireland Peace Process', *Eire-Ireland* 41.1–2 (2006), 262.

9 J. Wallach Scott, 'Gender: A Useful Category of Historical Analysis', *American Historical Review* 91.5 (1986), 1053–75.

10 J. Lorber, *Gender Inequality: Feminist Theories and Politics* (3rd edn, New York, 2005), 9–11.

11 Confortini, 'Galtung, Violence, and Gender'.

12 Cynthia Enloe, *Bananas, Beaches, and Bases: Making Feminist Sense of International Politics* (Berkeley, CA, 1990); Sandra McEvoy, 'Loyalist Women Paramilitaries in Northern Ireland: Beginning a Feminist Conversation about Conflict Resolution', *Security Studies* 18.2 (2009), 282.

13 See M. Zalewski et al., 'Celebrating Twenty Years of British Gender and IR', *International Feminist Journal of Politics* 11.3 (2009), 305–33; and works by Joshua S. Goldstein, Christine Sylvester, Ann Tickner, Laura J. Shepherd and Sandra Whitworth.

14 M. Hammond-Callaghan, 'United Nations Security Council Resolution 1325', in Nigel Young et al. (eds), *International Encyclopaedia for Peace* (Oxford, 2010). Also, see C. Cohn et al., 'Women, Peace and Security: Resolution 1325', *International Feminist Journal of Politics* 6.1 (2004), 130–40; F. Hill et al., 'Non-governmental Organizations' Role in the Buildup and Implementation of Security Council Resolution 1325', *Signs: Journal of Women in Culture and Society* 28.4 (2003), 1255–69.

15 Gawerc, 'Peace-building: Theoretical and Concrete Perspectives', 439; C. de la Rey and S. McKay, 'Peace-building as a Gendered Process', *Journal of Social Issues* 62.1 (2006), 141–53.

16 Gawerc, 'Peace-building: Theoretical and Concrete Perspectives', 439; de la Rey and McKay, 'Peace-building as a Gendered Process', 143; Elisabeth Porter, 'Women, Political Decision-making, and Peace-building', *Global Change, Peace and Security* 15.3 (2003), 254–62.

17 de la Rey and McKay, 'Peace-building as a Gendered Process', 143–44.

18 L. Racioppi and K. Sullivan See 'Engendering Democratic Transition from Conflict: Women's Exclusion in Northern Ireland's Peace Process', *Comparative Politics* 38.2 (2006), 189; C. Cockburn, *From Where We Stand: War, Women's Activism and Feminist Analysis* (London, 2007).

19 Porter, 'Women, Political Decision-making, and Peace-building', 249–50; also see E. Porter, *Peacebuilding: Women in International Perspective* (London and New York, 2008).

20 Confortini, 'Galtung, Violence, and Gender', 61–84; Porter, 'Women, Political Decision-making, and Peace-building'; A. Smyth, 'Paying our Disrespects to the Bloody States We're in: Women, Violence, Culture, and the State', *Journal of Women's History* 7.1 (1995), 190.

21 United Nations Security Council Resolution 1325 (2000), Adopted by the Security Council at its 4213th meeting on 31 October 2000, http://daccessdds.un.org/doc/ (accessed 16 March 2011).

22 C. Chinkin, and H. Charlesworth, 'Building Women in Peace: The International

Legal Framework', *Third World Quarterly* 27.5 (2006), 937–57; V. M. Moghadam, 'Peacebuilding and Reconstruction with Women: Reflections on Afghanistan, Iraq and Palestine', *Development* 48.3 (2005), 63–72.

23 C. Cohn, H. Kinsella and S. Gibbings, 'Women, Peace and Security: Resolution 1325', *International Feminist Journal of Politics* 6.1 (2004), 130–40, and Hammond-Callaghan, 'United Nations Security Council Resolution 1325'.

24 S. E. Cooper, 'Peace as a Human Right: The Invasion of Women into the World of High Politics', *Journal of Women's History* 14. 2 (2002), 211–25 (202).

25 B. Roberts, 'Women's Peace Activism in Canada', in Linda Kealey and Joan Sangster (eds), *Beyond The Vote: Canadian Women and Politics* (Toronto, 1989), 276–306. Also see R. Roach Pierson (ed.), *Women and Peace: Theoretical, Historical and Practical Perspectives* (London, 1987).

26 F. Early, 'Feminisms Influence on Peace History', *Atlantis* 25.1 (2000), 3–10; Harriet Hyman Alonso, 'Why Women's Peace History?', *Peace and Change* 20.1 (January, 1995), 48–52; Cooper, 'Peace as a Human Right'.

27 S. Roseneil, *Disarming Patriarchy: Feminism and Political Action at Greenham* (Buckingham, 1995).

28 S. E. Cooper, 'The Subversive Power of Peace History', *Peace and Change* 20.1 (1995), 61.

29 H. Alonso, 'Why Women's Peace History?'; also see A. Swerdlow, *Women Strike for Peace: Traditional Motherhood and Radical Politics in the 1960s* (Chicago and London, 1993).

30 Roseneil, *Disarming Patriarchy*.

31 C. Cockburn, *The Space between Us: Negotiating Gender and National Identities in Conflict* (London, 1998); Roseneil, *Disarming Patriarchy*; Roberts, 'Women's Peace Activism in Canada'.

32 R. Cullen Owens, 'Women and Pacifism in Ireland, 1915–1932', in M. Valiulis and M. O'Dowd (eds), *Women and Irish History* (Dublin, 1997), 228. Also see B. Gray and L. Ryan, 'The Politics of Irish Identity and the Interconnections between Feminism and Colonialism', in R. Roach Pierson and N. Chaudhuri (eds), *Nation, Empire, Colony: Historicising Gender and Race* (Bloomington, 1998), 121–38.

33 Cullen Owens, 'Women and Pacifism in Ireland, 1915–1932', 238.

34 Cullen Owens, 'Women and Pacifism in Ireland, 1915–1932'; D. Hearne, 'The Irish Citizen, 1914–1916: Nationalism, Feminism and Militarism', *Canadian Journal of Irish Studies* 18.1 (1991), 10.

35 Cullen Owens, 'Women and Pacifism in Ireland, 1915–1932'.

36 Cooper, 'Peace as a Human Right'.

37 A. Carter, *Peace Movements, International Protest and World Politics since 1945* (London and New York, 1992), 19.

38 J. Ruane and J. Todd, *The Dynamics of Conflict in Northern Ireland* (Cambridge, 1996), 91–92.

39 S. Sharoni, 'Rethinking Women's Struggles in Israel-Palestine and the North of Ireland', in C. O. N. Moser and F. C. Clark (eds), *Victims, Perpetrators or Actors? Gender Armed Conflict and Political Violence* (London, 2001), 85–98.

40 Gawerc, 'Peace-building: Theoretical and Concrete Perspectives'; S. Roseneil, *Disarming Patriarchy: Feminism and Political Action at Greenham* (Buckingham, 1995).

41 M. Hammond-Callaghan, 'A tender flower ... to be carefully nourished': The Northern Irish Women's Peace Movement, Gender Order, State Security and the Cold War, 1970–76', in D. Urquhart and G. McIntosh (eds), *Irish Women at War* (Dublin, 2010).

42 M. Hammond-Callaghan, 'Peace Women and Peace-Building in Northern Ireland: Gender, Discourse And "Difference"', *Canadian Women's Studies / Les Cahiers De*

La Femme (special issue on 'Women and Peace-building') 22.2 (2003), 28–35; idem, 'Surveying Politics of Peace, Gender, Conflict and Identity in Northern Ireland'; idem, 'A tender flower ... to be carefully nourished'.

43 S. B. Hyatt, *Accidental Activists: Women and Politics on a Council Estate* (Amherst, 1991), 4, cited in Monica McWilliams, 'Struggling for Peace and Justice: Reflections on Women's Activism in Northern Ireland', *Journal of Women's History* 6.4/7.1 (1995), 21.

44 Early, 'Feminism's Influence on Peace History'.

45 R. Fairmichael, *The Peace People Experience* (Belfast, 1987), 1–29.

46 See D. Keogh and M. H. Haltzel, *Northern Ireland and the Politics of Reconciliation* (Cambridge, 1994.); M. T. Love, *Peace Building Through Reconciliation in Northern Ireland* (Hants, 1995); M. Power, *From Ecumenism to Community Relations: Inter-Church Relationships in Northern Ireland, 1980–2005* (Dublin, 2007)

47 M. Hammond-Callaghan, 'Surveying Politics of Peace, Gender, Conflict and Identity in Northern Ireland: The Case of The Derry Peace Women in 1972', in A. O'Day and N. C. Fleming (eds), *Ireland and Anglo-Irish Relations Since 1800: Critical Essays. III. From the Treaty to the Present* (London, 2008); idem, 'A tender flower ... to be carefully nourished'.

48 For example, J. Bowyer Bell, *The Irish Troubles: A Generation of Violence, 1967–1992* (Dublin, 1993); and T. P. Coogan, *The IRA* (London, 2000); as discussed in M. Hammond-Callaghan, 'Gender, Difference and the Politics of Location: Situating Women's Peace Activism in Northern Ireland and Quebec, Canada, in Conflict and Crisis, 1970–1972' (unpublished PhD, National University of Ireland, Dublin, 2004).

49 Both were recipients of the Nobel Peace Prize in 1977.

50 Fairmichael, *The Peace People Experience*.

51 M. Corrigan Maguire, *The Vision of Peace: Faith and Hope in Northern Ireland* (Maryknoll, NY, 1999); Fairmichael, *The Peace People Experience*.

52 Fairmichael, *The Peace People Experience*; also, see N. McCafferty, 'The Peace People at War', *Goodnight Sisters: Selected Articles of Nell McCafferty* (Dublin, 1987), 104–40; and McWilliams, 'Struggling for Peace and Justice', 13–39.

53 Hammond-Callaghan, 'A tender flower ... to be carefully nourished'; *Women Together Newsletter* 1, Belfast, December 1971 (Linen Hall Library [hereafter LHL], Belfast, Northern Ireland Political Section, Box 1, 'Peace and Reconciliation Groups', file 206); D. Bleakley, *Sadie Patterson: Irish Peacemaker* (Belfast, 1980); and M. Geelan, 'Women's Contribution as Peacemakers in Northern Ireland: A Case Study of Women Together' (unpub. MA thesis, Peace Studies, University of Ulster, Coleraine, 1999).

54 *Irish News*, 27 November 1970 and *Belfast Newsletter*, 19 February 1971.

55 *Belfast Newsletter*, 19 February 1971.

56 *Irish Independent*, March 1971 and *Belfast Newsletter*, 2 December 1971.

57 J. Vellacott, 'A Place for Pacifism and Transnationalism in Feminist Theory: The Early Work of the Women's International League for Peace and Freedom', *Women's History Review* 2.1 (1993), 46.

58 *Women Together Newsletter* 3, Belfast, Autumn 1972.

59 *Women Together Newsletter* 1, Belfast, December 1971.

60 See Correspondence of the UK representative in Belfast, the Home Office at White-hall, and the Community Relations Commission Director: 'Hywel Griffiths, Director', c. Apr. 1971; H. Griffiths to Miss Murnaghan re. Women for Peace Movement, 12 Nov. 1970 (Public Records Office of Northern Ireland, PRONI, CREL 4/2/9); 'Visit to Belfast', 6–11 Jan. 1972; and Howard Smith to J. T. A. Howard-Drake, 31 Jan. 1972 (The National Archives, TNA, 'Women Together and Other Women's Organizations', CJ4 1548, 17 Jan. 1972–24 June 1977).

61 Lord Windlesham's meetings with WT, 21 June 1972; 26 July 1972; and 30 Mar. 1973 (TNA, 'Women Together and Other Women's Organizations', CJ4 1548, 17 Jan. 1972–24 June 1977)

62 de la Rey and McKay, 'Peace-building as a Gendered Process', 141.

63 *Women Together Newsletter* 1, Belfast, December 1971 (LHL, Belfast, Box 1, 'Peace and Reconciliation Groups', file 206).

64 'Women Together, Project Material', Leslie Haslett, Chairman of WT, June 1977 (TNA, 'Women Together and Other Women's Organizations', CJ4 1548, 17 Jan. 1972–24 June 1977); interview with 'Joan' (pseudonym), Belfast, 7 July 1999.

65 Author's interview with 'Mary' (pseudonym), Belfast, 19 June 2000 in Hammond-Callaghan, 'Gender, Difference and the Politics of Location'.

66 Hammond-Callaghan, 'Surveying Politics of Peace, Gender, Conflict and Identity in Northern Ireland'; A. Kerr, 'The Derry Peace Women', in Adrian Kerr, Paul Hippsley and Declan Carlin (eds), *Perceptions: Cultures in Conflict* (Derry, 1996), 40–43.

67 *Irish Times*, 24 June 1972 and *Daily Mail*, 24 June 1972.

68 Author's interview with 'Deirdre' (pseudonym), Derry, 3 Dec. 2000 in Hammond-Callaghan, 'Gender, Difference and the Politics of Location'.

69 *Irish Times*, 24 June 1972.

70 K. Beckwith, 'Mapping Strategic Engagements: Women's Movements and the State', *International Feminist Journal of Politics* 9 (2009), 318.

71 Thanks to Frances Early (History Department, Mount Saint Vincent University) for helping me to come to this insight.

72 Ward, 'Gender, Citizenship, and the Future of the Northern Ireland Peace Process', 263; *Women Together Newsletter* 1, Belfast, December 1971 (LHL, Belfast, Box 1, 'Peace and Reconciliation Groups', file 206); and interview with 'Deirdre' (pseudonym), Derry, 3 Dec. 2000.

73 Beckwith, 'Mapping Strategic Engagements: Women's Movements and the State', 318.

74 Hammond-Callaghan, 'A tender flower … to be carefully nourished'.

75 J. V. Gottlieb, 'Right-Wing Women in Women's History: A Global Perspective', *Journal of Women's History* 16.3 (2004), 107; K. E. Nielson, 'Doing the "Right" Right', *Journal of Women's History* 16.3 (2004), 168–72.

76 Ward, 'Gender, Citizenship, and the Future of the Northern Ireland Peace Process', 270.

77 Nielson, 'Doing the "Right" Right', 171.

78 Racioppi and Sullivan See, 'Engendering Democratic Transition from Conflict', 196–99; Ward, 'Gender, Citizenship, and the Future of the Northern Ireland Peace Process', 271–72. Also see R. Taillon, *NI Women's Organizations' Experiences of EU Funding Programmes, Survey Report* (Belfast, October 2002); B. Hinds, 'Women Working for Peace in Northern Ireland', in Yvonne Galligan, Eilis Ward and Rick Wilford (eds), *Contesting Politics: Women in Ireland, North and South* (Boulder, CO, 1999), 113; Katherine Side, 'Snapshot on Identity: Women's Contributions Addressing Community Relations in a Rural Northern Irish District', *Women's Studies International Forum* 28.4 (2005), 315.

79 Ward, 'Gender, Citizenship, and the Future of the Northern Ireland Peace Process', 274.

80 Cockburn, *The Space between Us*, 83.

81 M. Hill, *Women in Ireland: A Century of Change* (Belfast, 2003), 229.

82 See K. Fearon, *Women's Work: The Story of the Northern Ireland Women's Coalition* (Belfast, 1999); K. Fearon and M. McWilliams, 'Swimming against the Mainstream: The Northern Ireland Women's Coalition', in C. Roulston and C. Davies (eds), *Gender, Democracy and Inclusion in Northern Ireland* (Hampshire, 2000),

117–37; Monica McWilliams and Avila Kilmurray, 'Athene on the Loose: The Origins of the Northern Ireland Women's Coalition', *Irish Journal of Feminist Studies* 2.1 (1997), 1–21; and C. B. Rynder, 'The Origins and Early Years of the Northern Ireland Women's Coalition', *New Hibernia Review* 6.1 (2002), 44–58.

83 Fearon and McWilliams, 'Swimming against the Mainstream', 119 and 124.

84 Hill, *Women in Ireland*, 228–31.

85 R. Whitaker, 'Gender and the Politics of Justice in the Northern Ireland Peace Process: Considering Roisin McAliskey', *Identities* 15.1 (2008), 6.

86 Fearon and McWilliams, 'Swimming against the Mainstream', 122–25.

87 Ward, 'Gender, Citizenship, and the Future of the Northern Ireland Peace Process', 275.

88 George Mitchel as cited in Fearon and McWilliams, 'Swimming against the Mainstream', 129.

89 Rynder, 'The Origins and Early Years of the Northern Ireland Women's Coalition', 50; Ward, 'Gender, Citizenship, and the Future of the Northern Ireland Peace Process', 275.

90 Hill, *Women in Ireland*, 232, and Ward, 'Gender, Citizenship, and the Future of the Northern Ireland Peace Process', 275.

91 Ward, 'Gender, Citizenship, and the Future of the Northern Ireland Peace Process', 283.

92 C. Cohn, H. Kinsella and S. Gibbings, 'Women, Peace and Security: Resolution 1325'; Laura J. Shepherd, *Gender, Violence and Security* (London, 2008).

93 Shepherd, *Gender, Violence and Security*; H. Hudson, 'Doing Security as Though Humans Matter: Feminist Perspective on Gender and the Politics of Human Security', *Security Dialogue* 36 (2005), 155–74; Chinkin and Charlesworth, 'Building Women in Peace: The International Legal Framework'; C. Cohn and C. Enloe, 'A Conversation with Cynthia Enloe: Feminists Look at Masculinity and the Men Who Wage War', *Signs: Journal of Women in Culture and Society* 28.4 (2003), 1187–1207.

94 Confortini, 'Galtung, Violence, and Gender', 350.

95 Ward, 'Gender, Citizenship, and the Future of the Northern Ireland Peace Process', 279.

96 M. Smyth, 'The Process of Demilitarization and the Reversibility of the Peace Process in Northern Ireland', *Terrorism and Political Violence* 16.3 (2004), 546 and 549–51.

97 C. Enloe, *Manoeuvres: International Politics of Militarising Women's Lives* (California, 2000).

98 Smyth, 'The Process of Demilitarization and the Reversibility of the Peace Process in Northern Ireland'; L. McEvoy, K. McEvoy and K. McConnachie, 'Reconciliation as a Dirty Word: Conflict, Community Relations and Education in Northern Ireland', *Journal of International Affairs* 60.1 (2006), 81–106; and McEvoy, 'Loyalist Women Paramilitaries in Northern Ireland', 262.

99 Racioppi and Sullivan See, 'Engendering Democratic Transition from Conflict', 204.

100 Gawerc, 'Peace-building: Theoretical and Concrete Perspectives'.

101 de la Rey and McKay, 'Peace-building as a Gendered Process', 150; B. Hamber et al., 'Discourses in Transition: Re-Imagining Women's Security', *International Relations* 20.4 (2006), 487–502; Marsha Henry, 'Gender, Security and Development', *Conflict, Security and Development* 7.1 (2007), 61–84.

102 Chinkin and Charlesworth, 'Building Women in Peace: The International Legal Framework'; Moghadam, 'Peace-building and Reconstruction with Women'; Ustina Dolgopol, 'Women Peace-building', *Australian Feminist Studies* 21.50 (2006), 257–73.

103 Gawerc, 'Peace-building: Theoretical and Concrete Perspectives', 436.

7

Encumbered by Data: Understanding Politically Motivated Former Prisoners and the Transition to Peace in Northern Ireland

Kieran McEvoy and Pete Shirlow

Introduction

Our previous work on politically motivated former prisoners (PMFP) has contended that the peace process in Northern Ireland has provided various and sustained examples of the role that PMFPs have played as both leaders of and agents in the delivery of conflict transformation. However, a more frequent and unsympathetic discourse directed at PMFPs remains tied to a representation of them as terrorist-inspired and insidious. As one academic has argued, when critiquing the approach of the authors, 'the obsession with labelling actions as political, obscures the fact that the republican and loyalist campaigns were fundamentally sectarian and terroristic and undoubtedly criminal'.[1]

Within that perspective, past violent deeds remain as the barometer against which PMFPs 'must' remain measured. Such an interpretation appears incapable of countenancing the positive role that PMFPs have played in upholding and delivering peace, stability and the promotion of non-violent practice precisely because they used to be 'terroristic' [sic]. While academics will continue to 're-fight' the conflict in scholarly journals, the real-life impact of such views are a daily experience for many PMFPs who grapple with the various consequences of the violence of the past. Moreover, many of the positive assessments of the significance and quality of PMFP work emanates from sources who would hardly be described as 'fellow travellers'.[2]

In conducting our research on ex-combatants and PMFPs, we have stressed continuously that we do not naively eulogise them[3] and unlike many who continue to rail against former combatants we are encumbered by data. We have made informed assessments as to the role that PMFP groups have played or continue to play by examining what they actually do. Either together or separately over the past two decades we have conducted literally hundreds of interviews and extensive survey work with ex-combatants and PMFPs, prison staff, police officers, policy-makers and others with knowledge or insights into this world. We have reviewed numerous official documents and publications as well as the scholarly literature. In discussing the 'warts and all' transformation of the principal paramilitary groups in Northern Ireland, we have acknowledged cease-fire breaches, criminality, punishment violence, sectarianism and a range of other brutal realities.[4] Despite that, we have nonetheless concluded that PMFP groups have been central to the gradual process of embedding conflict transformation in communities most affected by violence.

Perhaps by virtue of their proximity to the conflict, PMFP groups were arguably amongst the first constituencies to appreciate that the peace process would lead to new social, cultural and political relationships as well as the development of intra and inter-community linkages.[5] Based upon strong political identities and a respect for the rights of the 'other', rather than any imagined 'middle ground', PMFPs have been crucial in building a stable process on the ground.[6] Not-withstanding the activities of dissident Republicans, the fact that all of the major paramilitary organisations have now decommissioned most of their weapons and appear firmly committed to their own dissolution speaks directly to the leadership skills of former combatants.

The predisposition of sections of the media, academia and some unionist and nationalist politicians to focus almost exclusively upon individual acts of criminality undertaken by former combatants in recent times has, we would argue, obfuscated a more nuanced grasp of what is actually happening both within the PMFP groups themselves and also the communities in which they live and operate. It is now undeniable that, at leadership level, the IRA and the UVF\RHC have for more than a decade been involved in real and meaningful efforts to transform their respective organisations and by extension, the communities from which they emanate. Even within the historically more fragmented and criminogenic UDA,[7] as was acknowledged in the most recent report from the International Monitoring Commission,[8] conspicuous examples of real leadership have emerged.

This essay explores the ways in which the disputes concerning the nomenclature concerning prisoners and former prisoners have mapped onto the broader political struggles concerning 'the conflict about the conflict'.[9] It then explores the process of early release and reintegration as a 'critical juncture' in the trajectory towards conflict transformation. The essay also focuses on three particular areas of activity in which former prisoners have been involved as sites of 'putting reintegration into praxis', namely their role in the parallel processes of demobilisation and disarmament, dealing with the past and their recent involvement in developing an educational resource for young people both to better understand the conflict and to serve as a bulwark against future generations becoming involved in political violence. We conclude by drawing out some of the key themes from these experiences which, the authors suggest, offers a more grounded approach to reconciliation work more generally which may be of relevance to other transitional societies.

From political prisoners to politically motivated former prisoners

For some, the policy of criminalisation, formally adopted by the British government in 1976, resonated strongly with wider discourses and practices which sought to portray republicans and loyalists as pathological, misguided and thus criminal. Throughout the conflict, and even in its wake, the contests concerning the definitions applied to those imprisoned as a result of their involvement in political violence were so keenly fought precisely because they represented competing claims as to the legitimacy or not of that violence.[10]

Such wrangling is not unique to Northern Ireland. Groups such as Amnesty International historically adopted a fairly narrow view of political detainees as 'prisoners of conscience', who had not advocated or condoned acts of violence.[11] Others, using the International Humanitarian Law ('Laws of War') or extradition law framework, have used the term 'prisoners of war' to refer to those imprisoned for politically motivated acts.[12] As is evidenced by the fierce struggles over the terminology of those imprisoned as a result of the 'War on Terror', competing claims as to the relevance of the Geneva Conventions have themselves become a key ideological battleground rather than offered definitional clarity.[13] While prisoners themselves have historically self-referred as 'prisoners of war', and at different junctures did experience practical prison conditions akin to that status, in practice neither the British nor Irish governments have ever referred to them as such.

In Northern Ireland, successive British governments adopted a broadly instrumentalist approach to defining the actions of 'terrorists'. 'Terrorism' was defined from 1972 onwards as 'the use of violence for political ends and includes any use of violence for the purpose of putting the public or any section of the public in fear'. A terrorist was defined as 'a person who is or has been concerned in the commission or attempted commission of any act of terrorism or in directing, organising or training persons for the purpose of terrorism'.[14] Within such a technocratic framework, the admission that acts of 'terrorism' had 'political ends' meant nothing more than that such acts represented attacks on a societal value system. In essence, the issue of legitimacy remained vested in the state as the 'protector' and 'guarantor' of security.

The claims for a recognition of their political status by Republicans and Loyalists had different resonances in their respective communities. For nationalists, even those who were strongly opposed to the use of political violence, there appeared few difficulties in accepting the fact that such violence was in essence politically motivated.[15] Loyalists who engaged in violence clearly saw their actions as politically driven by the desire to maintain the union and 'defend their community'. 'Their' community on the other hand appeared to have a much more ambivalent position on accepting the political character of that violence or its Republican equivalent. For the unionist community, regarded here in its broadest sense, the use of violence by paramilitaries was (in public at least), deemed to be objectionable and an aberration that was distasteful in a 'decent' society.[16] In this depiction, members of the security/ state forces were not combatants but instead defenders of the state and its people. To deem them as combatants was to accept the Republican account of the conflict as a war and therefore to afford some legitimacy to paramilitary claims. The criminalisation discourse, with its view of terrorism as but one further category of criminal behaviour which sought to undermine both 'law and order' and the democratic state, resonated strongly within Unionism.

The acknowledgement in the Emergency laws that terrorism entailed the use of the violence for political ends was not extended to other important legislation. For example, Fair Employment legislation in Northern Ireland, which was established to prevent discrimination on the grounds of religion or political opinion, specifically excludes support for Loyalist or Republican violence. Under the Fair Employment Order (1998), which updated the existing legislation but retained the same wording, Article 2 (4) stipulates that 'any reference to a person's political opinion does not include an opinion which consists of or includes approval or acceptance of the use of violence for political ends connected with the affairs of Northern Ireland'. This legislation means that politically motivated prisoners can lawfully be debarred from employment on the grounds of their past support for political violence. That position, reiterated in a 2009 House of Lords decision in McConkey and Marks,[17] clearly represents a significant obstacle for former prisoners. In the colourful words of the applicants' barrister in that case, it arguably offers employers the potential to use legislation that was designed to outlaw discrimination at a time of extreme political violence as a 'bigots charter' with regard to politically motivated former prisoners in the changed context of a post-conflict society.

Prisoner release and reintegration as a 'critical juncture' in the peace process

Perhaps the defining issue in shaping negative attitudes towards former prisoners was the controversies surrounding the early release of politically motivated prisoners. Within the literature on historical institutionalism, there is an interesting concept referred to as a 'critical juncture' which is of direct relevance.[18] Broadly understood, critical junctures are key historical moments or processes in the history of an institution such as the prison service which become shorthand for a series of (often contested) meanings around which broader political, social and ideological struggles coalesce.[19] Thus, for example, the murder of Stephen Lawrence and the subsequent MacPherson Inquiry in Britain is widely accepted as a critical juncture in the history of British policing which became a metaphor for heated arguments about the meaning and prevalence of institutional racism in the police and British society more generally. Such critical junctures provide important historical and cultural narratives which shape and inform collective memory and political discourses.[20] The early release of prisoners and 'reintegration' was precisely such a critical juncture – a defining element of the Belfast Agreement which continues to be a key prism through which to view the competing understandings of the peace process as either conflict transformation or the appeasement of terrorism.

Under the early release provisions of the Belfast Agreement, to date, 452 prisoners have been released (197 loyalist, 242 republican and 13 non-aligned) early and on license under those provisions. Although these releases constituted 6% of all such persons imprisoned, the Life and Times Survey (2000)[21] indicated that a mere 12% supported or strongly supported the release of PMFPs compared to 61% who opposed or strongly opposed this policy. Within the same survey, 31% of Catholics compared to 3% of Protestants supported the release of such prisoners.

The evident ire of the Unionist community was palpable and became emblematic of the broader rejection of the acknowledgement of political motivation of the non-state combatant groups.[22] In addition to releases, the subsequent funding of PMFP groups as the logical outworking of the Agreement's commitments toward reintegration was also interpreted, especially within the unionist community, as 'rewarding the men of violence'.[23] One prominent feature of the attitude towards PMFPs that has emanated from the main unionist parties, has been a consistent linkage of the question of prisoner release and funding with regard to the treatment of victims of violence. The DUP, in particular, spoke often of the need for all Unionists to 'recoil with moral contempt' at the idea of prisoner release. Thus, a persistent theme amongst those who campaigned against early release was that of framing their position as those who spoke 'on behalf' of the victims of violence. As one of the authors has argued previously, this assumption of representing the voice of victims belied the fact that while of course many victims of violence were opposed to the early releases, victims did not speak with one voice on the issue.[24] Some high-profile victims actually spoke in favour of early releases. These include Joan Wilson (mother of Marie Wilson killed by the IRA in the Enniskillen bombing) and Colin Parry (father of Tim killed by the IRA bomb at Warrington). Mr Parry expressed his position in the following terms:

> Whilst it is offensive to have my son classed as collateral damage, I saw the prisoner release process as part of the Good Friday Agreement as being absolutely essential. I accepted that the position that both governments were taking, that without prisoner releases there would have been no deal.[25]

Despite the generosity and/or pragmatism of such individuals, negative discourses attached to PMFPs remain tied to the discursive and ideological competition regarding the meaning and reasons for violent conflict. As Brian Gormally[26] has argued, prisoners and former prisoners are at the most symbols of the anger people feel about the past, they are 'the perpetrators of numerous atrocities, the enemies of democracy and civilisation incarnate'. The general argument pertains that innocent victims groups are under-funded. As is well illustrated by Jim Allister, leader of the TUV,

> 'ex-prisoners' have been deemed as a marginal group, and therefore have been awarded priority status under the new Peace III Programme due to begin shortly. Should the Executive fail to reverse this approach, they will be adding great insult to those innocent victims of terrorist violence.[27]

Jim Allister's commentary related to the £9.2m received by PMFP groups between 1995–2003, from the Community Foundation for Northern Ireland (CFNI) and the European Special Support Programme for Peace and Reconciliation (Peace I and II). His commentary neglected to note that such funds represented less than one per cent of the total EU- and government-funded budget for peace and reconciliation work in Northern Ireland.[28] In comparative terms, the funding of victim-related work in Northern Ireland has been amongst the most financially well supported in the world of transitional justice.[29] The British government initially committed £18m towards victim issues between 1998 and 2001.[30] By 2006, a total of £44m had been allocated towards provision of services to victims.[31] Under Peace III, the needs of victims were slated to be addressed under Priority 1, 'acknowledging and dealing with the past', with a total budget for that Priority of £105m between 2007–2013.

Not all opposition to the funding of PMFPs has come from within Unionism. In 2007, Margaret Ritchie (an MLA from the nationalist Social Democratic and Labour Party) and the then Minister for Social Development tried to remove a grant provided by the Northern Ireland Office, during the suspension of the Northern Ireland Assembly, of £1.2m to the Conflict Transformation Initiative (CTI) project involving the Ulster Political Research Group (linked to the Ulster Defence Association [UDA]). Her reasons for doing so were explained as being tied to the failure of the UDA to decommission and that 'There is no excuse now for paramilitarism. It is time for all those who subject their communities to thuggery, extortion and violence, under the pretence of defending them, to get off the stage.'[32] In interview work with one of the authors, the UDA-aligned Ulster Political Research Group argued that they had and were involved in meaningful engagement with the Independent International Monitoring Commission and that their group had held nearly 40 meetings, over the previous three months, before the suspension of funds, with the police regarding crime and criminality. In a subsequent judicial review of the decision by Ms Ritchie to remove the funding to the CTI, the validity of that decision was subsequently struck down by the current Lord Chief Justice Sir Declan Morgan on the grounds that she had failed to consult properly with her Executive colleagues in making the decision.[33]

The SDLP had previously been engaged in quite vicious political struggles with Sinn Féin over projects concerning PMFPs. In that instance, tussles centred on the issue of community-based restorative justice programmes, many of which are managed and staffed by former IRA prisoners.[34] At that juncture in the peace process, before Republicans agreed to join the Policing Board, such struggles were a reflection of the political contest within nationalism concerning the timing of support for policing structures. Sinn Féin accused the SDLP of having 'jumped too soon' and the SDLP countered that the restorative justice projects represented an effort by Republicans to maintain their own 'private army' in the areas where they were strong.[35] In the case of the CTI funding of a UDA-linked project, where Sinn Féin were supportive of the funding of the project and the SDLP against, the mapping of the issue onto broader nationalist politics was none too subtle. PMFP were caught in a political cross-fire which was largely removed from any objective judgement as to the quality of the work engaged in.[36]

In sum, the process of release and reintegration of PMFPs has become a key battleground. Media attention, particularly from local tabloids, serves up a constant diet of stories concerning the involvement of paramilitaries and former prisoners in criminality.[37] What gets lost in the ensuing noise is that 12 years after the early releases began, of the prisoners released early, only 23, or 5%, have had their licences suspended.[38] By way of comparison, the recidivism rate for ordinary criminals in Northern Ireland is 48% within two years of their release from prison.[39] In general, PMFPs struggle to get news of their actual work beyond the confines of neighbourhood papers with many of their achievements and positive contributions remaining hidden from public attention. This fragmentation of knowledge and understanding, between the very localised and the more general, means that broader discussions in both popular and academic outlets concerning combatants, former combatants and PMFPs often appear frozen in the staid caricatures of good and evil.[40] In order to get beyond such stereotypes, it is necessary to consider further what PMPFs actually do.

Reintegration, conflict transformation and 'praxis'

Before examining in more detail the work of the PMFP projects, it is important to enter a further terminological caveat, in this instance concerning the term reintegration. Although the Belfast Agreement explicitly referred to the notion of reintegration,[41] in practice this concept is a loaded term for a number of overlapping reasons. Many PMFPs associate the term with 'ordinary' criminality rather than 'politically motivated' offending. As discussed above, for former prisoners who resisted state-driven criminalisation via their political struggle, sometimes to the point of death during the conflict, there is an understandable reluctance to accept this classification in the post-conflict era.[42] PMFPs argue that the term suggests a misunderstanding of the relationship between them and their communities and that they are an organic element of them.[43] The term reintegration implies otherwise and that they alone must change in order to 'fit back' into society. The term also fails to address the political origins of violence in the first place. It suggests a distinction between such individuals and some imagined 'normal' society to which these 'outcasts' may return now that they have 'seen the error of their violent ways'.[44] The term underplays the required removal of the structural causes of conflict such as discrimination, marginalisation and state violence.[45] Ultimately, the term reintegration assumes that something needs to be 'done to' or 'proscribed for' such individuals or groups rather than a process over which they determine stewardship.

The experience of reintegration efforts in Northern Ireland, both good and bad, is that PMFPs generally respond better to being treated as subjects with agency rather than objects to whom aid is delivered. Thus, appropriately nuanced discussions of PMFPs and their agentic-orientated approaches to reintegration are both feasible and necessary.

From the outset, the post-Agreement model for the reintegration of PMFPs was essentially a self-help model with the management and staffing of the PMFP programmes left largely to the former prisoners themselves.[46] Monies from the government and the EU were distributed via the Community Foundation for Northern Ireland, an experienced and well-respected local grant-giving organisation. After establishing an advisory committee made up of all the PMFP groups as well representatives of different agencies with historical experience of working with prisoners and their families, the projects were funded on a factional basis, broadly mirroring the allegiances of the different paramilitary organisations. These include:

- Coiste na n-Iarchimi became the umbrella organisation for former Provisional IRA prisoners;
- EPIC serviced former UVF and RHC prisoners;
- Prisoners Aid, later CHARTER, acted for former UDA\UFF prisoners;
- Teach na Failte acted for former INLA prisoners;
- and a range of programmes which catered for different smaller and non-aligned groups.

Although those groups have maintained their distinct roles and organisational form they have, as discussed below, developed a number of joint initiatives and a broad spectrum of activities that includes:

- challenging stereotyping with regard to sectarianism, racism, homophobia and sexism;
- undertaking diversionary work to discourage young people from engaging in sectarian, usually interface, violence;
- providing direct welfare and trauma counselling support;
- delivering employment-based training;
- supporting the social economy and self-help initiatives;
- developing and implementing community-based anti-poverty work;

- resolving disputes at interface areas and policing contested marches;
- upholding community-based restorative justice as alternatives to social-control violence;
- encouraging inter-community initiatives on dealing with the past including truth recovery;
- developing relations with state agencies, notably the PSNI;
- designing and supporting equality and human rights campaigning both with regard to the PMFP constituency themselves but also the communities in which they live and work;
- taking forward legal challenges to discriminatory policies and practices.

Given the limitations of space, we have opted to proffer detail on three specific areas of work which illustrate the nature and scope of the work undertaken. These are (a) decommissioning and demobilisation, (b) dealing with the past and (c) citizenship education in schools

Decommissioning and demobilisation

PMFPs have been at the forefront of key initiatives linked to the transformation of the paramilitary organisations themselves. In particular, the issue of the decommissioning of paramilitary weapons and the existence and function of such organisations have been central issues in the peace process over much of the past 15 years.[47] The disarmament and demobilisation elements of a transition from conflict are generally tied to providing mechanisms and finance to enable combatants to disassociate from their past activities and enter civilian life.[48] In most transitional societies, there is an emphasis on achieving these twin goals as quickly as possible to try to minimise the potential for individuals or factions to return to violence. However, as we have argued elsewhere,[49] often in such a process combatant organisations are viewed primarily as potential 'spoilers' who need to be quickly managed out of existence in order to neutralise their threat. In the Northern Ireland context, as has been repeatedly recognised by the International Monitoring Commission and others, retaining the paramilitary structures in place during the transition allowed for an orderly if time-consuming transition within the organisations towards non-violence.

Given the political sensitivities within the various organisations that decommissioning might be viewed as 'surrendering', it was perhaps inevitable that those with the credibility of significant jail time would be tasked with managing such difficult conversations and the related practicalities. On the IRA side, former prisoner and senior IRA commander Brian Keenan (now deceased) was the interlocutor with the International Independent Commission on Decommissioning over a number of years and Seanna Walsh (also an ex-prisoner) formally indicated the end of the IRA campaign as he read out the video statement indicating that the IRA had formally ordered an end to the armed campaign in 2005.[50] For the UVF, former prisoner Billy Hutchinson acted as the interlocutor and also was one of those who indicated that UVF decommissioning had occurred.[51] Similarly, most of those who were involved in the discussions and negotiations which led to the decommissioning of weapons by the INLA, UDA and the Official IRA were also PMFPs.[52]

As is detailed elsewhere, PMFP groups explicitly saw part of their function as creating 'safe spaces' within the respective activist communities where people could have frank and often critical conversations about the direction of their organisations while seeking to minimise the political impetus for damaging splits or schisms. Decommissioning, together with the decision to support policing structures in Northern Ireland (for Republicans), was always likely to present the greatest risks for such splits. The PMFP groups were key sites where heated and at times highly critical debates on such moves could take place amongst former comrades.[53] Indeed the shared bonds of the prison experience remain one of the most useful contemporary platforms to take forward outreach towards dissident organisations even when there is quite fundamental disagreement on broader political or 'military' direction. In conducting our research on these matters over the years, we have found a refreshing and well-informed awareness amongst funders and policy-makers of the bona fides and importance of the PMFP groups as vehicles to develop and sustain the necessary processes of weapons decommissioning and the transformation of paramilitary organisations. That faith has been rewarded by near year on year falls in conflict-related violence, casualties and death and, as noted above, the subsequent decommissioning of much of the weaponry, at least of the groups represented by PMFPs. In the 1990s, for example, 15.1% of all conflict-related deaths since 1968 occurred. This compares to 2.1% of all deaths falling in the period post-2000 (data supplied by the PSNI).

Dealing with the past

A number of those who negotiated the Agreement have suggested that the additional difficulties of establishing such a mechanism to deal with the past would have made the achievement of an agreement almost impossible.[54] That said, as Christine Bell[55] has argued, the Agreement did contain a number of mechanisms which might be described as 'piecemeal' elements of an approach to the past. These elements included the provisions discussed above for the release and reintegration of paramilitary prisoners, the provision of services to victims, the establishment of the Patten Commission on Policing, the Human Rights Commission, and a range of other measures – all of which were broadly geared towards addressing past consequences of the conflict.[56] However, in the absence of a formal institution tasked with a holist examination of the past, many local community and civil society organisations have attempted different ways of 'dealing with the past' themselves.

For example, by 2006 there were almost 150 different victims organisations in Northern Ireland, many of which were and are involved in 'dealing with the past' style work, often as part of broader counselling efforts.[57] More broadly, many other community or civil society projects have been engaged in a broad range of story-telling style programmes of work and local historical and commemorative projects. For example, an audit of story-telling style projects details 33 different projects involved in such work concerning the conflict in and about Northern Ireland.[58] There has also been an increasingly lively public debate concerning forms of conflict-related public commemoration in Northern Ireland with much of the most delicate work done on the ground (e.g. in negotiations concerning the replacement of paramilitary-style murals) conducted by locally based community and civil society organisations.[59] Local groups and civil society organisations have also had a long history of 'bottom-up' efforts at truth recovery.[60] Healing Through Remembering, the main Non-Governmental Organisation working in this field, have produced a range of material on truth recovery, acknowledgement, commemoration, a day of remembrance and other past-related materials which have significantly informed local and international debates on the subject.[61]

What is quite remarkable about many of these 'bottom-up' approaches to dealing with the past is the prominent involvement of PMFPs directly involved in such work across a range of projects and different styles of interventions. Perhaps most remarkable for current purposes is the work of the Ex-POW Consortium. In February 2007, the Community Foundation for Northern Ireland (CFNI) issued a limited call for applications to projects engaged in work which was designed to 'develop skills for addressing the past as a pathway to reconciliation'. Funding was provided under the European Union's Programme for Peace and Reconciliation (Peace II Programme). The Ex-POW Consortium emerged from a number of political ex-prisoner groups who desired to work together to skill up their members to consider the range of issues associated with 'dealing with the past'. This unique partnership included ex-prisoners and former combatants from Republican and Loyalist traditions – three Republican and two Loyalist Groupings. The ex-prisoner organisations involved were Coiste na n-Iarchimí, An Eochair, Teach na Fáilte, EPIC and Charter representing former prisoners from the Provisional IRA, the Official IRA ex-prisoners, the INLA, UVF and UDA. Those involved included members of organisations which had been previously involved not only in political violence against 'the other side' (e.g. Republican\Loyalist or Republican\State) but also intra-factional violence within the Republican and Loyalist communities. A key premise of the project was of the central role of ex-prisoners in taking forward discussions on dealing with the past both within their own organisations and in broader society.[62]

One of the most interesting aspects of the work engaged in by the groups was where individuals from different backgrounds led discussions on the different past-related events from their own perspective. Thus, for example, different members of the various Republican organisations facilitated discussions on the history of Republicanism, and the reasons behind various Republican splits and feuds. Similarly, Loyalist members provided personal accounts of the historical origins of the different Loyalist organisations. Other themed discussions included personal story-telling and structured seminars led by the participants on 'origins and motivation for involvement in political struggle', 'exploring personal and communal identities', 'the changing role of ex-prisoner groupings', 'is the conflict over ?', 'truth recovery' and a more general residential on 'dealing with the past'. The Consortium also made a significant impact at a number of events and conferences where the practical and symbolic contribution of former enemies engaged in collective efforts to deal with the past was widely viewed as extremely powerful. As an international delegate who attended the 'Whither Now after the War' Conference at Queens in 2007 (at which a number of the Consortium spoke) told one of the authors,

> It really is quite remarkable to see these guys who were once deadly enemies making real efforts to deal with the past in a constructive way. They weren't pretending to be the best of buddies. But nonetheless there was obviously a real effort to accommodate their different perspectives. It really was quite impressive.

The Ex-POW consortium also appeared highly self-conscious of the importance of a group of former combatants from diverse paramilitary and political backgrounds engaging in a concerted effort to explore their respective perspectives on the past. At a symbolic level, the message that such work was possible even amongst former sworn enemies was self-evidently powerful.[63] In terms of its practical work, the group engaged in a series of outreach events, conferences, seminars and meetings with a wide range of organisations. Again Ex-POW consortium members seemed to go out of their way to meet with groups and individuals who would not have been historically sympathetic to former prisoners, including different victims organisations, the Orange Order, former soldiers and members of the security forces and others. Quite apart from their capacity to exercise 'leadership by example' functions within their own constituencies about the possibilities of exploring their very diverse views on the past, many of those who took part in the Ex-POW programme also seemed very aware of their potential to exercise significant influence in the broader communities in which they lived.[64] As discussed above, it is precisely some of those who have both inflicted violence and indeed often been on the receiving end of it who have shown most willing in such grass-roots efforts to take forward difficult conversations about our troubled past in Northern Ireland.

From prison to peace: citizenship education in schools

The final example of PMFPs involvement in praxis-orientated conflict transformation we have chosen to focus upon is a recent initiative involving a diverse group of PMFPs, the Community Foundation for Northern Ireland (CFNI) and a number of people engaged in citizenship education in Northern Ireland. By way of background, in 2009 CFNI together with a number of PMFP organisations submitted a successful application for EU Peace III funding. Coiste, the network for former Provisional IRA prisoners, which has historically been the largest and (arguably) best organised of the PMFP groupings, successfully submitted an individual bid for funding of its network throughout Ireland, also in partnership with CFNI. However, the other programme discussed below, in which Coiste was also a stakeholder, also included provision for funding for the groups associated with the other factions including the INLA, Official IRA, UVF and UDA. This latter collective bid became known as the Prison to Peace Partnership Consortium. In addition to providing financial support for the individual groups and their respective centres and offices, the programme also contained provisions for work on collective themes around which the groups would work together, including Conflict Transformation and Peacebuilding, Social Change in the Community and Youth Development and Citizenship.

In 2009, as part of the commitment to the Youth Development and Citizenship theme, the Prison to Peace Partnership Consortium began working with a citizenship education specialist at the School of Education at Queens University. As we have argued elsewhere, a key element of the mobilisation efforts of the PMFP groups in Northern Ireland has focused on their assertion that they should be entitled to enjoy the rights and responsibility associated with 'full citizenship' in the changed polity.[65] What is particularly interesting about this project is the ways in which the traditional mobilisation efforts of PMFPs readily mapped onto themes contained in the Northern Ireland Curriculum. The local citizenship curriculum focuses on four themes; Human Rights and Social Responsibility, Diversity and Inclusion, Equality and Social Justice, Democracy and Active Participation.[66] All of these themes have featured prominently in the practical work and lobbying efforts of the PMFP groups.

That resonance was institutionalised when representatives from the five PMFP groupings worked over a period of months with the educationalist to produce this educational resource and the accompanying DVD. Over a total of nine sessions, the resource provides teachers with advice, activities and guidance which are designed to assist the students to explore a number of themes. Former prisoners from the different groups are interviewed on the DVD about their reasons for becoming involved in political violence, the prison experiences and the conflict transformation work of their groups. Over the course of their studies, students are expected to:

- develop an understanding of the term 'political ex-prisoner';
- consider the factors which influenced individuals' decision to become involved in the conflict;
- explore the reality of the prison experience and its impact on political ex-prisoners, their families and their communities;
- become familiar with the post-conflict work of political ex-prisoners in conflict transformation and community development;
- determine how young people could make a positive contribution in their own communities.[67]

As in other conflicted societies, it is a significant challenge to deliver a curriculum about past violence which is balanced, critical but also which does not seek to sanitise events which, although they may have occurred in the recent historical past, nonetheless often took place before the children were born.[68] In the Northern Ireland context, where only five per cent of children are formally educated in the 'Integrated' sector, the reality for the vast majority of children is that they must be educated about such events in either predominantly Catholic or State (Protestant) schools.[69] It was not until the late 1980s that the curriculum was required to reflect the political and sectarian divisions in the jurisdiction through the inclusion of the statutory cross-curricular themes of Cultural Heritage (CH) and Education for Mutual Understanding (EMU) in the Common Curriculum (Education Reform Order 1989). While intuitively few could dispute the objectives of these themes, in practice it is widely accepted even by strong advocates that that they had limited impact.[70] As Lesley McEvoy and Laura Lundy have argued, the weakness of these interventions was 'unsurprising' given the weak theoretical framework upon which EMU was based. EMU over-emphasised the nature and importance of individual prejudice, failed to acknowledge the political nature of the conflict or the role of the state as something more than as a 'neutral' umpire benignly refereeing between the two warring traditions, and it was bereft of any reference to human rights principles.[71]

Thus, as the citizenship curriculum evolved in Northern Ireland from 2006 onwards, the citizenship advisors for the local education and library boards, relevant policy-makers and the teachers who took forward the pilots developed a curriculum with a particular emphasis on human rights, social justice and other themes which took on board the established critiques of EMU.[72] The process also included NGO actors, human rights organisations, environmental groups and others whose 'place' as having a legitimate voice in the delivery of citizenship education was firmly established. In short, although it obviously was not designed with PMFPs in mind, a space was created for exactly the kind of intervention into the curriculum which was ultimately taken forward by CFNI and the Prisoner to Peace initiative.

The 'From Prison to Peace' resource was launched in June 2010 by current Sinn Féin Minister for Education Catriona Ruane who publicly committed her department to write to all schools encouraging them to utilise it in the delivery of the citizenship curriculum. Its potential importance is well captured by Bruce Robinson, Head of the Northern Ireland Civil Service, who states,

> What strikes me most about these materials is their reality. The real stories of the real lives of real people are reflected time and time again throughout the resource and I believe this is its key strength as an educational tool. In bridging the gap between yesterday, today and tomorrow, I believe this resource can only enrich the educational experiences of many young people throughout our society and encourage them to play a positive role in their community.

It is of course too early to tell what the overall impact of this resource will have in the schools of Northern Ireland or on the children who are taught about the past through its various learning schemes. CFNI and the Prisoner to Peace Consortium have plans to assist in the roll out of the resource to local schools, which will include (where requested) former prisoners coming into the schools to talk about their past experiences of conflict and imprisonment. Even by virtue of its development, it does again well capture the practical potential of PMFPs as agents of conflict transformation. As Harold Good, former President of the Methodist Church in Ireland, stated in his endorsement of the resource,

> As young people growing up in a much more peaceful Northern Ireland, it is difficult for you to imagine what it was like to grow up in the very violent years of the not-so-distant past. This is why this resource is so important, not least in helping you to understand how young people like yourselves were affected by the conflict and how so many, on both sides of our sadly divided community, became involved in the conflict and in violence ... This is why it is so important for you to hear their stories – so that you may be spared what they went through and that together with you we will now build a happy, fair and safe community for us all to share.

Conclusion

During the conflict in Northern Ireland, many academic and popular discourses on those engaged in political violence were arguably characterised by propaganda, pathology, criminality or a straightforward lack of intellectual rigour. For those of us working on conflict-related issues, it became something of a jokey truism that the only reliable sources for accuracy on the calibre of individual combatants or combatant organisations were private military or security assessments which occasionally leaked into the public domain.[73] Whilst we would be the last people to eulogise the accuracy or reliability of security or intelligence information in general, it is certainly no accident that occasional flashes of clarity used to permeate the smoke of battle from those who were tasked with understanding what was actually going on. It did not require that such security sources had sympathy with the violence of the paramilitaries, simply that they were required to make pragmatic judgements which were as objective as possible in order to do their jobs properly.

Transitions from violence require a similar cold-eyed approach to judging what is happening. In our work which has detailed the activities of PMFPs and ex-combatants over the years since the Agreement was signed, we have sought as much as possible to base our conclusions on data. Making informed and measured assessments as to what is going on in a transition from conflict requires access to the actors; confidence in one's abilities to analyse the data generated by as many sources as possible; political judgement in calibrating the nature, impact and trajectory of the transition; and finally, if positive judgements are made as to the bona fides of at least some of the key actors, a degree of human empathy with those who are genuinely committed to moving forward the transition. This does not entail a suspension of critical faculties. Quite the opposite, in fact. It is precisely in a context of solid relationships that have been built up over many years with PMFPs and former combatants that highly critical comments on policy or practice are most likely to be taken on board. It does, on occasion, require what critical scholars sometimes refer to as publicly 'speaking truth to power'. As Jonathan Simon has well articulated, speaking truth to power does not necessarily mean adopting a particular political ideology, rather it may be viewed as 'opening up new pathways of knowing and acting on certain social problems whose time has come'.[74]

As is evidenced in this chapter, the release and reintegration of PMFPs was such a critical juncture in the peace process in Northern Ireland. From our perspective, as is underlined in their contests against the discourses of residual criminalisation, their contribution to demobilisation and decommissioning, dealing with the past and the development of resources for the teaching of our children, the judgement of the two governments and those who signed the Agreement to support the release and reintegration processes has been vindicated. Despite the continued activities of dissident Republicans, and occasional flare-ups of Loyalist violence and criminality, Northern Ireland remains an example par-excellence of a successful process in the messy business of conflict transformation. Real conflict transformation is more than the signing and implementation of elite-level agreements. It requires individuals with credibility at grassroots level who are willing to do some of the least glamorous aspects of grassroots peacemaking in communities most affected by violence. Warts and all, reflecting on the larger picture as we progress well into the second decade of the transition in Northern Ireland, PMFPs have delivered such peacemaking, and then some.

Notes

1 C. McGrattan, '"Order Out of Chaos": The Politics of Transitional Justice', *Politics* 29.3 (2009), 164–72.
2 See Justice Oversight Commissioner, *Second Report of the Justice Oversight Commissioner* (Belfast, 2004); Justice Oversight Commissioner, *Third Report of the Justice Oversight Commissioner* (Belfast, 2005); Criminal Justice Inspectorate, *Northern Ireland Alternatives: Report of an Inspection with a View to Accreditation under the Government's Protocol for Community Based Restorative Justice* (Belfast, 2007); Criminal Justice Inspectorate, *Restorative Justice Ireland Report of a Pre-inspection of Schemes in Belfast and in the Northwest with a View to Accreditation under the Government's Protocol for Community Based Restorative Justice* (Belfast, 2007); International Monitoring Commission, *Eighteenth Report of the Independent Monitoring Commission* (London, 2008).
3 K. McEvoy and P. Shirlow, *'Beyond the Wire': Former Political Prisoners and Conflict Transformation in Northern Ireland* (London, 2008), and 'Reimagining DDR: Ex-combatants, Leadership and Moral Agency in Conflict Transformation', *Theoretical Criminology* 13.1 (2009), 31–59. For example, in June 2010, Northern Ireland witnessed the brutal murder of loyalist Billy Moffett on the Shankill Road apparently by the UVF, despite that organisation having apparently decommissioned all of its weapons. This event led to the resignation in protest of the UVF aligned Progressive Unionist Party (PUP) leader Dawn Purvis. Like Ms Purvis, we have never sought to 'defend the indefensible'; 'Purvis Quits PUP over Murder of Loyalist Moffett', 3 June 2010, http://news.bbc.co.uk/1/hi/northern_ireland/10222663.stm (accessed 16 March 2011).
4 K. McEvoy and H. Mika, 'Restorative Justice and the Critique of Informalism in Northern Ireland', *British Journal of Criminology* 42 (2002), 534–62; K. McEvoy, 'Beyond the Metaphor: Political Violence, Human Rights and "New" Peacemaking Criminology', in *Theoretical Criminology* 7.3 (2003), 319–46; K. McEvoy and P. Shirlow, 'Reimagining DDR: Ex-combatants, Leadership and Moral Agency in Conflict Transformation', *Theoretical Criminology* 13.1 (2009), 31–59, and P. Shirlow, J. Tonge, J. McAuley and C. McGlynn, *Abandoning Historical Conflict? Former Political Prisoners and Reconciliation in Northern Ireland* (Manchester, 2010).
5 For example, see M. Green, *EPIC Research Document No. 1: The Prison Experience: A Loyalist Perspective* (Belfast, 1998).
6 L. McEvoy, K. McEvoy and K. McConnachie, 'Reconciliation as a Dirty Word: Education in Northern Ireland', *Journal of International Affairs* 60.1 (2006), 81–107.
7 C. Crawford, *Inside the UDA: Volunteers and Violence* (London, 2003).
8 International Monitoring Commission, *Twenty-Third Report of the Independent Monitoring Commission* (London, 2010).
9 J. Ruane and J. Todd, *The Dynamics of Conflict in Northern Ireland: Power, Conflict, and Emancipation* (Cambridge, 2006).
10 K. McEvoy, *Paramilitary Imprisonment in Northern Ireland: Resistance, Management, and Release* (Oxford, 2001).
11 E. Kaufman, 'Prisoners of Conscience: The Shaping of a New Human Rights Concept', *Human Rights Quarterly* 13.1 (1991), 39–67.
12 C. Campbell, 'Extradition to Northern Ireland: Prospects and Problems', *Modern Law Review* 52.5 (1989), 585–621; R. Keightley, 'Political Offences and Indemnity in South Africa', *South African Journal of Human Rights* 9.3 (1993), 334–57.
13 K. J. Greenberg, J. L. Dratel and A. Lewis, *The Torture Papers: The Road to Abu Ghraib* (Cambridge, 2005).

14 The original definitions, replicated in later versions of the Emergency Provision Act and the Prevention of Terrorism Act, are taken from the legislation to enact Internment (discussed below), the Detention of Terrorists (NI) Order 1972, Art. 2 (2).

15 B. Girvin, 'National Identity and Conflict in Northern Ireland', in B. Girvin and R. Sturm (eds), *Politics and Society in Contemporary Ireland* (Aldershot, 1986); K. Cavanaugh, 'Interpretations of Political Violence in Ethnically Divided Societies', *Terrorism and Political Violence* 9.3 (1997), 33–54.

16 J. Galliher, and J. Degregory, *Violence in Northern Ireland: Understanding Protestant Perspectives* (New York, 1985).

17 See McConkey and Marks v. Simon Community (2009) UKHL 24 (2009). The House of Lords found in that case that the decision by the Simon Homelessness Charity not to employ two former mainstream IRA prisoners on the basis of their past support for violence was lawful despite the fact that both were now supporters of the peace process.

18 G. Capoccia and R. Kelemen, 'The Study Of Critical Junctures: Theory, Narrative, and Counterfactuals in Historical Institutionalism', *World Politics* 59 (2007), 341–69.

19 J. W. Hogan, 'Remoulding the Critical Junctures Approach', *Canadian Journal of Political Science* 39.3 (2006), 657–79.

20 J. W. Hogan and D. Doyle, 'A Comparative Framework: How Broadly Applicable Is a "Rigorous" Critical Junctures Framework?', *Acta Politica* 44.2 (2009), 211–40.

21 Life and Times Survey 2000, www.ark.ac.uk/nilt/2000/Political_Attitudes/ GFAPROP7.html (accessed 16 March 2011).

22 McEvoy, *Paramilitary Imprisonment in Northern Ireland*, 382.

23 B. Gormally, *Conversion from War to Peace: Reintegration of Ex-Prisoners in Northern Ireland* (Derry, 2001).

24 McEvoy, *Paramilitary Imprisonment in Northern Ireland*, 346.

25 P. Shirlow, B. Graham, K. McEvoy, F. Ó hAdhmaill and D. Purvis, 'Politically Motivated Former Prisoner Groups: Community Activism and Conflict Transformation' (2005 Report, unpublished), 23.

26 B. Gormally, *Conversion from War to Peace*, 5.

27 J. Allister, Submission on: Draft Programme for Government 2008–2011, Draft Budget 2008–2011, Draft Investment Strategy 2008–2018 (2008), 11.

28 Shirlow, et al., 'Politically Motivated Former Prisoner Groups', 12

29 K. McEvoy, *The Trouble with Truth: The Struggle to Deal with the Past in Northern Ireland* (London, 2011).

30 C. Gilligan, 'Traumatised by Peace? A Critique of Five Assumptions in the Theory and Practice of Conflict-Related Trauma Policy in Northern Ireland', *Policy and Politics* 34.2 (2006), 325–46.

31 B. McDougall, *Interim Commissioner for Victims Survivors, Support for Victims and Survivors, Funding by the Government* (Belfast, 2006).

32 M. Ritchie, Conflict Transformation Initiative – statement by Minister Margaret Ritchie, 2007, http://www.dsdni.gov.uk/conflict-transformation-initiative.htm (accessed 16 March 2011).

33 See Re Solinas Application (2009) NIQB 43.

34 K. McEvoy, and A. Eriksson, 'Who Owns Justice? Community, State and the Northern Ireland Transition', in J. Shapland (ed.), *Justice, Community and Society* (Willan, 2008), 157–90.

35 Social Democratic and Labour Party (SDLP), *The Issues Explained in a Nutshell* (Belfast, 2006).

36 For example, in the Solinas judgement, LCJ Morgan notes that Ms Ritchie 'made it clear that she had no criticism to make of Farset'. Farsett is the community development organisation which received the £135,000 monies as part of the CTI initiative.

37 J. McDowell, *Godfathers: Inside Northern Ireland Drugs Racket* (Dublin, 2001).

38 Northern Ireland Prison Service 2010, Early Releases. Available at http://www.niprisonservice.gov.uk/index.cfm/area/information/page/earlyrelease (accessed 16 March 2011).

39 Northern Ireland Prison Service 2003, *Resettlement Strategy* (Belfast, 2003).

40 J. Sluka, *Hearts and Minds, Water and Fish: Support for the IRA and INLA in a Northern Irish Ghetto* (Stanford, CT, 1991); D. Miller, *Don't Mention the War: Northern Ireland, Propaganda and the Media* (Belfast, 1994); P. Magee, *Gangster or Guerrillas, Representations of Irish Republicans in Troubles Fiction* (Belfast, 2001).

41 'The Governments continue to recognise the importance of measures to facilitate the reintegration of prisoners into the community by providing support both prior to and after release, including assistance directed towards availing of employment opportunities, re-training and/or re-skilling, and further education', The Agreement (Belfast, 1998), 26.

42 L. McKeown, *Out of Time: Irish Republican Prisoners, Long Kesh, 1970–2000* (Belfast, 2001).

43 As one PMFP told one of the authors, 'There's a misconception by people – academics and others, and especially the press – that these paramilitary groups come from the mountains. It's people that live next door, it's people within the community – it is the community. So they're not separate, they're not two separate entities. It is the community. They came from the community'; interview with Loyalist PMFP, 2 June 2008.

44 Coiste, *Processes of Nation Building: Cultural Diversity* (Belfast, 2003).

45 B. Gormally, S. Maruna and K. McEvoy, *Thematic Evaluation of Funded Projects: Politically-motivated Former Prisoners and Their Families* (Monaghan, 2007).

46 McEvoy and Shirlow, *Beyond the Wire*, 5.

47 G. Mitchell, *Making Peace* (Berkeley, 2007); J. Sluka, 'Silent but Still Deadly: Guns and the Peace Process in Northern Ireland', in C. Fruehling (ed.), *Open Fire: Understanding Global Gun Cultures* (Oxford, 2007).

48 K. Kigma, *Demobilisation and Reintegration of Ex-Combatants in Post-war and Transition Countries* (Eschborn, 2001); J. Gomes Porto, C. Alden and I. Parsons, *From Soldiers to Citizens: Demilitarisation of Conflict and Society* (Farnham, 2007).

49 McEvoy and Shirlow, 'Reimagining DDR', 35.

50 This video is available at http://www.youtube.com/watch?v=ALuHAd3SnYw&feature=related (accessed 16 March 2011).

51 See 'Loyalist Weapons Put beyond Use', *BBC Northern Ireland*, 27 June 2009.

52 *Irish Times*, 12 October 2009, *UTV News*, 6 January 2010, http://www.u.tv/news/UDA-decommissioning-confirmed (accessed 16 March 2011) and *BBC News*, 8 February 2010.

53 Gormally et al., *Thematic Evaluation of Funded Project*, 6.

54 McEvoy, *The Trouble with Truth*.

55 C. Bell, 'Dealing with the Past in Northern Ireland', *Fordham International Law Journal* 26.4 (2003), 1095–1147.

56 C. Harvey (ed.), *Human Rights, Equality and Democratic Renewal in Northern Ireland* (Oxford, 2001).

57 Gilligan, 'Traumatised by Peace?'.

58 Healing through Remembering, *'Storytelling' Audit: An Audit of Personal Story, Narrative and Testimony Initiatives related to the Conflict in and about Northern Ireland* (Belfast, 2005, updated 2007).

59 J. McCormick, and N. Jarman, 'Death of a Mural', *Journal of Material Culture* 10.1 (2005), 49–71.

60 B. Rolston, *Unfinished Business: State Killings and the Quest for Truth* (Belfast, 2000); K. McEvoy, *Making Peace with the Past: Options for Truth Recovery Regarding the Conflict in and about Northern Ireland* (Belfast, 2006).

61 See Healing through Remembering at www.healingthroughremembering.info *(accessed 16ᵗʰ March 2011)*.

62 B. Gormally and K. McEvoy, *Dealing with the Past in Northern Ireland 'from below': An Evaluation* (Belfast, 2009).

63 Gormally and McEvoy, *Dealing with the Past.*

64 For example, at one EX-POW Consortium session attended by one of the authors, a former Loyalist combatant spoke about what he regarded as his personal responsibility to relate with brutal honesty the reality of violence and imprisonment, particularly to a younger generation of loyalist activists who had comparatively little direct experience of political violence. His view was that the tendency of former combatants to focus upon the cameraderie and humour of their past experiences – what South African activists refer to as 'struggle nostalgia' (see E. Pietersen and F. Meintjies, *Voices of the Transition: The Politics, Poetics and Practices of Social Change in South Africa* [London, 2004]) – represented a danger that the past might become sanitised to such an extent that some young people might find it glamorous. He argued persuasively that it was incumbent on those who had experienced the real horrors of the past to be frank about their experiences to buttress against future generations becoming involved in political violence. This style of work is discussed further below.

65 McEvoy and Shirlow, *Beyond the Wire,* 26.

66 Education Curriculum Minimum Content Order Northern Ireland (2007).

67 Community Foundation for Northern Ireland, *From Prison to Peace, Learning from the Experience of Political Ex-prisoners in Northern Ireland: A Resource for Local and Global Citizenship at Key Stage 4* (Belfast, 2010), 9.

68 S. Warshauer-Freedman, D. Corkalo, N. Levy, D. Abazovic, B. Bronwyn Leebaw, D.Ajdukovic, D. Djipa and H. Weinstein, 'Public Education and Social Reconstruction in Bosnia Herzegovia and Croatia', in H. Weistein and E. Stover (eds), *My Neighbour, My Enemy: Justice in the Aftermath of Mass Violence* (Cambridge, 2004); S. Warshauer-Freedman, D. Kambanda, B. Lewis Samuelson, I. Mugisha, I. Mukashema, E. Mukama, J. Mutabaruka, H.Weinstein and T. Longman, 'Confronting the Past in Rwandan Schools', in Weistein and Stover (eds), *My Neighbour, My Enemy.*

69 T. Gallagher, *Education in Divided Societies* (Basingstoke, 2004).

70 For example, see A. Smith, 'Citizenship Education in Northern Ireland: Beyond National Identity?', *Cambridge Education Journal* 33.1 (2003), 15–32.

71 L. McEvoy and L. Lundy, '"In the Small Places": Human Rights Culture, Education And Conflict-Affected Societies', in J. Morison, K. McEvoy and G. Anthony (eds), *Judges, Human Rights and Transition* (Oxford, 2007).

72 L. McEvoy, 'Beneath the Rhetoric: Policy Approximation and Citizenship Education in Northern Ireland', *Citizenship and Social Justice* 2.2 (2007), 135–57.

73 Thus, for example, the famous description of Martin McGuinness as 'excellent officer material' by one Royal Marine Major who fought his IRA units in Derry in the early 1970s was often counter-posed to the public depiction as Mr McGuinness as a mindless 'godfather of terrorism' (see P. Bishop and E. Mallie, *The Provisional IRA* [London, 1987], 197).

74 J. Simon, 'Speaking Truth and Power', *Law and Society Review* 36.1 (2002), 37–44.

8

Loyalism and Peacebuilding in the 2000s[1]

Joana Etchart

Introduction

It could be argued that the Northern Irish conflict has been successfully settled by antagonistic groups entering a process of dialogue with one another. Yet, observers point that the process as it has been designed failed to develop a culture of democracy involving such mechanisms as debates, discussions, disagreement, compromission and cooperation. Besides, recent events led Wilson to conclude that the rationales provided by the paramlitaries still remain meaningful for many.[2] Some observers pushed the argument further by stating that a link existed between the way the peacemaking process had been designed and the increase in intercommunal tensions and violence. For example, Wilson and Wilford noted in 2003 that 'the sobering conclusion must be that at best the agreement has had a neutral effect on communal division – and, at worst, that perversely it has exacerbated it'.[3] The thrust of their argument was that some of the leading principles of the various peace agreements (notably the 1998 Good Friday Agreement and the 2006 St Andrews Agreement) did not question the segregationist culture prevalent in Northern Ireland.

In the same vein, I contend that the policy-making framework in which strategies aiming at building peace[4] have been designed has had an impact on the efficiency of the peace process in general. To all appearances, peace has not been stabilised. Different forms of violent or aggressive behaviours continue to exist. If traditional paramilitary activities lessened in the 2000s, Hansson stated in 2005 that 'young people in interface areas continue to be involved in sporadic outbreaks of violence or disturbances'.[5] Intimidation through street violence and rioting is still a prevalent form of social interaction. Leonard pointed out that in North Belfast they shared a 'sense of inevitability and permanence about the conflict'.[6] Mechanisms such as rioting still represent a necessary, efficient mode of action that permits to assert one's rights.[7] Peace, as it stands, remains fragile.[8] Different studies have shown that young people in deprived areas are still affected by cross-community tensions, sectarianism and social exclusion in the 2000s.[9] Intercommunal tensions have not decreased despite the ongoing process of political dialogue and an array of public policies aiming at improving community relations.

I previously studied one particular policy aiming at building peace in Northern Ireland bewteen 1969 and 1998 – the community relations policies – and concluded that, over the years, the policy-making framework consistently focused on some aspects at the expense of others. Most notably, peace initiatives in the community sector[10] and the objective of structural change[11] have been disregarded. One of the unforeseen consequences is that the feeling of marginalisation as expressed by some groups and individuals prevails and is even exacerbated on some occasions. The underlying assumption here is that the very conditions in which peacebuilding policies have been designed and implemented have generated unforeseen, paradoxical effects.

This essay will study peacebuilding initiatives launched at grassroots level by loyalists in the 2000s. I will analyse their impact on the community, as well as their strengths and weaknessses. Eventually, I will draw attention to the unequal relationship binding top-level and grassroots peacebuilding strategies and raise the question of the impact of that unbalanced relationship on the outcomes of the peace process in general.

Loyalists and the peace process in the 2000s

Peacebuilding is a general term encompassing a wide range of activities. In this essay, it refers to a particular sub-group of initiatives involving paramilitaries and seeking to reflect on and transform military modes of action and organisation. Such activities have developed in the 2000s, although my own doctoral thesis has shown that they also existed in the late 1960s and the 1970s. They were then called 'facilitation' activities and were led mainly, but not exclusively, by community workers employed by the Community Relations Commission (1969–1974).[12] The objectives of facilitation, also called 'political' peacebuilding in this essay, are twofold. They aim at transforming violent modes of action (based on intimidation) and they seek to find reliable, satisfactory ways of multiplying the links between the paramilitary activists and outside partners (paramilitary or non-paramilitary). This may be called 'structural' or 'political' peacebuilding. This essay will also shed light on an alternative form of peacebuilding developed by community activists and former combatants in loyalist areas, which aims at tackling social imbalances. It will be referred to as 'social' peacebuilding.

This essay will focus on two such projects developed separately in the 2000s on the one hand by members of the UDA's (Ulster Defence Association) think tank, the UPRG (Ulster Political Research Group),[13] and on the other hand by the PUP (Progressive Unionist Party) and the UVF (Ulster Volunteer Force).[14] This essay will show that particular forms of peacebuilding activities involving members of the loyalist paramilitary groups and local community groups have been set up in the 2000s. Two particular initiatives will be studied: the East Antrim Conflict Transformation Forum (EACTF, set up in 2005) and the Standing Northern Ireland Peacebuilding Process (SNIPP, launched in 2007).

In the situation that developed after the signing of the Good Friday Agreement (1998), loyalists sensed that their identity was in decline. There was a widespread feeling among unionists in general that they were losing ground in terms of cultural assertiveness in Northern Ireland.[15] They also felt increasingly dismayed as the peace process looked to them to be one-sided in favour of Nationalists. Besides, the wider context of the peace process involved the reconstruction in Northern Ireland of a political culture around the principles of power-sharing and cross-community accord at a regional level (power-sharing assembly). Loyalists felt that they were left behind from those developments.

Overall, loyalist leaders from a paramilitary background, and the working-class communities they seek to represent, suffer from multiple factors of marginalisation, political under-representation standing as one of the main debilitating elements. If overlooked, this issue can lead to nurturing antagonistic discourses and to lessening the chances of developing loyalist and nationalist exchanges. A leadership that remains isolated tends to encourage aggressive behaviours among its followers. Thus, for loyalist leaders, developing their own political credo and new forms of non-violent action in the 2000s is important in order to be able to engage in peace efforts.

Political under-representation in loyalist areas is due to internal as well as external factors. Externally, loyalist supporters, instead of voting for emerging loyalist community leaders, generally vote for members of the two main unionist parties, the UUP (Ulster Unionist Party) or the DUP (Democratic Unionist Party), believing it more important to preserve unionist unity in order to defeat republicanism, all the more so as Sinn Féin gradually became the largest nationalist party in Northern Ireland in the aftermath of the signing of the GFA. Under such circumstances, in the late 1990s and early 2000s, a majority of people in loyalist areas turned to the DUP for support, given that this was considered a more reliable alternative to an assuaged UUP, who accepted to deal with nationalists and the British and Irish governments to help establish the Northern Ireland Assembly and Executive.

The issues affecting the loyalist community became more pressing following the signing of the St Andrews Agreement in 2006. It was signed by representatives of the British and Irish governments and endorsed by the political parties of Northern Ireland, including the two main parties DUP and Sinn Féin, in order to set in place measures for the restoration of the Northern Ireland Assembly. DUP members agreed to abide by power-sharing principles in the Northern Ireland Assembly and to form a new Executive with the republicans, whereas the republicans agreed to support the new Police Service of Northern Ireland (PSNI), the courts and rule of law. Many loyalists felt betrayed by the DUP going into government with Sinn Féin as, since the signing of the Good Friday Agreement in 1998, the DUP had opposed all attempts at cross-community peacebuilding. Now, the DUP was going into government with Sinn Féin and many loyalists felt that they had been used by the DUP simply to gain electoral power.

Such a feeling of mistrust towards unionist and loyalist political represent-atives has been latent since the 1970s.[16] Sean Brennan underlines that 'many grassroots leaders in the loyalist community were suspicious of the DUP who were quick to use loyalist leaders at times of crises only to dismiss them as "gangsters" and "criminal drug dealers" when the crises had passed'.[17] Besides, scholars have shown that loyalist paramilitaries have tried, at different times since 1969, to develop a proper political expression in defiance of mainstream unionism.[18] For instance, the UVF set up a political party in 1979, the Progres-sive Unionist Party (PUP), whose members developed a discourse defending the interests of the Protestant working classes. Sarah Nelson argues that they 'wanted change, disliked overt sectarianism and sought to involve Protes-tant workers in an independent movement'.[19] Similarly, the UDA set in place a political party in 1981, the Ulster Democratic Party (UDP), which is now extinct, even though they still have a think tank called the Ulster Political Research Group (UPRG). However, historical developments since the 1970s have shown that there is limited ground for development for paramilitary leaders as political representatives. There are still many barriers preventing loyalist leaders from becoming elected representatives, which would eventu-ally enable them to become a stable political force. One of the main reasons for this is the fact that mainstream unionists have sought to marginalise them.[20]

Internal reasons render the situation more complicated. The study of the attempts made by loyalist paramilitaries to find political expression since the 1960s sheds light on a couple of peculiar aspects of loyalism. First, it appears that the loyalist leaders involved in the political initiatives mentioned above hold at times liberal views on such matters as power-sharing (both the UDP[21] and the PUP supported the Good Friday Agreement). Loyalist activ-ists involved in the PUP consider themselves to be 'progressive' on social and political issues.[22] They promote anti-sectarianism and pluralism.

But, when articulated, liberal loyalism does not gain systematic support either from the working-class communities it seeks to represent or from the members of the paramilitary groups from which it emanates. This is one of the main paradoxes of loyalism. McAuley explains:

> In promoting these views [in favour of the creation of a Council of the British Isles] the UDP took two seats through the special arrangements made around the Forum following the elections of 1996. When the first elections to the Northern Ireland Assembly eventually took place, however, the DUP failed to have any representative elected, whereas the PUP secured two seats. Moreover, the distance between the UDP and the electorate was apparent. Further, even within the UDA's own membership there was little evidence of support for the UDP.[23]

UDP's leadership became contested by less liberal members of the UDA. Graham Spencer also noted that the rhetorics of community defence were often manipulated by loyalist leaders to achieve an individual gain.[24]

On the republican side, Sinn Féin took part in the negotiations preceding the 1998 Agreement and supported its implementation. The IRA were also in favour of the GFA. They committed themselves to decommissioning their weapons and eventually began this process in 2001. The Independent International Commission on Decommissioning stated that the PIRA had fully decommissioned in September 2005. At first sight, one could expect such developments to nullify the *raison d'être* of the loyalist paramilitaries from the UVF and the UDA, as their action was partly prompted by the need to defend their people against republican violence. As this has largely been non-existant since the 1997 ceasefire (except for recent attacks by republican dissidents),[25] military action has become less relevant for loyalists. Recently, the International Decommissioning Body announced that both groups had completely decommissioned their weapons (the UVF in June 2009 and the UDA in January–February 2010). This raises the question of alternative modes of action and organisation for the loyalist leaders whose *raison d'être* has been linked to the existence of such paramilitary organisations.These factors shaped the situation in which peacebuilding activities developed between loyalist paramilitaries and local community groups.

However, whilst the political context has been important, another element has contributed to encouraging loyalist paramilitary leaders to get involved in peacebuilding activities. As a result of an increasing influx of European monies dedicated to peacebuilding, particularly through the Reconciliation for Sustainable Peace programme of Peace II from 2000, communities have been encouraged to 'develop strategies and activities which promote reconciliation as a means to sustaining peace'.[26] This has invigorated community activism, particularly in deprived areas, whether Nationalist or Unionist. Combined with a growing interest from scholars in the state of loyalism,[27] this has led to the emergence of clusters of people concerned with the issues affecting loyalist leaders and communities since the signing of the Good Friday Agreement in 1998. Through the examples of UDA's and UVF's engagement in peacebuilding, it will be argued that it is the rapprochement between loyalist paramilitary leaders and community activists that has enabled the former to engage in a 'structural' process seeking to transform their modes of action and organisation. Working in collaboration with community groups has enabled loyalist leaders to break out of isolation and to engage in peacebuilding. But what exactly does peacebuilding mean for UDA and UVF leaders?

Peacebuilding involving paramilitary leaders

Sensing that they would have to adjust to new circumstances in the near future, loyalist leaders within the UDA and the UVF separately started pondering alternative modes of action in the early 2000s. Three key issues were at stake, all revolving around the question of their position in the community as 'genuine', consented leaders, away from their former role as self-proclaimed protectors of the community. In order to address the issue of the legitimacy of their position as leaders in the post-GFA circumstances, loyalists had to reconsider their paramilitary *raison d'être*, address the problem of under-representation in political and public spheres and connect with the 'community', that is to say the people whom they sought to represent and lead. The initiatives that will be depicted in this study must be seen as attempts at dealing with the three issues simultaneously, sometimes leading to confusion as social and political objectives intermingle. For example, in November 2007, the UDA declared in their Remembrance Day Statement that

> At present up to 60% of our community do not vote or do not register to vote and languish in the top 10% [sic] of the most socially and economically deprived communities in the country. This leaves our people isolated, marginalised and open to exploitation and not able to defend ourselves from politicians who would seek to improve their political carriers [sic] and criminals in particular drug dealers.
>
> If we are to create a society where citizens feel they should not be defended by paramilitaries then we must have political structures that protect all the citizens and where politicians can not jump in and out of those political structures when it suits them to further their own political aims. The people must have confidence in the political structures and feel they will be defended if wronged. That feeling does not exist in our community.
>
> We feel that some Irish nationalist politicians along with others are intent on excluding our people from the new-shared [sic] future that is the over arching [sic] principle for the new Assembly. They are working at every turn to erode our British identity and undermining the Union. What we do recognise is that we must face these challenges within the law and through non-violent means. What compounds this situation is that we feel the majority of Unionist politicians are unable to defend our rights at present but recognise that politics in the new assembly are very much in transition.[28]

This extract illustrated the UDA's dual ambition to defy both republicans (who were the main nationalist party in the Assembly) and Unionist and Loyalist politicians from the main parties (the UUP and DUP). They were also willing to develop a new strategy in order to achieve the three objectives mentioned above (to end paramilitary activities, to engage in the wider political arena and to contribute to the development of their community).

According to the main line of work that was adopted, peacebuilding activities in loyalist spheres could take on either a 'social' or a 'political' hue. On the one hand, 'social' peacebuilding focused on the improvement of living conditions in deprived areas by setting in place local self-help projects. 'Political' peacebuilding, on the other hand, sought to investigate the question of the nature and state of leadership. This process might, in turn, reinforce the former combatants' commitment in a sustainable and long-term peacebuilding activity. It was implied that a better knowledge of leadership mechanisms would contribute to making the peacebuilding process meaningful and effective to those leaders who had felt excluded from it. 'Political' or 'structural' peacebuilding was analogous to what is also called, at times, 'facilitation'.

As we will now see, the conditions in which peacebuilding activities developed in the two loyalist spheres (the UDA and UPRG and the UVF and PUP) bore similarities. Both initiatives were designed and led by community leaders and they were the result of a rapprochement between loyalist combatants (or former combatants) and community activists in a context of changing circumstances.

As a first step, in the mid-2000s, the two paramilitary groups launched consultation processes within their rank and file to discuss the future of the organisations. An internal consultation was organised by the UVF in 2004.[29] Meetings were held to discuss the future of paramilitary activities. As Edwards indicates, 'This was undertaken in a variety of forums and ranged from one-to-one contacts between the leadership and the rank-and-file to larger "roadshow" gatherings in loyalist social clubs and bars.'[30] Eventually, the principles of conflict transformation were endorsed in 2004 and 2005 by the UVF and the PUP. At the same time, a community-based programme was set in place in East Antrim (a loyalist stronghold) in order to address the issues affecting local communities in Rathcoole, Monkstown, New Mossley, Carrickfergus and Larne. The overall aim was to deal with the conditions which gave rise to paramilitary activity by addressing the 'fears and anxieties'[31] of loyalist communities in those areas.

In parallel, in a statement issued in November 2004,[32] a group of loyalist leaders from the UDA assembled through the UPRG articulated new lines of action which were aimed at creating a situation whereby the UDA would no longer be required to exist as armed defenders of their community. This implied that they were seeking to create the conditions that would eventually invalidate the paramilitaries' mode of action. Around 2005, loyalist leaders within the UDA and the UPRG then decided to consult their members and engage in a process which would lead to the transformation of loyalism and contribute to a more peaceful society. A sample of opinions and reactions expressed during the consultation process were published by Farset Community Think Tank Project with the aim of opening up the debate to a broader section of the loyalist community and to mobilise them around the issue of the possible changes to their modes of action.[33] This led to the creation of a group called Conflict Transformation Initiative (CTI): Loyalism in Transition. According to CTI, the loyalist community faced a certain number of issues which had not been addressed by recent peacebuilding initiatives. They mentioned specifically the predominance of the feelings of disaffection and marginalisation within loyalist communities which had been growing since the signing of the GFA. They perceived that the structures and programmes set up following the Agreement did not take into consideration the needs of the loyalist community. CTI underlined the alienation of loyalist youth and ex-combatants. They also pointed out the absence of an effective political representation for local loyalist communities.[34]

Interestingly, Seán Brennan testifies that loyalist communities suffered from multiple factors of marginalisation owing to their image as 'paramilitaries'. He explains that

> What is often forgotten is that working class Protestant areas suffered as much from poverty, alienation and deprivation as Nationalist ones. People from these poor Protestant areas, especially paramilitaries and former politically motivated ex-prisoners were considered 'the lowest of the low, scum' even by other Protestants. They were social pariahs and felt abandoned.[35]

If finding a job and becoming 'electable' were difficult for many people living in loyalist communities, it was all the more so for former combatants (also called 'politically motivated ex-prisoners'). Precisely, the latter played an important role in triggering the consultation processes.[36] For instance, the PUP and the group of former prisoners, EPIC (Ex-Prisoners Interpretative Centre), started developing new strategies from the late 1990s. PUP representatives stated in the *Principles of Loyalism* (2002) document that 'The process started for many volunteers when they personally acknowledged that violent responses to conflict were simply leading us further and further into an unending cycle of violence and counter-violence. Upon their release from prison they committed themselves to non-violent activism.'[37]

As stated earlier, grassroots peacebuilding activities developed thanks to an increasing influx of European subsidies dedicated to peacebuilding. Between 2000 and 2004, the European programme for Peace and Reconciliation received a total allocation of 834 million Euros.[38] In Northern Ireland, 8,300 projects[39] had received grants by December 2004 both in Nationalist and Unionist areas.[40] As a consequence, grassroots initiatives flourished, particularly in deprived areas. Loyalist leaders themselves, under the influence of 'politically motivated' ex-prisoners, began to develop peacebuilding strategies mixing social and political objectives. Such projects provided employment for ex-prisoners. Seán Brennan explains:

> Many loyalists saw the positive impact grassroots conflict transformation projects were having in republican areas and wanted similar projects set up in their areas. Especially as grassroots conflict transformation projects

offered prospects of employment for former loyalist prisoners who were struggling to find jobs due to their prison records.[41]

As support to community groups increased thanks to European programmes, so did their working ambit. Accordingly, a rapprochement took place between community activists and loyalist leaders from the UVF and PUP and the UDA and UPRG and led to the launch of different processes aiming at transforming loyalism: the UVF got involved in the East Antrim Conflict Transformation Forum (EACTF) and the UDA and UPRG in the Standing Northern Ireland Peacebuilding Process (SNIPP). We shall now look more closely at each initiative.

The East Antrim Conflict Transformation Forum (EACTF)

In the early 2000s, community worker Kelly Haggarty and Billy Mitchell from LINC (Local Initiatives for Needy Communities), a Belfast-based community group linked to the Church of the Nazarene (Evangelicals), devised a conflict transformation strategy for loyalist areas in East Antrim. Haggarty explains:

> Billy [Mitchell] was absolutely passionate and committed to conflict transformation, he wanted to affect a change in the wider East Antrim constituency (which was my area of work at the time). Billy also had credibility within the ranks of the UVF, as well as the PUP. That, coupled with our in-depth knowledge and capability, created a perfect platform from which to project the theories and practices of conflict transformation to a wider, more inclusive audience.[42]

Other practitioners in conflict transformation joined in. So did the local Battalion Commander of the UVF. A local East Antrim Commander explained:

> I would buy into that [EACTF] approach 100%. The PUP, at the minute, I don't think it is going anywhere: it hasn't got support from our own people. Many of the younger ones in the UVF simply don't vote. There is a fear of putting your name on the electoral register and fear of having their benefits taken away. The DUP has no interest in us – the UUP has no interest – so practically we have no voice. The only voice therefore is through the community work. We have been neglected and marginalised over the years. It's up to us now to devise and develop our own programmes; it's up to us to help our own people in the area.[43]

In February 2005, the East Antrim Conflict Transformation Forum (EACTF) was set up in order to address local needs affecting loyalist communities in Rathcoole, Monkstown, New Mossley, Carrickfergus and Larne. A focus group, bringing together founding members (Haggarty, Mitchell, Bloomer, Edwards and the battalion commander for the UVF) oversaw the work of the East Antrim Conflict Transformation Forum (EACTF). The Focus Group brought together 'active paramilitaries, former UVF prisoners, PUP members, community activists, and "critical friends" from faith-based groups and academia'.[44] Its mission was 'To establish and co-ordinate a strategic plan to help enrich and enhance the quality of life for people living within loyalist communities. To help address and remedy those negative aspects of loyalism that undermines [sic] the security, safety and social and economic development of their communities.'[45] Academics and observers from the civil society were also welcome in the process: 'The Focus Group will seek to encourage Critical Friends from civic society to assist it in developing its strategy by providing critical analysis, drawing in appropriate expertise and evaluating the process.'[46]

After its inception, the Focus Group claimed that 'over 100 people' were 'actively involved'[47] in their activities. According to a progress report, their main areas of work entailed securing funding[48] in order to employ a coordinator and to provide resources for local groups, but also organising dialogue sessions and standing conferences involving community workers, loyalist leaders, observers and representatives from statutory bodies.[49] This was in line with what has been described here as 'social' peacebuilding[50] and corresponded to the method of community development as it was originally advocated in the 1970s by members of the Northern Ireland Community Relations Commission (1969–1974). At that time, the Commission's first director Hywel Griffiths introduced the approach of community development (CD) in Northern Ireland. This encouraged people most affected by conflicts to engage in an analysis of their problems, to define who had responsibility for such problems and to design non-violent modes of action that might contribute to improving their conditions. The overall goal of Griffiths' strategy consisted in strengthening some aspects of the community (social, economic, environment) in order to be able to reach out to other communities who faced the same difficulties.

In Northern Ireland, this meant encouraging community groups in republican and loyalist areas to share their experiences and eventually work together. Even though the Commission was disbanded abruptly in 1974, this approach of community development continued to exist, albeit in many different forms, much of it through some of the Community Relations Commission's (1969–1974) former field workers. Thus, the principles of community self-help and empowerment, which had been advocated by members of the Commission in the 1970s and have remained a benchmark for many, resurfaced in loyalist areas in the changing circumstances of the 2000s.

The Standing Northern Ireland Peacebuilding Process (SNIPP)

The UPRG and UDA leaders also sought external help and expertise to conduct their own transformation initiative in the early 2000s. They got in touch with grassroots activists involved in community development and conflict resolution in Belfast, namely the Farset project and MICOM, who were regarded as a trustworthy form of grassroots leadership. MICOM's objective then became to 'design, set in place, and facilitate the transition process'.[51]

MICOM (Moldovan Initiative Committee of Management) originated in the 1990s when Joe Camplisson, a conflict resolution expert from Belfast, got involved in a peacebuilding experience in a former region of the Soviet Union which had become an independent country, Moldova.[52] Now a sovereign state, Moldova is engaged in an armed conflict with the separatist region of Transdniestria (supported by Russia). Camplisson soon assembled a group of people in Northern Ireland to help Moldovans and Transdniestrians enhance peacebuilding efforts. The approach was based on a principle dear to John Burton,[53] according to which the people most affected by the conflict have to go through a preliminary stage of problem definition. That is part of the 'analytical method' of conflict resolution. It is through their own analysis that participants in peacebuilding can perceive what the problems are. Camplisson adds, 'Often it boils down to significant identity needs, which are not necessarily expressed through political, social or economic issues, but through the symbols which people want to have in place. So the question becomes one of how they can satisfy those identity needs without coming into conflict with others.'[54]

MICOM's director Camplisson involved community leaders from Belfast, mainly loyalists, to assist him in helping Moldovans and Transdniestrians experience an assisted needs analysis. The group called Local Community Initiative (LCI) conducted conflict resolution workshops based on John Burton's idea of an analytical method, as it has been depicted above.[55] Then, Camplisson's team in Moldova invited members of the Moldovan and Transdniestrian groups to visit Northern Ireland in March 1996.[56] At that stage, many community leaders and political representatives from both sides in Northern Ireland were involved. As a result of their engagement in this work, the group LCI strengthened and started asking itself if and how the methods applied in Moldova could be workable in Northern Ireland.

Given that MICOM invited grassroots activists and former combatants from Northern Ireland to assist in the Moldovan initiative, MICOM became a natural partner for the loyalist leaders who sought to engage in a similar transformation process in their own area in the 2000s. A key element of that partnership lay in the relationship of trust that had gradually developed between members of MICOM and some loyalist leaders throughout the 1990s and early 2000s. This background description of the main actors of the SNIPP initiative enables us to grasp a very important aspect related to the involvement of most SNIPP participants in some sort of grassroots activism in Northern Ireland since the 1960s. Joe Camplisson, for instance, has been involved in different sorts of grassroots activities, such as facilitation between paramilitaries of both sides, since 1969. He was also a member of the initial team of field workers in the first body to deal with issues of conflict, community relations and deprivation in Northern Ireland, namely the Northern Ireland Community Relations Commission (1969–1974). Thus, most, if not all, of the leaders of the peace-building processes involving loyalist paramilitaries in the 2000s have been active at grassroots level in initiatives aimed at long-term peacebuilding. It must be stressed that, when trying to develop links with outside partners, loyalist leaders sought help from local community workers and not from public bodies promoting peace and cross-community work. This shows that despite benevolent messages of reconciliation being spread by bodies such as the Community Relations Council, mainstream peacebuilding programmes may bear some limitations as to their ability to reach out to isolated communities and their leadership. The examples depicted in this essay also demonstrate that it is important for some forms of marginalised leaderships to develop mechanisms favouring empowerment and self-help away from mainstream peacebuilding techniques.

In October 2006, loyalist leaders in the UDA and the UPRG organised an international conference in Belfast to announce openly the UDA's involvement in a conflict resolution process.[57] In October 2007, an event was organised in Belfast which marked a new stage in the process towards building up an embryonic conflict transformation process among loyalist leaders from the UDA and UPRG. Alan Bell, a local peacebuilding, business and community activist on the interface for many years, tells about the circumstances that contributed to generating a conflict transformation process:

> I was approached in January 2007 by a man I have known for many years, Dr Joe Camplisson, who has been involved in conflict resolution work here, Palestine and Israel, Moldova and Transdniestria, and more recently Armenia and Azerbaijan. He had been asked by some leading loyalists to assist them in their attempt to break away from their past as they were concerned about the effect that their actions had had and were still having on their communities.
>
> At this time I was involved in organising a return visit by Tony Brown, an African American lecturer from the Mennonite College of Hesston University in Kansas. Tony, although a classically trained singer, discovered many years ago that the Spirituals have a wonderful effect on people and Tony sings these and speaks to them.
>
> Dealings with the Loyalists in January 2007 were all hush hush but it was considered that quite possibly by the time of Tony's proposed visit in October 2007, things would have moved on sufficiently to contemplate a gathering at Taughmonagh Social Club to which Republicans could be invited (Taughmonagh is a large Loyalist housing estate). The decision was taken to go with that idea and to engage Tony for the event. Our great local singer, songwriter and peace activist, Tommy Sands was also engaged.[58]

The event organised in October 2007 was considered a success because organisers managed to assemble people from different backgrounds: there were republicans, ex-prisoners from both sides, former combatants, politicians, community workers and church/media/government representatives. Besides, those attending the event were eager to repeat the experience. A formal group came out of that, called the Standing Northern Ireland Peacebuilding Process (SNIPP). Their aims were thus described by Joe Camplisson in April 2008: 'SNIPP is the cornerstone of a local community orientated self help attempt at ending sectarian conflict and its causes. It is an inter-denominational, cross/cultural component within a MICOM facilitated Community Development strategy aimed at conflict resolution.'[59]

From an organisational point of view, SNIPP did not follow a clear pattern of development and was commanded by no definite structure. The loose constitution of the process implied constant organisational evolution. The process existed as long as key members remain involved in it, key members being members of the UDA, UPRG, MICOM, Conflict Transformation Initiative, Taughmonagh Social Club, Dublin Busmen, Ainsworth Community Association and the Religious Society of Friends (Quakers). They were staunchly committed to setting up a process of some sort which would help loyalist leaders in the UDA and UPRG to enhance their organisational skills. They also wanted to make the process viable in the long term and were looking for ways of piloting it. Joe Camplisson stressed that 'event funding to date has been piecemeal'[60] as costs were usually absorbed by representatives from the groups aforementioned.[61] There were some peripheral members of the process whose participation was sought after: government representatives, members of the republican community and members of the community in general (community workers, civil servants, political activists and so on). If the focus was on 'political' peacebuilding, the UDA and UPRG also launched a 'social' programme to address specific issues affecting marginalised loyalist communities. Vulnerable people such as young people and those living at interface areas were to be assisted in developing their organisational skills in order to learn how to address their difficulties. Empowerment and social improvement were at stake.

By engaging in peacebuilding processes designed by themselves, the loyalist leaders were addressing the issues of social exclusion and violence. They were thus playing an important role in rendering aggressive mechanisms such as rioting obsolete by providing alternative forms of action.

Assessment

Different as they were in shape, the initiatives launched separately by the two loyalist groups shared a certain number of identical features. For instance, they were supported by community groups whose work was respected by the loyalist leaders. A trusting relationship enabled them to launch new modes of action implying collaboration with outside partners. It is important to stress that loyalist leaders in the UVF and the UDA sought help from community groups whom they trusted. This rapprochement led the loyalist leaders to develop an elaborated philosophical discourse on their method. For instance, loyalist activists involved in the EACTF initiative developed their own understanding of what peacebuilding encompassed. They advocated the method of conflict transformation (as opposed to conflict resolution), highlighting the fact that the cessation of violence did not necessarily entail peace. PUP representatives claimed that

> Peace building for the genuine loyalist is not about achieving a result for loyalism through non-violent means. Nor is it merely about resolving conflict through the politics of non-violence. It is not even about achieving agreement through non-violent means. It *is* about seeking a commitment to developing creative alternatives to violence through dialogue with the enemy. It is crucial therefore that both current and former participants in the conflict are regarded as key resources in the peace building process. They are not mere recipients of imposed solutions but an essential part of the transforming, healing and restorative process. They must, however, be sincere in their desire for both non-violence and the democratic process.[62]

Regarding the theoretical background of the SNIPP initiative, its underpinning theory was based on John Burton's human needs theory.[63] According to this theory, ethno/religious/political conflicts arise from the denial and frustration of basic human needs. Basic needs can be related to identity issues and/or to social, economic, cultural, educational, health, political, environmental and security conditions. Those needs have to be addressed. Precisely, in Northern Ireland, there is a feeling that some questions have been left unanswered by the macro peacebuilding efforts. Here the new SNIPP initiative aimed at complementing existing peacebuilding advancements. In fact, it sought to address some tacit gaps in the understanding of what makes a resolution process efficient in the sense that it effectively addresses the problems and needs that nurture violent conflicts. In a recent conversation, Joe Camplisson highlighted 'the importance of having a comprehensive characterisation of the nature of that leadership which is instrumental in bringing countries into war, and generating movement toward internecine violent conflict'.[64] SNIPP was based on the belief that positive modes of action, based on development and change, would contribute to eradicating the underlying causes of conflict. This libertarian philosophical background revealed the importance of the contribution made by leaders from community groups. Thus, one might link the peacebuilding work depicted here with the successful decommissioniong of weapons completed by loyalist groups in 2009 and 2010.

However, some observers might think, in a deterministic tone, that the modes of thinking and acting of loyalist leaders in Northern Ireland will not change, as they are inescapably shaped by past events and culturally inherited mindsets. On one previous occasion, following the strike organised in 1974 by the Ulster Workers' Council, leading members[65] of the UDA developed an interest for the work done by community activists.[66] At that time, they were attempting to fortify their leadership in the community. But their interest in community work gradually waned and Nelson argues that it was only a calculated move.[67] Should the enthusiasm shown by loyalist leaders in the 2000s be seen as a tactical move to provide a new *raison d'être*? Or was it a genuine attempt at creating solid partnerships with the community sector? Those questions cannot be answered at this stage.

SNIPP and EACTF, as tools for change, could also be regarded as over-optimistic and dismissed as utopian. Being at the intersection of heterogeneous groups, social and/or identity differences stood as barriers to easy, flowing working relationships. For instance, SNIPP's work was slowed down by a series of disheartening circumstances. If the organisation of the first event happened without trouble, the second event, which was planned outside a loyalist area in the Sarsfield's GAA Club in January 2008, had to be brought back to loyalist Taughmonagh in May because of what Joe Camplisson describes as 'security fears'. A new event was then planned for September 2008, again in a nationalist area with people from Moldova joining in to give a presentation on the conflict with Transdniestria, accompanied by musicians. However, this event was cancelled as well. Alan Bell narrates the events leading to the cancellation:

> On the morning of 17th September, the day of the Sarsfield event, an article appeared in the Irish News giving notice of the event. It was to have appeared inside the paper, but instead, it was emblazoned across the front page: **'UDA boss' McDonald to speak at Belfast GAA club**. On seeing this, a few members of the GAA club cancelled the event, stating that the club had not been fully informed of its content. Although other members did not agree that this was correct, the event was nevertheless cancelled.[68]

This brings about many questions: Was this simply a series of unfortunate circumstances? Were some members of the community afraid of developing a mission of transformation in the loyalist areas? In the republican areas? Those questions remain unanswered but the events confirm that 'spoiler groups'[69] exist. It could also be assumed that resistance to change comes from outside institutions (media, churches, government, political parties or state intelligence services). Making the peacebuilding process last was a challenge facing SNIPP and EACTF. Some groups of people within loyalist communities most affected by the conflict did not want to see changes happening and would fight those changes. Reasons for this were varied. Seán Brennan assumes very accurately that 'some are crude sectarian views. Others fear that change will remove them from self appointed leadership or "gate keeper" roles in their community.'[70] Indeed, if the main force to an efficient peacebuilding effort lies within the grassroots activists, so do possibly its main detractors. Moreover, members of SNIPP and EACTF were mostly amateurs in the field of conflict resolution and conflict transformation. It was a learning curve, with its share of mistakes, frustration and disenchantment. All the same, SNIPP and EACTF could become extinct if some of its leaders decided that they had nothing to gain from the process any longer.

Precisely, Joe Camplisson recently specified that some key members of SNIPP dropped and that his position as facilitator may no longer be tenable.[71] Moreover, Kelly Haggarty indicated that she, 'and the original members of the EACTF Focus group and critical friends, have now left the project, as far as we are concerned it is dead'.[72] This is partly due to leadership issues within the local UVF group, who remained with no battalion commander for months. As a consequence, members of the paramilitary group started to withdraw from the EACTF and the rapprochement between all the different actors gradually disintegrated. But Kelly Haggarty lays emphasis on causes that are related to the question of power:

> We were becoming a dangerous thing to the bureaucrats that had power, be that the police, security forces, politicians, civil servants or even other community groups or organisations. We had the hearts and minds of a certain constituency, and this scared the hell out of some people. We were giving a voice and a new-found sense of effectiveness to a once powerless and apathetic community.[73]

Interestingly, this shows that despite a general consensus on the necessity of encouraging peacebuilding at all levels, initiatives enhancing local empowerment do not receive systematic support from decision-makers.[74]

All in all, the difficulties underlined here shed light on the elusiveness of the task that was undertaken by SNIPP and EACTF alike. Numerous people in Northern Ireland have continually set to the task of bringing people together and changing modes of action and thinking, from political representatives in the government (who established the Community Relations Council in 1990) to grassroots activists who have unremittingly engaged in peacebuilding activities even at the height of the Troubles in the 1970s and 1980s. Few have attempted to engage former paramilitary leaders. SNIPP and EACTF were no straightforward answer to the difficulties depicted previously. The task at hand was big and the process complex. As peacebuilding initiatives, however, they contained some unprecedented advantages as they were based on the assumption that peacebuilding activities led at grassroots level could contribute to the stabilisation of peace. How so?

EACTF and SNIPP sought to transform the modes of action of those who participated in the conflict. As we have seen, in Northern Ireland, loyalist leaders in the UVF and the UDA tried since the mid-2000s, in two separate initiatives, to develop a process which would lead to responding to key issues through non-violent ways. The processes offered opportunities to find mechanisms that would help respond to their needs efficiently because they were wanted by, conducted by and aimed at the community which has suffered from the conflict and who once participated in it. In that regard, SNIPP and the EACTF implied many advantages for loyalist leaders who could discuss sensitive issues,[75] engage their communities in a process of development away from traditional modes of violent action and thought and, eventually, spread a more positive image of loyalists in Northern Ireland. They offered innovative ways of accompanying and supporting the development of a solid loyalist leadership. This was in line with the theoretical approach of conflict transformation, which differs from more traditional 'conflict resolution' methods. It is considered that 'resolution' focuses on bringing the conflict to an end and deters initiatives of change. Conflict transformation, on the contrary, seeks to shed light on the elements that render a conflict violent. This understanding then permits those who were engaged in the conflict to find ways of transforming their role in the conflict into a more positive process leading to change in society. It has been noted that peacebuilding in loyalist spheres developed as a result of a process of rapprochement between loyalist paramilitary leaders and community groups. Loyalist leaders had much to gain from this collaborative work: it provided a means of maintaining a status of leadership in the community and, by helping devise a new project, dispensed a *raison d'être*. Through this transformation process the conditions which had given rise to violence were slowly being eliminated.

But this means that political, paramilitary and administrative groups must undergo structural changes. This remains a difficult, unnatural task to take on. For instance, the objectives of conflict transformation sometimes became secondary to loyalist leaders whose main preoccupations remained linked to security issues. Despite the declarations that their arsenal had been destroyed (the UVF's in June 2009 followed by the UDA's in January 2010), the issue of security has remained critical. Loyalist paramilitary leaders kept a prominent role in addressing it.[76] Despite recent peace agreements, successful decommissioning processes and the setting up of constitutional provisions in Northern Ireland, the situation is such that conflicts may arise at any time and at different scales, regional or national. Many members of SNIPP and EACTF have repeatedly stressed that peace remains fragile. In such circumstances, the help of loyalist leaders is requested at times when tensions are likely to lead to confrontations, particularly during the marching season. On such occasions, they act as mediators to try and marshal potential rioters. So, the question of defence still arises sporadically. Demilitarisation, slow-moving as it has been, has nonetheless led loyalists to framing differently their protective call to defend the interests of their community. Tools such as community development and conflict transformation, developed in collaboration with community activists, provided alternative modes of action which were considered accurate and effectual by some loyalists in the UDA and the UVF at a given time. The processes of conflict transformation depicted here arouse interest because of the commitment and hard work of those involved, and also due to the originality of the work that was undertaken with former paramilitary leaders. They will undoubtedly hold the attention of activists who are busy enhancing peace efforts in countries undergoing a situation of conflict elsewhere in the world.

But initiatives advocating structural change require strong support. My recent doctoral study on community relations programmes (1969–1998) showed that, since the 1970s, policy-makers in Northern Ireland generally tended to discard programmes or initiatives advocating structural change and prefered to focus on cultural transformation through educational programmes. The study concluded that peace efforts became less efficient if one of the two elements was dismissed.

Moreover, community-led peacebuilding initiatives such as EACTF and SNIPP focused on the understanding of conflict as it was felt and expressed by people who had been affected by it. Transformational processes favour participation from below. Such scholars and practitioners as Curle have come to realise that 'it is essential to consider the peacemaking potential within the conflicting communities themselves'.[77] It seems necessary to help community leaders to design a process of conflict transformation that they will then lead. This is what John Paul Lederach calls 'indigenous empowerment'.[78] This empowerment in a loyalist context in Northern Ireland might have led to strengthening a grassroots leadership and to mobilising it around the task of peacebuilding. Lederach[79] argues that traditionally peacebuilding was monitored by top- and middle-level leaders who saw grassroots leaders and their communities as 'the problem'. The former considered themselves to be outsiders who designed solutions to the conflict affecting people 'below'. But Lederach places grassroots leadership at the centre of peacebuilding and argues that solutions are more viable in the long term if they are indeed designed by people from below. This, however, remains difficult to grasp in Northern Ireland as local, regional or national forces act as 'spoiler groups' against the development of self-help initiatives aiming at building peace.

The study of the loyalist peace initiatives sheds light on some of the main shortcomings of the policy-making and peacebuilding frameworks in Northern Ireland. Since the 1970s, British policy-makers have tended to consider that peace would develop somehow naturally in Northern Ireland when political representatives from antagonistic groups would manage to share power in a regional assembly. Basically, in a pragmatic way, it was thought that peace would develop indirectly from political agreements between rivals. To that end, in the 1990s and 2000s, peace*building* policies have tended to serve the political motive of furthering peace*making* efforts. That is one of the reasons why, feeling that they were being manipulated, some sections of the Northern Irish community grew suspicious of official programmes promoting reconciliation and prefered to work in collaboration with community leaders in the field of peacebuilding. But transformational work undertaken by grassroots activists has been considered at best as secondary, at worst as suspicious by decision-makers because of their appraisal of the notion of empowerment. This, in turn, has tended to further ostracise those at the margins. Consequently, the peacebuilding policies have generated paradoxical effects. Moreover, it appears that the notion of balance between the different actors contributing to peace (high, middle and low ranges) remains an illusion, as initiatives emanating from independent sources – that is, not controlled by policy-making infrastructures – are clearly undervalued. This imbalance might explain why the peace process in general lacks efficiency and how it might even nurture the conflict, albeit indirectly.

Notes

1 The author wishes to thank the members of SNIPP for their participation in this project (in particular Joe Camplisson, Alan Bell and Seán Brennan) as well as Kelly Haggarty (née Robinson), who is the former coordinator of EACTF.

2 R. Wilson, 'Northern Ireland: Guns, Words and Publics', 16 March 2009, www. opendemocracy.net/article/northern-ireland-guns-words-and-publics (accessed 22 November 2010).

3 R. Wilson and Wilford, *A Route to Stability: The Review of the Belfast Agreement* (Belfast, 2003), 11.

4 The author makes a distinction between the processes of peace*making* and peace-*building*. Peacemaking is the process of shaping a settlement between disputing parties. Negotiations and third-party mediation are used to reach peace agreements. This must be followed by long-term peacebuilding – the process of reconciliation.

5 U. Hansson, *Troubled Youth? Young People, Violence and Disorder in Northern Ireland* (Belfast, 2005), 27.

6 M. Leonard, *Children in Interface Areas: Reflections from North Belfast* (Belfast, 2004), 105.

7 Leonard, *Children in Interface Areas*, 44.

8 Recently, in 2009 and 2010, dissident Republican groups launched attacks on Army barracks and against officers of the Nothern Ireland's reformed police.

9 See S. McAlister, P. Scration and D. Haydon, *Childhood in Transition: Experiencing Marginalisation and Conflict in Northern Ireland* (Belfast, 2009).

10 Despite Lederach's recommendation that initiatives from the grassroots, middle range and top level complement each other. See J. P. Lederach, *Building Peace: Sustainable Reconciliation in Divided Societies* (Washington, DC, 1997), 84.

11 A process of transformation might focus on two different objects: culture or structure. Cultural change encompasses working on such issues as identity, social relationships and perceptions of self and others. Structural change will deal with political mechanisms (or modes of action), structures (structures enabling participation for instance) and the issue of leadership. See, for instance, D. Bloomfield, *Peacemaking Strategies in Northern Ireland, Building Complementarity in Conflict Management Theory* (Basingstoke, 1997), 93.

12 Jim Fitzpatrick, proprietor of the *Irish News* since 1983, interviewed by the author (28 September 2005). Leading members of the Community Relations Commission (1969–1974) also arranged secret gatherings for paramilitary leaders (author's interview with Hywel Griffiths, 8 April 2005). See also the report of such a gathering: Community Conference Council 1974, *Report on Port Salon Conference 13th, 14th, 15th September, 1974* (Belfast, September 1974, unpublished).

13 The predecessor of the UPRG emerged in 1978 as the New Ulster Political Research Group. This political think tank was established by the UDA to reflect on the development of their political views.

14 The UDA and the UVF were set up under different circumstances and by different people. On the one hand, the UVF emerged in 1966 in the face of an alleged threat of a republican upheaval in Northern Ireland in the year of the fiftieth commemoration of the 1916 Easter Rising and also because Unionist Prime minister O'Neill was considered too liberal. See S. Bruce, *The Edge of the Union, the Ulster Loyalist Political Vision* (Oxford, 1994), 4. On the other hand, the UDA was set up in 1971, at a time when a major crisis had developed in Northern Ireland with people demanding equal civil rights for all and criticising the unfair policies of the Unionist parliament. This caused mayhem on the streets. It is in that specific context that the UDA emerged. At the beginning, groups of people started to assemble in their areas to protect the community. They were called vigilante groups. See S. Nelson, *Ulster's Uncertain Defenders, Protestant Political, Paramilitary and Community Groups and the Northern Ireland Conflict* (Belfast, 1984), 82. Vigilante groups progressively became better organised and eventually merged into a unique group in 1971. This was the UDA. The idea of protecting and defending one's community was at the heart of their motivations.

15 See Graham Spencer, 'The Decline of Ulster Unionism: The Problem of Identity, Image and Change', *Contemporary Politics* 12.1 (2006), 45–63, and *The State of Loyalism in Northern Ireland* (Basingstoke, 2008).

16 On loyalists' historical mistrust of unionist political leaders, see Bruce, *The Edge of the Union*; Nelson, *Ulster's Uncertain Defenders*; Peter Shirlow and Mark McGovern (eds), *Who Are 'The People'? Unionism, Protestantism and Loyalism in Northern Ireland* (London, 1997); and Susan McKay, *Northern Protestants: An Unsettled People* (Belfast, 2000).

17 Seán Brennan, community development worker, in an interview with the author (5 November 2008) and a series of e-mails with the author since then. He is employed by Intercomm in North Belfast and is a member of the North Belfast Conflict Transformation Forum.

18 Since the 1970s, loyalist leaders have repeatedly sought to transform loyalism into a consistent movement with its articulate political and social credo. But loyalist attempts to gain political representation have failed. For further developments, see D. Miller, *Queen's Rebels: Ulster Loyalism in Historical Perspective* (Dublin, 1978); A. Edwards and S. Bloomer, *A Watching Brief? The Political Strategy of Progressive Loyalism since 1994* (Conflict Transformation Series, 8; Belfast, 2004). For more details, see J. W. McAuley, 'Whither New Loyalism? Changing Loyalist Politics after the Belfast Agreement', *Irish Political Studies* 20.3 (2005), 323–40; A. Edwards and S. Bloomer (eds), *Transforming the Peace Process in Northern Ireland: From Terrorism to Democratic Politics* (Dublin, 2008); and Spencer, *The State of Loyalism in Northern Ireland*.

19 Nelson, *Ulster's Uncertain Defenders*, 136.

20 Nelson, *Ulster's Uncertain Defenders*, 181–92.

21 See A. Edwards, 'Abandoning Armed Resistance? The Ulster Volunteer Force as a Case Study of Strategic Terrorism in Northern Ireland', *Studies in Conflict and Terrorism* 32.2 (2009), 325.

22 See Edwards and Bloomer, *A Watching Brief?*

23 McAuley, 'Whither New Loyalism?', 325–26.

24 Spencer, *The State of Loyalism in Northern Ireland*, 246.

25 Some dissident republicans reject the Good Friday Agreement and hold an uncompromising stance on the objective of Irish unity and independence. They assemble in two paramilitary organisations called Real Irish Republican Army and Continuity Irish Republican Army. They are still active.

26 European Commission, *EU Programme for Peace and Reconciliation in Northern*

Ireland and the Border Region of Ireland 2000–2006, Operational Programme (Brussels, 2004), Chapter 6.6, 114.

27 See Edwards, 'Abandoning Armed Resistance?'; McAuley, 'Whither New Loyalism?'; Edwards and Bloomer (eds), *Transforming the Peace Process in Northern Ireland*; Spencer, *The State of Loyalism in Northern Ireland*; and C. Mitchell, 'The Limits of Legitimacy: Former Loyalist Combatants and Peace-Building in Northern Ireland', in *Irish Political Studies* 23.1 (2008), 1–19.

28 Ulster Defence Association, *Remembrance Day Statement*, 11 November 2007, www.cain.ulst.ac.uk/othelem/organ/uda/uda111107.htm (accessed 28 March 2010).

29 For further details, see East Antrim Conflict Transformation Forum's website at http://changeeastantrim.org/background.html (accessed 16 March 2011); Aaron Edwards and Stephen Bloomer, 'Democratising the Peace in Northern Ireland: Progressive Loyalists and the Politics of Conflict Transformation', http://www.linc-ncm.org/CTP_12.pdf (accessed 8 June 2009); and Edwards, 'Abandoning Armed Resistance?'.

30 Edwards, 'Abandoning Armed Resistance?', 156.

31 East Antrim Conflict Transformation Forum, www.linc-ncm.org/old/eactf.html (accessed 17 March 2010).

32 The statement is mentioned and described in Community Think Tanks Project, *Conflict Transformation Initiative, Loyalism in Transition: 1, A New Reality?* (Island Publications, 79; Newtownabbey, 2006), 7.

33 Community Think Tanks Project, *Conflict Transformation Initiative*.

34 Community Think Tanks Project, *Conflict Transformation Initiative*, 19–22.

35 Author's interview with Seán Brennan, 5 November 2008.

36 On the constructive role of ex-prisoners in peacebuilding, see K. McEvoy and P. Shirlow, 'Re-Imagining DDR: Ex-Combatants, Leadership and Moral Agency in Conflict Transformation', in *Theoretical Criminology* 13 (2009), 31–59; and P. Shirlow, B. Graham, K. McEvoy, F. Ó hÁdhmaill and B. Purvis, *Politically Motivated Former Prisoner Groups: Community Activism and Conflict Transformation* (Belfast, 2005).

37 Progressive Unionist Party, *Principles of Loyalism, An Internal Discussion Paper* (Belfast, 2002), 43.

38 531 million Euros were provided by the European Commission: *EU Programme for Peace and Reconciliation. Annual Implementation Report 2004* (Belfast, 2005), 4. The amount was topped up by British and Irish governments according to the principle of additionality.

39 Trutz Haase, *Community Uptake Analysis of Peace II* (Belfast, 2005), 8.

40 Nationalists receive 51.4 per cent of approved funding and Unionists 48.6 per cent. This does not necessarily mean that there is a bias in the distribution of funds in favour of Nationalists. According to a study on differentials in community uptake, Nationalists are generally more deprived and tend to apply for funds more readily. See Haase, *Community Uptake Analysis of Peace II*, 7.

41 Interview with Seán Brennan.

42 Kelly Haggarty in a series of messages exchanged between January and April 2010. Kelly Haggarty, formerly coordinator of EACTF (2005–2009), is now employed by the Greater Shankill Partnership Board.

43 Quoted in Edwards, 'Abandoning Armed Resistance?', 158.

44 According to Billy Mitchell (former loyalist combatant and ex-prisoner) quoted by Edwards, 'Abandoning Armed Resistance?', 158.

45 Kelly Haggarty, Programme Co-ordinator EACTF 2005–2009, 'East Antrim Conflict Transformation Forum Provide and Environment for Progressive Loyalism to Grow', http://www.changeeastantrim.org (accessed 9 June 2009).

46 East Antrim Conflict Transformation Forum, www.linc-ncm.org/old/eactf.html (accessed 17 March 2010).

47 East Antrim Focus Group, 'Progress Report' (2006), www.linc-ncm.org/old/focus. html (accessed 17 March 2010).

48 According to Kelly Haggarty, the EACTF 'acted solely on a voluntary capacity'; however, the money that was already coming into the area was used to fund community development projects in the loyalist areas covered by the EACTF's strategy. Messages from Kelly Haggarty, January to April 2010.

49 East Antrim Focus Group, 'Progress Report'.

50 Members of the PUP have been responsible for developing a more 'political' form of peacebuilding. See Progressive Unionist Party, *Principles of Loyalism* and the website, www.pup-ni.org.uk/home/ (accessed 21 November 2009).

51 Joe Camplisson, 'MICOM, UDA De-Militarisation Process Development' (Belfast, Farset Community Development Project, 2006, unpublished).

52 Author's Interview with Joe Camplisson, 3 November 2008.

53 John Burton is an expert in conflict resolution. On 'assisted analysis', see J. Burton, *Deviance, Terrorism and War, The Process of Solving Unsolved Social and Political Problems* (Oxford, 1979), and for MICOM's experience in Moldova, see M. Hall and J. Camplisson, *From Conflict Containment to Resolution: The Experiences of a Moldovan-Northern Ireland Self-Help Initiative* (Newtownabbey, 2002).

54 Joe Camplisson, quoted in Farset Community Think Tanks Project, *Conflict Resolution, the Missing Element in the Northern Ireland Peace Process* (Newtownabbey, 1999), 9.

55 See Community Think Tanks Project, *Conflict Resolution*.

56 Community Think Tanks Project, *Conflict Resolution*, 13.

57 See list of participants in Community Think Tanks Project, *Conflict Transformation Initiative, Loyalism in Transition: 2, Learning from Others in Conflict* (Newtownabbey, 2007), 4.

58 A. Bell, 'Report to Ulster Quarterly Peace Committee "Open Day" Gathering Held at South Belfast Meeting House', 11 October 2008, unpublished.

59 J. Camplisson, 'SNIPP Profile, Draft by Joe Camplisson', Unpublished, April 21 2008, 1.

60 E-mail message from Joe Camplisson, 13 November 2009.

61 The Community Relations Council also provided funding as well as Quaker groups (the Irish Quaker Faith in Action and the Robert and Kezia Stanley Chapman Trust), as stated by Bell in 'Report to Ulster Quarterly Peace Committee "Open day" Gathering'.

62 Progressive Unionist Party, *Principles of Loyalism*, 43–44.

63 John Burton developed an approach to conflict resolution based on the needs theory. Needs theory holds that deep-rooted conflicts emerge out of the denial of one or more basic human needs, such as security and identity. See J. Burton (ed.), *Conflict: Human Needs Theory* (London, 1990), and J. Burton and F. Dukes (eds), *Conflict: Readings in Management and Resolution* (London, 1990).

64 Interview with Joe Camplisson and a series of e-mails since then.

65 Such as Andy Tyrie and Glen Barr. See D. Anderson, *Fourteen May Days: The Inside Story of the Loyalist Strike of 1974* (Dublin, 1994).

66 Nelson, *Ulster's Uncertain Defenders*, 194.

67 *Irish Times*, 13 July 1976.

68 Bell, 'Report to Ulster Quarterly Peace Committee "Open day" Gathering'.

69 St Bloomer, 'Bridging the Militarist-Politico Divide: The Progressive Unionist Party and the Politics of Conflict Transformation', in Bloomer and Edwards (eds), *Transforming the Peace Process in Northern Ireland*, 110.

70 Interview with Seán Brennan.

71 Joe Camplisson in a message dated 28 July 2010.

72 Messages from Kelly Haggarty, January to April 2010.

73 Messages from Kelly Haggarty, January to April 2010.

74 This was already the case in the 1970s when community development programmes encouraging self-help practices and community empowerment were regarded as highly suspicious by local and regional political representatives.

75 For example, workshops were organised by SNIPP focusing on Prejudice Reduction (October 2007 at Taughmonagh Social Club) and Transforming our Communities (May 2008 at Taughmonagh SC, too).

76 See N. Jarman, 'Ordering Transition: The Role of Loyalists and Republicans in Community-based Policing Activity', in Bloomer and Edwards (eds), *Transforming the Peace Process in Northern Ireland*, 133–47.

77 A. Curle, *Another Way: Positive Response to Contemporary Conflict* (Oxford, 1996), 96.

78 J. P. Lederach, *Preparing for Peace: Conflict Transformation across Cultures* (New York, 1995), 212.

79 Lederach, *Building Peace.*

9

Civil Society, the State and Conflict Transformation in the Nationalist Community

Kevin Bean

A violence from the past?

Serious rioting during the 2010 loyal order marching season prompted a predictable debate about Northern Ireland's political future in general, and the condition of the nationalist community in particular. Whilst there was a broad consensus that the disturbances, however severe, did not signal a return to the 'bad old days of the Troubles', there was little agreement about their underlying causes and significance. International media coverage, for example, evinced surprise at a turn of events that challenged a widely accepted 'international ideology of Northern Ireland' as a radically changed and stable region.[1]

For some, the violence could simply be condemned and dismissed as 'recreational rioting' by bored teenagers: using the trope of anti-social behaviour, they blamed feckless parents and a feral youth out of control.[2] Leading politicians from the DUP and Sinn Féin, whilst pursuing their own, distinct agenda, largely agreed with the PSNI's analysis that 'sinister elements' were at work behind the scenes. In the wake of the transfer of policing and justice powers to Stormont, the politicians claimed that dissident republicans opposed to 'dialogue, negotiation and accommodation' had orchestrated the fighting and were manipulating young people, thereby handing on 'the baton of hatred ... to another generation'.[3]

Other commentators, however, suggested that the causes of the violence were more fundamental, being located in a continuing and unresolved sectarian conflict and segregated ways of living. According to this view, the response of the authorities, cracking down on the rioters whilst failing to address the root causes, demonstrated 'the futility of seeking to forge a peaceful future in a deeply divided society without challenging the under-lying basis of those divisions'.[4]

A common feature of the debate about the riots within the Belfast media was the view that sections of the nationalist community increasingly felt excluded from Northern Ireland's new dispensation and that these feelings of alienation would only be strengthened by growing unemployment and cuts in public expenditure.[5] Thus, whilst in one sense the events in Ardoyne were indeed expressive of 'a violence from the past', they also, perhaps, revealed the shape of things to come.[6]

That is not how the political establishments in Britain and Ireland viewed Northern Ireland following the successful implementation of the Good Friday Agreement. Whether addressing issues of community cohesion in Burnley, taking on drug-dealers in Jamaica or the Taliban in Afghanistan, the Northern Ireland peace process has been regularly cited as a successful model that could be applied to a wide range of conflicts throughout the world.[7] This went beyond mere political rhetoric. For example, Northern Irish politicians met their Iraqi counterparts to discuss reconciliation and capacity building in civil society, whilst the PSNI contributed to rebuilding the shattered nation by training its new police force.[8]

A key theme of this transferable model of peacebuilding has been engagement with extremists, through inclusive dialogue, ultimately leading to an 'historic compromise' between long-standing enemies. The desired outcome, the incorporation of former radical insurgents into a liberal democratic polity, was to be realised through the conversion of former terrorists into conventional politicians. The Peace Process offered, in the words of former Secretary of State for Northern Ireland Shaun Woodward, 'a spectacular transformation' resulting from 'the historic acts of leadership that have been taken by unionists, nationalists and republicans ... in establishing a Northern Ireland which is about a genuine shared future'.[9]

The rhetoric of a 'shared future' has become a central trope in Northern Irish public life demonstrating that this 'spectacular transformation' was expected to be more than a marriage of convenience between the political leaders of rival ethnic blocs. The language of conflict transformation and conflict resolution suggests a new beginning of peacebuilding and collective reconciliation rather than a mere 'management of enmity'.[10] These masternarratives were most frequently and most eloquently expressed by Tony Blair who argued that the peace process

> teaches us the value of a civic society where ancient divisions can be healed. Today, engagement and dialogue have shattered the depressing status quo of the past. 'Working together', once dirty words, is now the basis of a new future that offers hope in place of war ... The majority rejected the old ways ... the fundamental lesson of Northern Ireland for us all ... [is that] ... [t]here is no place in the 21st century for narrow and exclusive traditions. It underlines the supreme importance in the modern world of understanding our dependence on one another, for future progress.[11]

The aim of this chapter is to investigate how accurately these and other narratives of conflict transformation describe the experience of 'peacebuilding' for the nationalist population over the last twenty years. Given the defining role of the British state, such a discussion will inevitably focus on the nature of the relationship between the state and civil society in Northern Ireland, and the ways that this has shaped both the politics and social structure of the nationalist community since the 'long peace process' began in the 1980s. It will conclude by assessing whether British strategy is essentially one of conflict management or conflict transformation, and how it will impact on the future of the nationalist community in Northern Ireland. However, beyond this specific context the discussion also touches on some of the most significant questions in contemporary politics internationally: namely, how can political elites rebuild their authority and legitimacy in the face of increasing challenges, and in what ways do these attempts impact on the relationship between the state and civil society.

Rediscovering civil society

Mr Blair's rhetorical essay to define a grand narrative for peacebuilding highlights some common themes in both the academic literature and popular perceptions of conflict resolution. His confident exposition of 'the lessons of Northern Ireland' attributes the success of the peace process to its roots in 'civic society' rather than seeing it as largely the creation of the political elite or the state. Although arguing that courageous political leadership had been necessary and, indeed, essential at times, for Tony Blair the key dynamic for success was located in the community: defined as 'the majority [who] rejected the old ways', it was ordinary people whose yearning for peace engendered grassroots engagement and constructive dialogue.[12]

It is easy to dismiss Blair's assessment as simply the rhetorical stock in trade of a consummate politician, an example, perhaps, of the necessary nonsense that was such an essential feature of the peace process. The rhetoric was, after all, rather familiar. British politicians had used the language of community since the late 1960s to rationalise various attempts at political settlement or explain how the 'moderate majority' could defeat the 'men of violence'.[13] Likewise, in the early days of the Troubles there had also been something of a focus on 'community relations', modelled on British race relations policy, as a means of resolving conflict in Northern Ireland.[14] These older themes were, of course, to re-emerge during the peace process in the 1990s, in a new context in which politicians and policy-makers were to place a very different emphasis on the discourse of civil society and conflict transformation.

However, there were novel aspects to Blair's argument and language that may help illuminate the origins, modalities and goals of peacebuilding in Northern Ireland. In particular, by using a 'bottom-up' discourse of political change rather than a 'top-down' language of elite accommodation, his speech suggests that peace processes are designed to *transform* rather than *manage* conflict, and that 'civil society' rather than the state is the driving force. This way of applying the discourse of civil society was not unique to Northern Ireland: from the Middle East to Eastern Europe, similar concepts were increasingly deployed in the 1990s to explain and theorise the new international phenomenon of peace processes. In particular, analysts, such as Lederach, who stressed the significant distinction between conflict *trans-formation* and conflict *management*, argued that 'bottom-level actions' in 'capacity building and empowerment, human rights and development work' were key ingredients for the successful resolution of a peace process.[15] Where peace processes were largely state-centred and elite-driven, it was argued, they would be less likely to succeed because, as Lederach put it, 'Building peace in today's conflicts calls for long-term commitment to establishing an infrastructure across all levels of a society … that empowers the resources for reconciliation from within that society and maximises the contributions from outside.'[16]

What lay at the heart of this approach was a particular understanding of the relationship between the state and civil society. While conflict transfor-mation practitioners could be critical of political initiatives on the basis that they were 'driven by a need to find quick fixes and solutions to complex, long-term problems rather than a systematic understanding of peace-building as a *process-structure*', they did not underestimate the key role that politicians or the state could play.[17] On the contrary, as Mary Kaldor puts it, whilst '[c]ivil society has an important humanitarian role to play in conflicts … [it] can only be sustained in the framework of a rule of law', which is ultimately upheld by the state.[18] Likewise, Lederach's 'peacebuilding pyramid' model also suggested that a strong partnership between the top leadership and civil society – perceived as the middle range and grassroots 'community' leadership – was absolutely essential for effective peace building.[19]

This emphasis on understanding and re-defining the relationship between the state and civil society was not confined to those who theorised and practiced peacebuilding. The new discourse of civil society, expressed in a language of renewed partnership, reveals broader anxieties among political leaders and policy-makers in the 1990s as they sought ways to re-engage polit-ically and restore legitimacy to the state, in the face of domestic challenges of an increasingly disenchanted population.

These issues not only exercised the Blair government in Northern Ireland, but were central domestically to the implementation of the 'Third Way' and its attempt to develop a new, if rather loose, form of progressive politics, 'beyond left and right'.[20] Furthermore, this interest in the relationship between civil society and the state, and the implications for public policy, was not limited to Tony Blair or confined to British public life: from the early 1990s the discourse of 'civil society' was growing in significance internationally as politicians and theorists tried to come to terms with the changes ushered in by post-Cold War politics.[21]

The intensity of these theoretical and political discussions often revealed radically diverging understandings of the nature and function of civil society.[22] Whilst most agreed that 'civil society refers to uncoerced associational life distinct from the family and the institutions of the state, [and is thus] … distinct

from, yet in a particular relationship with, the state', the character and significance of this 'particular relationship' remained problematic for both policy-
makers and political scientists alike.[23]

The form of this 'particular relationship' had been discussed as a problematic in political theory since the eighteenth century, usually with a focus on
questioning how far the state defines and shapes civil society, and the forces
that determine the boundaries of the relationship.[24] Similar issues were also
clearly present in contemporary accounts, even if not posed as starkly as in
the classical literature. The common starting point was that the state and
civil society formed two parts of the one societal whole. Thus, because they
delineated each other's boundaries and determined each other's functions,
not only could they not be completely separated, but also they could only be
fully understood *individually* through their symbiotic relationship, one to the
other.[25]

Contemporary theorists attempted to strengthen the state by either renew-
ing the partnership with civil society or by mobilising civil society to transform
the relationship without negating or dethroning the state's social power. For
example, Robert Putnam's widely influential response to concerns about the
health of this relationship suggested that civil society was a 'school of citizenship'.[26] Drawing on the American experience and older ideas of civic republican virtue, he argued that associational life was a vital foundation of the state,
producing the common values essential to bind together a liberal democracy.[27]

Similarly, Giddens responded to a widely perceived crisis of democracy
and state legitimacy with a new rhetoric of governance and partnership which
became central to British government policy initiatives in the 1990s and 2000s.
His calls for the devolution of authority and functions from the state to civil
society sought to strengthen a sense of collective autonomy through citizen
participation.[28] Critics, however, suggested that far from devolving power,
these kinds of partnerships were more a process of incorporation which broke
down or blurred the distinction between state and civil society, and ultimately
strengthened the state at the expense of civil society.[29]

If some saw civil society as a sphere that could support the state, others
stressed its transformative potential. Whereas Putnam believed that civil
society was the *manifestation* of a healthy polity, the experience of the 1989
revolutions in Eastern Europe suggested to some that civil society was in fact
an historical agent that could become *instrumental* in creating this healthier
society.[30] Habermas, for example, argued that civil society could be strengthened and made politically more effective through the process of developing 'the public sphere'.[31] He suggested that new social movements, which
empowered the citizen through forms of participatory democracy, performed
vital functions both in holding the state to account and developing the public
sphere as a medium for political change.[32]

With the decline of ideologically inspired modernist and class-based
politics from the late 1980s, many activists increasingly began to see 'civil

society' as an instrument for implementing radical change *within* the political system without necessarily overthrowing the state or radically remodelling society.[33] Whether among the political class or political activists, to those who lamented the loss of the 'sense of mass belonging which characterized European and American politics from the late 19th century' and were trying to find 'collective ideals around which we can gather', this discourse of civil society seemed to fill a deep political and spiritual void after 1989.[34]

Thus, by the 1990s, in both theory and practice, the concept of civil society had undergone a significant revision. It had become increasingly politicised and acquired en route a normative as opposed to a purely analytical character. In moving from academic description to political prescription, the political elite increasingly identified 'civil society' with 'a good society', said to be grounded in 'values such as social justice, solidarity, mutuality and sustainability'. Civil society also functioned as 'the public sphere where ... people and organisations discuss common interests, deliberate solutions to problems, or find ways of reconciling differences'.[35] This perspective endowed 'civil society' with a transcendent character and a sense of potential agency, which could potentially be applied to the business of transforming deep-rooted conflict, whether in former Yugoslavia, South Africa, Israel/Palestine or Northern Ireland. In the case of ethno-national conflicts, it was often suggested that the re-building of cross-community associational structures and networks would lead to a strengthening of 'bridging social capital', which 'united' communities and prevented conflict. In this way, the supposed 'universalism' of civil society could act as a mechanism for transcending the particularism of communal division.[36]

No longer defined simply as a mediating civil space or limited to a site of potential contestation, civil society had become a distinct ideological project and an actor in its own right, endowed with its own distinct values and sense of agency that might 'shape our world, and ... make the transition from an age of "me" to an age of "we"'.[37] In rhetorically minimising the role of the state in this way, the dominant discourses of the Third Way and ultimately the Big Society appeared to confer on 'civil society' the capacity to break free of, and be no longer defined by, the state.

This was 'civil society' characterised as both an idealised abstraction and a substitute for politics as traditionally and ideologically conceived.[38] However, the experience of government in the 1990s showed that far from a withering away of the state as the political rhetoric suggested, quite the opposite was occurring.[39] Behind the discourse of community empowerment it was actually the state, rather than an idealised model of civil society, that was growing ever more assertive and better able to mould the shape of public life.[40]

Civil society and the state in Northern Ireland

This contradiction was to become quickly apparent in Northern Ireland, too. Tony Blair's call for increased citizen participation initially resonated with long-established, locally based traditions of activism which lent support to his belief that civil society in Northern Ireland was capable of transcending 'narrow and exclusive traditions' by uniting citizens 'working together … for future progress'.[41] These quite disparate forces included a labourist tradition which believed class politics could transcend division; advocates of integrated education that saw religious segregation as a cause of conflict; localised cross-community and religious groups whose mediation initiatives aimed to build trust between communities; as well as high profile campaigns such as the Peace People in the 1970s.[42]

Outside of high politics and secret diplomacy, a wide range of initiatives developed from the late 1980s that appeared to firmly root the peace process in the soil of civil society. Originating beyond the political establishment and formally autonomous from government, community organisers and peace activists were frequently given an official imprimatur and used as evidence of popular support for political change. For those who believed that civil society had the potential to transform conflict, its importance went beyond the potential to support critical engagement and dialogue with political actors.

To some extent these kinds of activities, from the Opsahl Commission hearings to discussions between republican and loyalist community activists, did constitute a Habermasian public sphere, which influenced significant aspects of public life and policy formation.[43] Citing as evidence factors as diverse as the 1992 Opsahl Commission, the 1998 Referendum's Yes campaign and the political influence of the grassroots women's movement, a number of commentators optimistically suggest that civil society had been, and could continue to be, a significant force for the 'bottom-up promotion of political accommodation'.[44] Following the public sector spending crisis of 2010–2011, these arguments have been extended beyond peacebuilding to include initiatives designed to mobilise community and voluntary sector capacity and influence policy-making and resource allocation.[45] With some 4,700 organisations, with assets totalling £737.5 million, a workforce of 26,737 and nearly 90,000 volunteers, Northern Ireland's voluntary and community sector in particular is frequently regarded as just such a positive force for conflict transformation, active civic involvement and social integration.[46]

However, this account of civil society as a spontaneously formed, unifying social space is open to challenge, just as much in Northern Ireland as elsewhere. For, in spite of the language of community empowerment, the state remained the dominant force in political and public life, acting as an arbiter between the parties and becoming a focal point for the allocation of resources between communities. In many ways, far from ceding power to civil society, as Tony Blair's rhetoric suggests, the peace process actually strengthened the position of the state in society. This dominance illustrates the continuing power of the contemporary state and its ability to develop and reproduce a political and social hegemony based on consent rather than coercion.[47] The terrain for the manufacture of this consensus is civil society with the mechanisms of repro-duction located in the newer forms of 'soft power' rather than in the tradi-tional 'hard power' of armed bodies of men.[48] Thus,

> The definition of state power needs to be widened beyond its traditional forms to include the penumbra of para-state structures and intermediate layers surrounding the core state ... [T]his flexible architecture, with its ill-defined boundaries between state and civil society ... [determines] the construction of consent ... [much more] than repression and social control.[49]

These conciliatory features of the 'post-modern state' were brought fully into play by the application of the Blair government's 'Third Way' agenda to Northern Ireland.[50] Drawing on an established strategy of 'peace through prosperity', these strongly communitarian policies were designed to rearticu-late the relationship between the state and civil society using the discourse of 'community' and 'social inclusion' to promote the idea of the peace process as a bottom-up development based upon cross-community reconciliation.[51] Although sharing a number of the hybrid characteristics of the contemporary British state, Northern Ireland's new dispensation enjoyed its own distinc-tive form of 'multi-level and multi-form governance' deriving much of its character from the 'quangocracy' established during the long Direct Rule period, overlaid with new patterns of partnership that developed between the state and the community and voluntary sector through the 1990s.[52] An added impetus to this process was the increasing formalisation of the voluntary and community sector, reconstituted as 'the third sector' through the dynamics of managing European Union-funded Peace programmes, which incorporated the social policy objectives of Blairite 'joined-up' government.[53]

In line with established international conflict transformation models, the community and voluntary sector, although clearly rooted within the deeply entrenched divisions of Northern Ireland's communal blocs, were given key roles as middle range actors in the peace process.[54] These assumptions about the progressive potential of civil society were also central to the Bosnian peace process from the mid-1990s onwards. European Union policy-makers argued that in the former Yugoslavia

> civil society will be instrumental in the gradual emergence of a pluralistic and democratic society ... NGOs are ... destined to play an important role in this post-conflict situation as they have vast potential for transcending the fault-lines of society through the creation of new partnerships and alliances. They can moderate and mediate in addressing the relevant needs of society, not always within the realm of the state.[55]

Comparable hopes were entertained for Northern Ireland. In this case the strategy was predicated on the hope that a specifically neutral cross-community space would emerge from cooperation within the third sector, giving rise to a new type of civil society that could transcend sectarian division.[56] Entering into mainstream political rhetoric throughout the peace process, these aspirations to foster progressive change at community level were made manifest in the institutions established by the Good Friday Agreement, as well as in a broad range of policy initiatives from education through to economic development.[57] Being driven by the imperative for 'equality' enshrined in section 75 of the 1998 Northern Ireland Act, and shaped by deepening partnerships between the state and 'civil society', the polity that developed after 1998, with its Civic Forum, Human Rights and Equality Commissions, clearly represented much more than simply 'Sunningdale for slow learners'.[58]

The balance of power between the state and civil society can also be read in the conduct of the peace process itself, where conflict between the 'warring parties' was essentially managed through a diplomatic process, directed by the British and Irish governments and supported by the United States. Far from the healing of ancient divisions, the strategic and political aims of the governments had been long established (at least since Sunningdale, if not earlier), just as the institutional parameters of any settlement were fixed by the minimum requirements of the local political elites.[59] As Taylor astutely observes, the process was 'brokered through ethno-national elite-level group-interested bargaining between party leaderships' with no real popular engagement or dialogue in the public sphere about the form the new dispensation would take.[60] Political choreography and 'spin' took the place of serious debate.[61] That 'constructive ambiguity' and 'political lying' were deemed such an essential part of the peace process suggests to some critics that governments and political leaders were more interested in manipulating opinion than convincing the population of the merits of their case.[62]

Similar criticisms are made of the consociational institutions and forms of politics that emerged from this micro-managed process. The Agreement, it is argued, reinforced the essentialist politics of ethno-national solidarity and the maximisation of communal advantage, precluding universalist alternatives based on common citizenship or class.[63] Public life was likewise rigidly shaped by the discourse of 'the two traditions' alongside the notion of parity of esteem enshrined in the terms of the Good Friday Agreement. For those who advocated a transformational process, Northern Ireland's new dispensation 'defied the norms of international peace-making by disdaining moderation and embracing extremism, marginalised civic actors while rewarding ethnic protagonism and widened the gulf between the political arena and civic society'.[64]

'Actually existing civil society'

The central challenge facing the British state from the beginning of the Troubles has not been peacebuilding or conflict transformation, but how to restore its authority and reconstitute some form of hegemony over the nation-alist population. The balance between the military, political and economic instruments within British government strategy may have varied over this forty year period, but its general aims remained constant throughout.[65]

The exact composition of this strategy at any given time was largely deter-mined by the severity of the challenge that the state was facing and the changing nature of the nationalist community from which the challenge sprang. The threat initially posed by the Provisionals during their founding moment represented a serious challenge to the legitimacy of the state in Northern Ireland, which had already lost a great deal of ground amongst significant sections of the nationalist population by the early 1970s. The unstable condi-tions of this period provided an impetus for grassroots collective action reflec-tive of 'a community in revolt, rather than a hermetically sealed secret society of gunmen and bombers'.[66] For many nationalists, the young in particular, this was a time in which the shackles of state authority were thrown off: 'we realized that they were not all powerful ... we had no-go areas and we had an armed organization. All this resulted in a discussion about what could replace it.'[67] In this qualitatively transformed atmosphere, the revolutionary challenge to the hegemony of the British state in Northern Ireland was fundamentally greater than the mere bullets and bombs of the Provisional IRA.

This period of revolutionary crisis did not last long. By the mid-1970s, the collective mobilisation that gave rise to the Provisionals had receded while the British army managed to contain the IRA's military campaign to 'an accept-able level of violence'. British policy now began increasingly to focus on more permanent forms of stabilisation and the development of a 'normal' type of hegemony by the state. Politically this took the form of a series of initiatives in the 1970s and 1980s designed to undermine support for militant republi-canism, counter nationalist alienation from authority and bolster alternative constitutional politics.[68] The specific details of these policies varied, but the overall framework was consistent. Throughout this period, British govern-ments attempted to address nationalist aspirations for a role in government alongside implementing policies to remedy specific grievances concerning discrimination and fair employment.[69]

From the late 1980s, in a policy context of containment rather than con-frontation, the 'economic and social war against violence' began to emerge as the most important instrument available to British governments in pursuit of their normalisation strategy.[70] If the immediate aim was to counter the republican analysis of Northern Ireland as a 'failed state', through driving forward solid social and economic progress, the policy was to have much wider long-term political and social implications, especially for the nationalist population. As one Secretary of State for Northern Ireland put it, 'We all know that better security and economic policies are interlinked. There is no future for Northern Ireland as an economic wasteland, no future for Northern Ireland through terrorism and no future in a political vacuum; we need action on all fronts.'[71] 'The action', when it came, was strongly influenced by policy models developed in Britain to regenerate shattered, post-industrial cities and communities through initiatives designed to rebuild 'prosperity, pride and normality'.[72] The result was an ambitious programme of social engineering, beyond mere counter-insurgency, that aimed to remodel social and economic life in Northern Ireland and begin the 'reinvention of urban Ulster as normal, placeless and able to hold its own in a competitive global economy'.[73]

One of the reasons such an ambitious economic and social strategy seemed feasible was the dominant position of the state in the political economy of Northern Ireland. The overwhelming economic and political weight of the state in the region's life can be seen in the extent of British subvention to support public services, as well as high levels of public sector employment.[74] Even after the reductions of public expenditure from 1998 as a consequence of the 'peace dividend' the state still retained a disproportionately greater role in Northern Ireland than in the rest of the United Kingdom.[75] Most importantly, the state's ability to mediate the impact of a globalising economy had given it the power to transform Northern Ireland's society beyond recognition over the previous 25 years. Consequently, the region has emerged as an almost textbook example of a normalising post-industrial economy dependent on service industries and the public sector to sustain employment and living standards.[76] The political significance of this social weight has been intensified by the politics of the peace process, with increased segregation and heightened communalisation in public life meaning that 'the economy has, and continues to be an instrument for political contestation and social control' deployed by the British state.[77]

British policies throughout this period demonstrate how states might use economic and social change as part of peacebuilding strategies.[78] In Northern Ireland these changes had a radical and largely unforeseen impact on the political and social structure of the nationalist community. For example, one significant result of this strategy of engagement was the development of a new nationalist middle class employed in the public sector, alongside the emergence of a new class of nationalist business and social entrepreneurs.[79] This 'new Catholic money' has been much commented on, giving rise to assessments that in the new Northern Ireland 'Catholics are part of the establishment as never before'.[80] The impact of the rising nationalist bourgeoisie has been linked by some commentators to political de-mobilisation and a deepening rapprochement between a new nationalist elite and the state. Furthermore, it was argued that the communal loyalties of this new middle class might weaken and thus create a barrier to the further electoral success of Sinn Féin. However, this rather mechanistic argument about the impact of social change on identity has proved unsustainable, as Sinn Féin has continued to make electoral inroads into this middle-class nationalist electorate.[81]

If this aspect of state strategy appears to have been unsuccessful in weakening Provisionalism, other factors have had a much greater influence on its political and social base. For example, nationalist civil society in general, and community organisations in particular, became increasingly oriented towards the British state (and the European Union) for funding and resources.[82] The community sector has played a particularly important role in nationalist civil society, reflecting both an historically strong communal, self-help tradition re-enforced by the powerful collective mobilisation of the early period of the Troubles, as well as wielding significant contemporary social and economic power.[83] As once autonomous groups were drawn further into the orbit of the state, they increasingly found their activities largely shaped by its official priorities.[84] One critic of what she dismissively calls 'the peace industry' argues that this dynamic, largely driven by European Union, British and Irish government grants totalling over £1 billion since 1994, has created a 'huge dependency culture in the community and voluntary sector'.[85] As the state now increasingly shaped the terrain, so it defined the agenda for nationalist civil society.[86] The impact was as much ideological and cultural as material.

These developments in civil society were also mirrored by an institutionalisation process within Provisionalism. Since the Provisionals had deep roots in the nationalist community, with membership drawn from the same milieu as community activists (frequently being the same individuals), similar processes of organisational formalisation and engagement with the state were perhaps inevitable. Whilst republican critics have blamed the corruption of individual leaders for Sinn Féin's movement into mainstream politics or attributed its betrayal of republican principles to the 'fatal embrace' of electoral politics, the political and organisational transformation of Provisionalism is arguably as much a product of the social and economic forces and British state strategy that has transformed the nationalist community as a whole since the late 1980s.[87]

One of the paradoxes of the British state's strategy to rebuild its authority and establish its hegemony over the nationalist population is that not only did it fail to destroy its Provisional opponents, it actually strengthened them. This was partly an accidental by-product of social and economic change, but it also suited British interests to use the Provisionals – shorn of their republicanism – as partners in the peace process and interlocutors who could guarantee the future stability of the new dispensation. Sinn Féin's utility as partners for the state derived not so much from its electoral mandate, but rather in the structures of power that the Provisionals had built up in nationalist civil society, many of which reflected the characteristics of the state. Northern Ireland's new polity demonstrated the eventual success of the state in restoring its dominance, albeit at the price of recognising republicans – sans republicanism – as partners in governance. The Provisionals had likewise maintained their position as the leaders of the nationalist community, but at the cost of abandoning their challenge to the British state and their own claims to ideological hegemony.

A crisis of all societies

If one party to the Northern Ireland peace process can be said to have achieved its aims, then it is the British state. It has restored its dominance in the region and successfully managed a long-running conflict by coopting its former opponents as partners in governance. This governmental partnership is mirrored in nationalist civil society by the strength of the state's influence over the voluntary and community sector. Apart from a handful of republican dissidents, the British state's position now appears unassailable: when even its former enemies in Sinn Féin are prepared to give its rule a high degree of consent, it no longer requires much coercion to enforce its will.

Yet the triumph is not unalloyed. Tony Blair's appeals to an idealised 'civil society' betray a fundamental lack of confidence and sense of belief at the heart of the contemporary state and British political class. In his 'vision' of the peace process there is no sense of authority or clear project beyond pragmatic management, whereas British governments in the 1970s were committed to the defence of their state and prepared to utilise all the resources at their command to do so. Contrast the confident assertion of state interest in a 1979 *Times* editorial with the uncertainties of contemporary political rhetoric: 'The differences so stubbornly insisted upon in Ulster concern the most fundamental of all political issues: allegiance, national identity, the legitimacy of the state ... These are issues which are usually disposed of only when one side prevails decisively over the other.'[88]

Paradoxically, Sinn Féin politicians were presented with similar challenges to their authority by growing support for the dissidents from sections of alienated nationalist youth.[89] Appeals by Provisional leaders to 'the nationalist community' or a similarly ill-defined 'civil society' were attempts comparable to those of Tony Blair to re-engage with an increasingly disillusioned and disengaged nationalist electorate. These challenges to legitimacy showed how the politics of Northern Ireland seemed to be pervaded by a permanent sense of crisis which never quite tipped over the edge into a major collapse. Possibly, this stable instability is inevitable in a polity structured by an Agreement which leaves open for the foreseeable future the major questions about the constitutional status of the state.

Certainly, local politicians have learned to live and thrive in this uncertain climate, for example using controversies about contentious parades to either mobilise support or alternatively identify the enemy in an annual sham fight. Likewise, vital social and economic issues such as public housing and the distribution of other social goods continue to be refracted through communal frames.[90] This has led to widespread cynicism that Northern Ireland's political class as a whole are simply going through the motions. Despite the unresolved issues that remain at the heart of the region's politics there seems to be an emptiness at the centre of these parliamentary disputes and a lack of real substance to the 'contending' ideologies. If, as some still claim, politics in Northern Ireland are the continuation of war by other means it is by no means clear what the war is really still about.

However, it is in this very localism that a much deeper crisis in public life and a challenge to the very idea of the political is revealed. As one distinguished historian has described the politics of the post Cold War world,

> It was not a crisis of one form of organizing societies, but of all forms. The strange calls for an otherwise unidentified 'civil society', for 'community' were the voice of lost and drifting generations. They were heard in an age when such words, having lost their traditional meanings, became vapid phrases. There is no other way to define group identity, except by defining the outsiders who were not in it.[91]

For both the British state and Northern Ireland's political class, these attempts to re-engage with the population illustrate an underlying crisis of authority at the heart of their political projects. Thus, far from being a backward and exceptionalist outpost, the declining ideological legitimacy and mutual exhaustion embodied in the new language of civil society makes Northern Ireland very much part of the disorientated mainstream of contemporary liberal democratic societies.

Notes

1 D. Godson, 'The Real Lessons of Ulster', *Prospect* (November, 2007), 32–37. For some examples of international reaction, see *Hindustan Times*, 13 July 2010, and *El País*, 14 July 2010.

2 M. Simpson, '"Theme Park" Rioting Raises Old Fears', *BBC News Northern Ireland*, 14 July 2010, http://www.bbc.co.uk/news/uk-northern+ireland-10642001?: (accessed 15 July 2010).

3 First Minister Peter Robinson and Deputy First Minister Martin McGuinness quoted in Henry Chu, 'Northern Ireland leaders urge calm, denounce violent Belfast protests', *Los Angeles Times*, 15 July 2010, http://www.latimes.com/news/nationworld/world/la-fg-northern-ireland-riots-201007 (accessed 15 July 2010).

4 C. Heaney, 'Belfast Peace Will Come When a Shared Future Is Forged', *Guardian.co.uk*, 14 July 2010, http://www.guardian.co.uk/commentisfree/2010/jul/14/belfast-peace-shared-future/print (accessed 15 July 2010).

5 For example, David Ford, Northern Ireland's Minister of Justice, interviewed on BBC Radio Four's *Today* programme on 14 July 2010, specifically linked the Ardoyne riots to social deprivation and a belief amongst 'some nationalists that they had been left behind by the peace process'.

6 Nuala O'Loan, 'A violence from the past', *The Guardian*, 14 July 2010.

7 Elevate East Lancashire, 'Case Study-Community cohesion work-promoting good relations', http://www.audit-commission.gov.uk/housing/marketrenewal pathfinders/

goodpractice (accessed 15 July 2010), *The Guardian*, 26 May 2010 and 13 July 2010.

8 'N.I. Politicians Advise Iraqis on Reconciliation', *Spiegel Online International*, 9 April 2007, http://www.spiegel.de/international/world/0,1518,503732,00.html (accessed 19 March 2011), and *Belfast News Letter*, 4 August 2004.

9 William Graham, 'Woodward Praises Political Leadership', *Irish News*, 21 March 2008.

10 P. Bew, *Ireland: The Politics of Enmity, 1789–2006* (Oxford, 2007), viii.

11 T. Blair, 'Values and the Power of Community', speech given at the University of Tübingen, 30 June 2000, http://www.weltethos.org/dat-english/00_1-blair.htm (accessed 30 April 2010).

12 The Tübingen speech focuses on these communitarian themes, central to the 'Third Way' project, in an attempt to promote them as a coherent and internationally relevant ideology.

13 See, for an example of this political rhetoric, M. Rees, *Northern Ireland: A Personal Perspective* (London, 1985).

14 M. Power, '"Merely a Diversion in the Absence of a Real Policy": Community Relations Policy in Northern Ireland 1969–1975', unpublished paper given at the Centre for Contemporary British History, University of London conference, 'Reassessing the Seventies', 8 July 2010.

15 S. Buchanan 'Transforming Conflict in Northern Ireland and the Border Counties: Some Lessons from the Peace Programmes on Valuing Participative Democracy', *Irish Political Studies* 23.3 (2008), 390. I am grateful to Dr Buchanan for drawing my attention to the problems of defining conflict transformation and conflict management (unpublished paper given at the Political Studies Association of Ireland annual conference, Galway 2009).

16 J. P. Lederach, *Building Peace: Sustainable Reconciliation in Divided Societies* (Washington, DC, 1997), xvi.

17 Lederach, *Building Peace*, 28 (my emphasis).

18 M. Kaldor, *Global Civil Society: An Answer to War* (Cambridge, 2003), 135.

19 For a useful summary of Lederach's 'peace-building pyramid' model, see Buchanan, 'Transforming Conflict in Northern Ireland and the Border Counties', 391.

20 A. Giddens, *Beyond Left and Right: The Future of Radical Politics* (Cambridge, 1994).

21 For the continuing importance of the debate about the reinvigoration of civil society in Britain, see *Daily Telegraph*, 18 July 2010; P. Blond, *Red Tory: How Left and Right Have Broken Britain and How We Can Fix It* (London, 2010); and T. Judt, *Ill Fares the Land: A Treatise on Our Present Discontents* (London, 2010). For an introduction to the international dimensions of the debate on civil society, see S. Roginsky and S.Shortall, 'Civil Society as a Contested Field of Meanings', *International Journal of Sociology* 29.9/10 (2009), 473–87.

22 For examples of the range of the debate, see J. Keane (ed.), *Civil Society and the State: New European Perspectives* (London, 1988), and J. Keane, *Civil Society: Old Visions, New Images* (Cambridge, 1998).

23 S. Chambers and J. Kopstein, 'Civil Society and the State', in J. Dryzek, B. Honig and A. Phillips (eds), *The Oxford Handbook of Political Theory* (Oxford, 2006), 363–64.

24 M. Edwards, *Civil Society* (Cambridge, 2004).

25 J. Cohen and A. Arato, *Civil Society and Political Theory* (Cambridge, MA, 1992).

26 Chambers and Kopstein, 'Civil Society and the State', 371.

27 R. Putnam, *Bowling Alone: The Collapse and Renewal of American Community* (New York, 2000). For the importance of ideas of civic virtue, see also W. Kymlicka, *Contemporary Political Philosophy: An Introduction* (Oxford, 2002), 285–326.

28 Giddens, *Beyond Left and Right*.

29 K. Bean, *The New Politics of Sinn Féin* (Liverpool, 2007).

30 S. Osborne, 'Review Article – Reflections on Civil Society', *Local Government Studies* 28.4 (2002), 123.
31 J. Habermas, *Between Facts and Norms: Contributions to a Discourse Theory of Law and Democracy* (Cambridge, MA, 1996), 367.
32 Habermas, *Between Facts and Norms*, 370.
33 C. Farrington, 'Models of Civil Society and Their Implications for The Northern Ireland Peace Process', in Christopher Farrington (ed.), *Global Change, Civil Society and the Northern Ireland Peace Process* (Basingstoke, 2008), 123-27.
34 *London Review of Books*, 10 June 2010.
35 Commission of Inquiry into the Future of Civil Society in the UK and Ireland, *Making Good Society: Summary of Final Report of Commission of Inquiry into the Future of Civil Society in the UK and Ireland 2010*, www.futuresforcivilsociety. org (accessed 30 April 2010).
36 For examples of the theoretical discussion concerning 'bonding' and 'bridging' social capital, see Farrington, *Global Change*, 131.
37 Commission of Inquiry into the Future of Civil Society in the UK and Ireland, *Making Good Society*, 2.
38 See, for example, R. Sennett, 'The asbo is an icon of New Labour's Negligence', *Guardian*, 30 July 2010, http://www.guardian.co.uk/commentisfree/2010/jul/30/ asbo-icon-new-labour-negligence (accessed 31 July 2010).
39 D. Clements, A. Donald, M. Earnshaw and A. Williams (eds), *The Future of Community: Reports of a Death Greatly Exaggerated* (London, 2008).
40 A. Callinicos, *Against the Third Way* (Cambridge, 2001).
41 Blair, 'Values and the Power of Community', 2000.
42 For the Northern Ireland Labour Party, see A. Edwards, *A History of the Northern Ireland Labour Party: Democratic Socialism and Sectarianism* (Manchester, 2009); for integrated education, see, F. O'Connor, *A Shared Childhood: The Story of the Integrated Schools in Northern Ireland* (Belfast, 2002), and J. Bardon, *The Struggle for Shared Schools In Northern Ireland: The History of All Children Together* (Belfast, 2009); for religiously based peace activism, see M. Power, 'Building Communities in a Post-Conflict Society: Churches and Peace Building in Northern Ireland since 1994', *The European Legacy* 10.1 (2005), 55-68; and, for the Peace People, see C. McKeown, *The Passion of Peace* (Belfast, 1984).
43 For the impact of the Opsahl Commission, see A. Pollak (ed.), *A Citizen's Inquiry: The Opsahl Report on Northern Ireland* (Dublin, 1993), and A. Guelke, 'Civil Society and the Northern Ireland Peace Process', *Voluntas: International Journal of Voluntary and Nonprofit Organizations* 14.1 (2003), 61-78. For examples of dialogue between republicans and loyalists, see M. Hall, *Seeds of Hope* (Newtownabbey, 2000).
44 Guelke, 'Civil Society and the Northern Ireland Peace Process', 61 and 72-74. See also M. Potter, 'Women, Civil Society and Peace-Building in Northern Ireland: Paths to Peace through Women's Empowerment', in Farrington (ed.), *Global Change, Civil Society and the Northern Ireland Peace Process*, 142-58. For voluntary and community activism, see S. Byrne, 'Consociational and Civic Society Approaches to Peacebuilding in Northern Ireland', *Journal of Peace Research* 38 (2001), 327-52; Northern Ireland Council for Voluntary Action (NICVA), *Dialogue Paper Four: Role of the Third Sector in Building a More Tolerant Society*, www.nicva.org (accessed 15 July 2010) and n. 37.
45 NICVA, *Centre for Economic Empowerment-Background*, 17 December 2010, http://www.nicva.org/news/jobs-nicva (accessed 19 March 2011).
46 NICVA, *State of the Sector V 2010, and Dialogue Paper One: The Role of the Third Sector in Civic Life, Democracy and Governance*, www.nicva.org (accessed 15 July 2010).

47 B. Jessop, *State Power* (Cambridge, 2008), 2–12; M. Smith, *Power and the State* (Basingstoke, 2009), 89–108.

48 E. Hobsbawm, *The Age of Extremes: The Short Twentieth Century, 1814–1991* (London, 1995), 31–40.

49 Bean, *The New Politics of Sinn Féin*, 17.

50 A. Giddens, *New Thinking for New Times* (Belfast, 1995).

51 B. Murtagh, 'The URBAN Community Initiative in Northern Ireland', *Policy and Politics* 29.4 (2001), 431–46.

52 J. Morison, 'Democracy, Governance and Govermentality: Civic Public Space and Constitutional Renewal in Northern Ireland', *Oxford Journal of Legal Studies* 21.2 (2001), 287–310. See also, C. McCall and A. Williamson, 'Governance and Democracy in Northern Ireland: The Role of the Voluntary and Community Sector after the Agreement', *Governance* 14.3 (2002), 363–83.

53 R. Taylor, 'The Belfast Agreement and the Limits of Consociationalism', in Farrington (ed.), *Global Change, Civil Society and the Northern Ireland Peace Process*, 191. For the specific impact of European Union programmes, see Buchanan, 'Transforming Conflict in Northern Ireland and the Border Counties'.

54 S. Byrne and C. Irvin, 'Economic Aid and Policy Making: Building the Peace Dividend in Northern Ireland', *Policy and Politics* 29.4 (2001), 413–29.

55 Dialogue Development, *Survey of Bosnian Civil Society Organisations: Mapping, Characteristic, and Strategy* (Copenhagen, 1997).

56 R. Wilson, 'From Violence to Intolerance: Ethno-Nationalism and the Crowding Out of Civic Life', in Farrington (ed.), *Global Change, Civil Society and the Northern Ireland Peace Process*, 209–10.

57 Farrington, *Global Change*, 121–23; see also, Northern Ireland Executive, 'Minsters Announce Consultation on Review of the Civic Forum', 28 May 2008, http: //www. northernireland.gov.uk/new/news-ofmdfm/news-ofmdfm-may-2008/new   ... : (accessed 2 August 2010).

58 See Northern Ireland Act 1998 (c. 47), Part VII Human Rights and Equal Opportunities, http://www.opsi.gov.uk?acts/acts1998/ukpga_19980047_en_7 (accessed 30 April 2010). For the impact of these institutions, see M. Adshead and J. Tonge, *Politics in Ireland: Convergence and Divergence in a Two-Polity Island* (Basingstoke, 2009). For the role and significance of the voluntary and community sector as well as the European Union-funded Peace programmes, see NICVA, *State of the Sector* and *Dialogue Papers on the Third Sector 1–4*, www.nicva.org (accessed 15 July 2010), and Buchanan, 'Transforming Conflict in Northern Ireland and the Border Counties'.

59 D. Horowitz, 'Explaining the Northern Ireland Agreement: The Sources of an Unlikely Constitutional Consensus', *British Journal of Political Science* 32.2 (2002), 193–220.

60 Taylor, 'The Belfast Agreement and the Limits of Consociationalism', 190.

61 P. Dixon, 'Political Skills or Lying and Manipulation? The Choreography of the Northern Ireland Peace Process', *Political Studies* 50 (2002), 725–41.

62 A. Aughey, 'The Art and Effect of Political Lying in Northern Ireland', *Irish Political Studies* 17.2 (2002), 1–6.

63 Taylor, 'The Belfast Agreement and the Limits of Consociationalism', 183–87.

64 Wilson, 'From Violence to Intolerance: Ethno-Nationalism and the Crowding Out of Civic Life', 199.

65 P. Neumann, *Britain's Long War: British Strategy in the Northern Ireland Conflict, 1969–98* (Basingstoke, 2003).

66 T. McKearney, 'Putting the Provos in Context', *Sunday Business Post*, 7 August 2005; D. McAdam, 'Symposium on the Dynamics of Contention', *Mobilization* 8.1 (2001), 43.

67 Republican activist Feilim Ó hAdhmaill, quoted in Bean, *The New Politics of Sinn Féin*, 53.
68 H. Patterson, *Ireland since 1939: The Persistence of Conflict* (London, 2007), 248–60.
69 For example, the Sunningdale (1973) and Anglo-Irish (1985) Agreements addressed these political demands whilst legislation the Fair Employment Act 1989 dealt with discrimination in employment which was a particularly important issue for nationalists and republicans.
70 R. Needham, *Battling For Peace* (Belfast, 1998), 1.
71 Lord Prior, quoted in F. Gaffikin and M. Morrissey, *Northern Ireland: The Thatcher Years* (London, 1990), 62.
72 P. Hadaway, 'Cohesion in Contested Spaces', *Architects' Journal* 214.17 (November 2001), 40.
73 Murtagh 'The URBAN Community Initiative in Northern Ireland', 432.
74 For an overview of the importance of the public sector in Northern Ireland, see Oxford Economics/Economic Research Institute of Northern Ireland, *Cutting Carefully – How Repairing UK Finances Will Impact NI: A Report for NICVA*, July 2010.
75 D. O' Hearn, 'How Has Peace Changed the Northern Ireland Political Economy?', *Ethnopolitics* 7.1 (2008), 101–18.
76 C. Coulter and M. Murray (eds), *Northern Ireland after the Troubles: A Society in Transition* (Manchester, 2008).
77 P. Shirlow, 'The Economics of the Peace Process', in C. Gilligan and J. Tonge (eds), *Peace or War? Understanding the Peace Process in Northern Ireland* (Aldershot, 1997), 133.
78 The Portland Trust, *Economics in Peacemaking: Lessons from Northern Ireland*, May 2007.
79 F. O' Connor, *In Search of a State: Catholics in Northern Ireland* (Belfast, 1993), 16.
80 Dr John Reid MP, Secretary of State for Northern Ireland, 'Becoming Persuaders: British and Irish Identities in Northern Ireland', speech given at the Institute of Irish Studies, University of Liverpool, 21 November 1999.
81 J. Evans and J. Tonge, 'Social Class and Party Choice in Northern Ireland's Ethnic Blocs', *West European Politics* 32.5 (2009), 1012–30.
82 Some 45 per cent of the voluntary sector's income came from government funding in 2010. '£1bn Worth of Cuts Will Be Felt for a Generation, Warns Report', *Belfast Telegraph*, 26 July 2010.
83 C. de Baróid, *Ballymurphy and the Irish War* (London, 2000).
84 F. Cochrane and S. Dunne, *People Power? The Role of the Voluntary and Community Sector in the Northern Ireland Conflict* (Cork, 2002). For examples of the range of activities of these groups and the impact of British state funding, see the Annual Reports of the Ashton Centre, http://www.ashtoncentre.com/aboutus.php, and the Upper Springfield Development Trust, http://uppersprongfield.com/funders.html (accessed on 2 August 2010).
85 Fionnuala Meredith, 'Putting a price on peace?', *Irish Times*, 10 January 2006.
86 A similar process of internalisation can also be seen in the impact of the equality and fair employment discourse of the Fair Employment Act 1989 on Sinn Féin's policies. See Bean, *The New Politics of Sinn Féin*, 30–33.
87 'Adams accepts British police', *Saoirse*, November 2006.
88 *Times* editorial, 1979, quoted in Irish Freedom Movement, *The Irish War: The Irish Freedom Movement Handbook* (London, 1987), 29.
89 *Daily Telegraph*, 18 July 2010.
90 See, for example, the sectarian and territorial dynamics that underpin the controversy surrounding the planned re-development of a former British base in North Belfast reported in *Belfast Telegraph*, 17 March 2011.
91 Hobsbawm, *The Age of Extremes*, 11.

10

Examining the Peacebuilding Policy Framework of the Irish and British Governments

Sandra Buchanan

Since 1986 approximately €2.95 billion has been spent in Northern Ireland and the Border Counties funding conflict transformation initiatives through the IFI, Peace I and its successor Peace II and the INTERREG I, II and IIIA programmes, largely through social and economic development.[1] The IFI was set up in 1986 by the Irish and UK governments through the Anglo-Irish Agreement with the twin objectives of promoting social and economic advance and encouraging contact, dialogue and reconciliation between the two communities in Northern Ireland and on both sides of the Border. Funded by the United States, the EU, Canada, Australia and New Zealand, it formally ceased operations in 2010.[2] Peace I was set up in the wake of the 1994 IRA and loyalist ceasefires to support peace and reconciliation in Northern Ireland and the Border Counties, largely through social and economic development activities. Funded by the EU and the Irish and British governments, it covered the period 1995–1999, with Peace II continuing this work from 2000–2004 and the Peace II Extension covering the period 2005–2006 (Peace III, covering the period 2007–2013, is currently underway). INTERREG was initially set up by the EU in 1991 to assist weaker internal border areas in dealing with the Single Market and has been restructured over the years with INTERREG III primarily concerned with promoting sustainable and integrated cross-border development.

However, despite their successes[3] the collective lessons of these three tools have highlighted how, for a variety of reasons, a range of unnecessary difficulties arose for all levels of society in their attempts to transform the region's conflict over the last two decades,[4] demonstrating the ad hoc approach of the transformation process and therefore of this expenditure, as neither the Irish nor British governments possessed a comprehensive conflict transformation policy framework to strategically guide the process. Certainly, the British government had made some policy statements relating to various aspects of peacebuilding from a (international) development aid perspective, but not relating to the transformation of the conflict on its doorstep.[5] In the Irish context, a formal conflict transformation policy is also absent, reflected in the location of brief allusions to peacebuilding, mixed up with discussions on conflict resolution and prevention, within the development cooperation field.[6]

However, to sustain peace over the long term, a policy framework and planning operating at a strategically integrated level in both jurisdictions is necessary.

This essay asserts that these difficulties resulted from a lack of specialist knowledge and understanding of conflict transformation theory and processes due in part to the non-existence of a (government) conflict transformation policy framework and further reinforced by a strategic conflict transformation planning deficit. This was particularly so for those charged with the development, management and implementation of the region's conflict transformation process (through these tools) and consequently so for those at the grassroots. It is a particularly striking issue when one considers that conflict transformation is a long-term process. For any long-term process to work, policy guidelines and planning are essential; policy guidelines and planning operating at a strategic level, inclusive of the wide range of individual and organisational interests at all levels of society and in both jurisdictions is even more essential – it could have ensured that these difficulties were avoided, or, at the very least, curtailed.

Theoretically, conflict transformation has received increasing attention in recent years. However, as Ryan notes, 'the growth in the use of the term has not always been matched by greater precision and clarity'.[7] Its emergence from a number of pre-existing traditions within the broad field of conflict management has created a definitional morass: in most of the academic literature it is often mixed up with the terms conflict management and conflict resolution frequently referring to the same strategies. This presents a considerable challenge: the core difficulty facing it is that 'its jump to prominence ... has outpaced the development of its meaning in clearly understood policy and operational terms' resulting in practice terms, 'in a relative absence of consensus among governments on the question of appropriate implementation'.[8] This was clearly evident in the Northern Ireland and Border Counties context where, for example, the EU's role accentuated a clear lack of 'a strategic understanding of conflict management or a substantive understanding of what peace and reconciliation mean. Beyond the generic concepts ... there was no strategy for what the funding would deliver.'[9]

However, while no single conflict transformation model can be identified, some conceptual clarification can be provided if one places conflict transformation within the overall conflict management framework of conflict settlement, resolution and transformation. Within this framework, conflict settlement implies that conflict is a zero-sum game and peace is viewed in purely negative terms, with no set objective of longer-term positive peace or social justice. The ultimate aim is a cessation of violence that will lead to some sort of political settlement, involving top-level actors such as political, military and religious leaders. As a strategy purely concerned with a final result or settlement of the conflict and not with its underlying root causes, it is problematic, presenting a conflict of interest – if the root causes are not resolved, the final result that conflict settlement is concerned with will not be sustainable.

Conflict resolution aims not to eliminate conflict as such, but to eliminate the violent and destructive manifestations of conflict that can be traced back to the unmet needs and fears of the conflict parties. It is primarily concerned with the promotion of horizontal relationships between actors of relatively equal status, principally mid-level actors. However, this strategy is also problematic: being mainly concerned with the elimination of the causes of conflict rather than with the actual conflict itself, while only involving one level of society, will not enable the resolution to be sustainable. A sustainable strategy is required that eliminates both the root causes of conflict and the conflict itself while involving all levels of society.

Thus, conflict transformation builds upon these strategies as it is concerned with addressing the root causes of conflict over the long term and, more particularly, promoting conditions that create cooperative relationships both horizontally and vertically, principally by furthering vertical relationships between conflicting actors of relatively unequal status. Its particular focus on empowering grassroots actors sets it apart from other conflict management methods. A sense of local ownership is critical to any long-term sustainment of peace. Viewed this way, protracted violent conflicts are primarily the result of unequal and suppressive social and political structures (structural violence) and conflict is therefore seen as a positive agent for fundamental social change. Thus, while settlement implies a final end and resolution implies the process of finding a solution to a problem, to transform implies bringing about a deeply profound change of the conflict or the socio-political system in which it is rooted. The applicability of conflict transformation, rather than conflict resolution or settlement, is much more useful for transforming societies immersed in protracted social conflict into societies which embrace a relative peace. It is an essential part of the conflict management toolkit because, as Lederach observes,

> there are significant gaps in our capacity to build and sustain peace initiatives ... the gaps emerge from a reductionism focused on techniques driven by a need to find quick fixes and solutions to complex, long-term problems rather than a systemic understanding of peace-building as a process-structure.[10]

This essay therefore seeks to examine the learning from this region for practitioners and policy-makers nationally and internationally. Having briefly outlined the three conflict transformation tools in question, it will examine some of the unnecessary difficulties the transformation process experienced through them. It will then consider the implications a lack of specialist knowledge, a lack of policy and a strategic planning deficit have had for this region's conflict transformation process and also for transformational practice more generally, making the case for a strategic policy framework at government level, thus avoiding unnecessary difficulties in future process implementation.

Unnecessary difficulties

While difficulties are to be expected with such complex process implementation, particularly over the long term, a policy framework may have ensured
that many of the difficulties were avoided or, at the very least, curtailed.
These included *inter alia* theoretical misunderstandings and definitional
and conceptual confusion, overlooking the root causes of the conflict, overly
complex delivery structures, excessive bureaucracy, gap funding periods,
listening to and involving civil society, enabling accessibility and, critically,
sustainability issues.[11] While it is not possible to individually examine these
difficulties, a closer examination of some will further the case for a policy
framework.

Overlooking the root causes

In terms of overlooking the root causes of the conflict, what was remarkably
clear after five years of Peace I, for example, was that whilst the programmes
certainly attempted to address the root causes of the conflict, they really did not
succeed despite the fact that 'there was an attempt in the Peace I programme
to take a risk with regard to looking outside of the box with regard to the
causes ... [However,] it didn't do it in a well thought out [way] underpinned
by a very clear rationale'.[12] While this failure is generally accepted, it is not
surprising when one examines the political context within which this particular tool found itself – in 1995, when Peace I first began, negotiations were still
over three years away from a political agreement on the conflict. Moreover,

> given the fact that the Good Friday Agreement talks didn't address it [root
> causes of the conflict] either ... perhaps because the politicians at that stage
> realised they would never get to agreement if they did start [discussing the
> causes of the conflict], perhaps the Peace programme reflected it.[13]

However, as this is a critical element of transformation practice, for those
at the coalface of the conflict, such as working-class Protestant areas, it was
disappointing: 'nobody wanted to attack the real problem ... there was good
work done through the Peace I money ... but it never actually looked at the
real causes of conflict ... There was lip-service paid to it. But that was all ... the
basic problem of conflict here has never been examined.'[14] Certainly the Peace
programmes, particularly Peace I, brought those at the grassroots 'a sense of
ownership of their area and brought people a sense of working together to try
and look at a problem ... [However,] the underlying problem is we still have
poverty, we still have unemployment'.[15]

Complex delivery structures and excessive bureaucracy

Difficulties associated with overly complex delivery structures and excessive
bureaucracy were also clearly illustrated by the Peace programmes, particularly in comparison to the IFI. One of the major weaknesses of the first

programme was its inability to provide clear and basic programme and monitoring information. Such large amounts of funding required financial accountability and transparency. However, audit and monitoring information requirements increased (and changed) as the programme progressed, often frustratingly required (by the EU and their managing agents) retrospectively, not only for project promoters mid-project, but also for Intermediary Funding Bodies (IFBs) who managed the funding, some years after projects had been completed. Moreover, these requirements were disproportionate to the grant size, unfairly required regardless of the amount.

Additionally, some of the Peace I programme measures were described by the prior appraisal as complex and untidy – they were not well understood and, particularly in Northern Ireland, there was a multiplicity of delivery bodies for Peace I (64) and II (56), with different application periods, criteria and points of access, amounting to what the House of Commons Northern Ireland Affairs Committee termed an 'appalling complexity'.[16] While the necessity for such a multiplicity of delivery bodies, particularly IFBs, in terms of enabling an unprecedented level of grassroots participation in the transformation process has been noted elsewhere,[17] the downside was the associated complexities. In Northern Ireland, the wide range of decentralised and locally based delivery mechanisms, on top of numerous government departments, in comparison to the much simpler set up in the Border Counties whereby the funding was largely managed by one IFB (Area Development Management/ Combat Poverty Agency [ADM/CPA]), seemed totally unnecessary.

The move to Peace II was characterised by excessive bureaucracy, to the extent that it distracted attention away from the programme's overarching aims and fixed attention instead on operational delivery. The application process became a source of disempowerment for many as the lack of capacity in the voluntary and community sector and the need for adequate and properly trained support was simply disregarded:

> for many communities and sectors in the early stages of development the challenge of accessing Peace II funding was too great. In particular, the onerous application and project selection criteria often prevented the involvement of low capacity groups and sectors most in need of support.[18]

Application forms were excessively long, complex and repetitive and contained a somewhat unrealistic requirement (for those without the resources and skills to do so) for part completion online, the result of being centrally driven and controlled, ignoring previous experiences of IFBs. Thus the House of Commons Northern Ireland Affairs Committee concluded:

> the creation and dissemination of these forms was a shambles. As far as we have been able to ascertain, no one person or department took responsibility for the overall requirements being put upon the bodies seeking grants: but many organisations seem to have had a hand in adding to and complicating the application forms.[19]

Moreover, the gathering of monitoring and reporting information became one of the main thorns in the sides of project promoters, worsening considerably under the second programme, so much so that it acted as a deterrent to many prospective applicants.[20] As one grassroots project promoter noted, '[the Peace programmes] are a nightmare, absolute and total nightmare, the bureaucracy that's involved in them ... a ludicrous situation ... Peace II ... has lost the plot in bureaucracy.'[21] IFBs were also placed in a difficult position – it was noted that the bureaucracy

> often posed a quandary for Intermediary Funding Bodies who are faced with the potentially contradictory demands of being bold and imaginative in their funding policies, while being cautious and overly regulatory in their administrative procedures. One of the clear differences between ... Peace I ... and Peace II is that funding bodies ... are being left with little independence in deciding on the administrative procedures to be adopted.[22]

Sustainability Issues

Some of the most disconcerting difficulties related to the issue of sustainability: there was simply no provision made by either government for sustaining the transformation efforts enabled by these tools. If project or, indeed, process sustainability is not possible then successful transformation becomes questionable. Efforts by one Peace I IFB, the Community Foundation for Northern Ireland (CFNI) to raise the issue of appropriate exit strategies were unsuccessful, leaving it to conclude unsatisfactorily, 'sustainability was to be an issue confined to the individual project level and the intermediary funders'.[23] Moreover, the CFNI found that the biggest demand from groups who had availed of Peace I funding 'was for an extension of their current work on the basis that the initial funding time period was unrealistic to address issues of social exclusion and peacebuilding in any realistic manner'.[24] Their experience starkly highlighted the reality for many project promoters who viewed sustainability as unrealistic for social inclusion projects, particularly when one considers that 'community development and innovations by its very nature is not self-sustaining ... you don't make a programme sustainable in three, four, five years. You have to be in it for the long haul.'[25]

This issue was not helped either by the sustained two year gap funding period that existed between Peace I and II; projects that ran from Peace I to Peace II clearly had a considerably higher impact in their local communities.[26] Moreover, 44% of Peace I projects completed their task, 31% were sustained through additional funds, 10% were mainstreamed, 9% became self-sustaining and 6% continued on a smaller scale. In comparison, 'most [Peace II] projects would not be able to become self-sustaining, particularly those which are targeted at disadvantaged groups ... The potential implications for both governments are significant if a large number of projects require further funding to exist beyond Peace II.'[27] Sustainability is a serious challenge which, in the case of Peace II it was argued, 'cannot be left to the end ... as it is simply not a "closure" issue. Resources will have to be identified otherwise much of what has been created under Peace II will simply disappear.'[28] However, while a number of the Peace II measures became sustainable by virtue of government mainstreaming, it became evident that many would simply not continue. Moreover, while many grassroots actors had long ago accepted that 'some of the best and most needed projects are not sustainable',[29] attempts, particularly by IFBs, to persuade those at the top to accept this were not easy: 'a lot of them should and could be taken on in mainstream government programme[s] ... but ... that's a real challenge to try and get existing authorities ... to ... take that on board'.[30] This appeared incredible to practitioners: 'its huge that sustainability was never questioned ... the question was asked of community groups about sustainability – I don't think that the same question was put to either governments around how they would be assisting their investment.'[31] Although the Peace programmes were not set up to fund the voluntary and community sector, a fact recognised by them,[32] it would appear that they often had little choice but to rely on it. There is no doubt that this was quite damaging, not only to this sector, but to the overall success of the Peace programmes. In the Border Counties, for example,

> it took Peace funding money in a lot of instances to allow the community/voluntary sector to develop and then ... when Peace I, Peace II started getting withdrawn, they didn't have anywhere else to go, so certainly ... there would have been a certain level of dependency developed on the Peace programme.[33]

Essentially,

> the biggest issue is the fact that there isn't that mainstream budget line, there isn't an acknowledgement for the need for specific peacebuilding work ... people will want to categorise it in what they know, rather than in something new and it's going to be a real issue going forward.[34]

Therefore, 'intervention from government ... hasn't been forthcoming';[35] the cat and mouse game played by government, in terms of long-term sustainability of the process, clearly illustrates the difficulties faced by grassroots actors and IFBs alike who attempted to progress sustainability:

> you try to address sustainability – you send in groups ... to talk to [the Department of] Social, Community and Family Affairs or ... Health and ... they are willing to consider funding ... But then with government cutbacks it never happens ... and the governments are always saying 'if you can get Peace funding we'll delay ours' ... we [IFB] get blackmailed into giving it for another year because you're still hoping it's going to be mainstreamed ... It's that bit of hope that ... maybe ensures that the funding keeps coming on a drip sort of feed from the Peace programme ... a lot of that has been going on ... there is just no other structure there to fund.[36]

The issue was not helped either by bureaucratic thinking at the top level:

the [Peace I] projects were supposed to be sustainable [but] people didn't really believe ... their letters of offer couldn't exist beyond 2001. It had to end because that's when funds ended and there was no assurance of another programme. But projects did not act ... that's where the fault was ... projects were not sufficiently clear that there would be no more money ... people had applied their own expectations to this ... so you had these people who thought it was the Peace programme's job to fund the community and voluntary sector ... the child care sector ... the social economy sector and it wasn't the Peace programme's job to do any of those things.[37]

The difficulties associated with sustainability are clearly symptomatic of a lack of strategic thinking from government. As one mid-level project promoter noted,

It's the bridge between ... the visionary Europeans who said we'll set up a Peace Programme to help the Irish peace process and the hard nosed British and Irish ... who don't want to spend extra money ... there's no link between the first saying to the second 'we've spent a billion euros on this thing over the last ten years. Could you now at least take the successful examples of this and bring them on further with your money?' ... it is extraordinary that the Irish government which is supposed to be committed in its consti- tution to Irish unity, had got no thoughts about this area ... about ... the long-term ... this is work towards Irish unity however you define it, unity of people ... coming together. You don't have to be a Provo or a republican ... and there is no thinking in Dublin about this.[38]

Subsequently, the region's conflict transformation process is dependent on hope and European efforts, rather than strategic government policy. Thus, in terms of the Peace programmes, 'the government's ... short-term view from the start and the management of that in some ways became *ad hoc*, it began to be directed partly by the projects. But what the projects would identify needed to be known at the beginning ... not the middle.'[39] Consequently, there does not appear to be any commitment to transformation beyond a narrow political framework.

Involving civil society

Finally, in terms of difficulties associated with involving civil society, the early days of the IFI and INTERREG I and II demonstrated the harm caused to the transformation process by the lack of civil society involvement. In both cases, very little consultation had taken place beforehand, demonstrating no vertical or horizontal capacity development or integration. In terms of the IFI, for example, its first chairman C. E. B. Brett noted, 'I do not think that the purpose or potentialities of the Fund had been at all clearly worked out even before it came into existence. Its objects and functions were diffuse; even the primary objectives ... constituted a tall order, on a not unlimited budget.'[40] The consequent harm to the process clearly manifested itself in the main difficulty the Fund had to contend with from the beginning – strong hostility from the

Unionist community who saw the funding invariably as a 'slush fund' and American 'blood-money',[41] firmly believed to be an attempt to bribe Unionists into accepting the Anglo-Irish Agreement. Continuous criticism of the Fund was maintained from the Agreement's signing in November 1985 until after the Fund was activated in September 1986, persisting in the same vein well after the Fund had found its feet.[42]

While these criticisms suggest that not all levels of society were involved by the Fund in the transformation process, they have been strongly (and consistently) denied.[43] Unfortunately, however, it was very much the case that in its early years, Unionists were actively discouraged from getting involved with or applying to the Fund for grants and therefore missed out extensively, leading later to discrepancies being pointed out between the two communities in relation to the Fund.[44]

In the case of INTERREG, research by Laffan and Payne[45] and O'Dowd and Corrigan on the INTERREG I programme found that many felt a 'lack of consultation, information and technical assistance were features of the centralised management of INTERREG I'.[46] This lack of civil society involvement was reflected in the projects it funded, containing limited cross-border cooperation. A European Court of Auditors report was particularly critical of the Ireland/Northern Ireland projects:[47] effectively, many of them took the form of parallel rather than interrelated projects on either side of the border with little direct connection between them. Indeed, like Laffan and Payne, O'Dowd et al. also concluded that in this case, 'the whole process has little direct democratic accountability to national electorates, and especially not to those living in border areas'.[48] Essentially, 'cross-border co-operation remained weakly institutionalised and INTERREG I achieved limited results'.[49]

Research by Shirlow and McEvoy also highlights how neither government funded the many prisoner support groups, key actors in the region's conflict transformation process, which developed in the wake of the 1994 ceasefires. Instead, this role was taken on by the Peace programmes, leading one former loyalist prisoner to note that 'If the government had funded that and taken on its responsibilities, it could have developed something which could have been more powerful and more influential in terms of strengthening and cementing the peace process.'[50] Moreover, having been funded, in the main by the EU Peace programmes, the absence of government support also leaves them with an unsustainable and therefore doubtful future.

The implications of the current situation are serious: it is questionable whether Northern Ireland is a truly post-conflict society – it may be more accurate to refer to it as a transitional society between war and peace. While Northern Ireland is no longer, in the main, a directly violent society, it remains structurally and culturally violent: it is persistently polarised and is becoming increasingly racist and sectarian. Moreover, with a number of the key transformation tools in the region having either ended (IFI) or received considerably reduced funding levels (Peace III and INTERREG IV), after enabling an unprecedented level of civil society actor involvement in the transformation process, their diminution brings with them the danger of the process being left to elite-level actors only.

The above examples illustrate that a policy framework requires serious consideration if conflict transformation efforts to date are to be sustained and other regions enabled to learn from this experience. The arising implications for practice will now be examined.

Implications for practice

Lack of specialist conflict transformation knowledge and understanding

The definitional morass surrounding the conflict transformation field can seriously impede practice. Having no single conflict transformation model in existence, coupled with multiple definitions and understandings, the prospects for successful implementation can be left open to countless and needless problems. For example, ADM/CPA only began providing Peace-funded project promoters with a working definition of reconciliation (that devised by Hamber and Kelly, consisting of five interconnected strands),[51] one of the many processes of conflict transformation, twelve years into the implementation of the programmes, as it moved from its second phase into its third phase. Moreover, author interviews have suggested a distinct lack of knowledge of conflict transformation theoretics within government, subsequently creating a misunderstanding of the practice engaged in. Indeed, this lack of understanding has been highlighted by Hamber and Kelly who have bemoaned how the SEUPB 'adopted a simplified version of our working definition' for the Peace II extension, whereby

> applicants have to argue how their project furthers reconciliation in relation to at least three of the strands which are scored. The risk of this approach is that a dynamic conceptualisation of reconciliation could become mechanised and compartmentalised, and another 'tick-box exercise'. We envisaged the five strands of reconciliation as being deeply interdependent and any reconciliation process should consider how it furthers reconciliation holistically and not based on a selection of strands.[52]

Of particular concern is the invitation a lack of understanding of the conceptual basics gives to governments to shun their responsibilities in relation to meeting some crucial transformation requirements, such as fundamental changes to oppressive social and political structures, furthering horizontal and vertical relationships and strategically planning their management and implementation over the long term. Moreover, it can leave the door open to a top-down only approach rather than a grassroots-led approach that receives top-level encouragement and support. This was clearly evident in the move from Peace I to Peace II, whereby the programme moved from focusing largely on social inclusion due to the influence of civil society and the EU, to focusing largely on economic development due to the influence of the Assembly and the absence of the EU.

While it can also act as an excuse for government interference or worse, non-action, a lack of specialist knowledge and understanding can also lead those charged with process management and implementation to actually believe that they are delivering peacebuilding anyway, which can oftentimes be more dangerous than non-action. Thus, Smith has argued that

> if there is any lack of clarity about peacebuilding, there will be a tendency to slip into a default mode of the concepts, approaches and vocabulary of normal (i.e. peace-time) development. This tendency may be particularly strong if the concepts and terminology of peacebuilding are unclear, as indeed they are.[53]

Responsibility for this conceptual confusion largely lies with the fact that the conflict transformation field is still a developing one requiring clarification as it grows and progresses. However, clarification in the Irish and British context is considered urgent as it is certainly a contributory source of a strategic policy and planning deficit in the region.

Non-existent transformational policy framework

What is glaringly absent from this case study is an overarching policy structure at government level. The lack of specialist knowledge and understanding discussed stems in part from both governments' distinct lack of conceptual peacebuilding thinking on the issue. The criticisms levelled at the Peace programmes for failing to discuss the core issues of the conflict, the funding gap between Peace I and II, difficulties surrounding implementation timetables experienced by both the Peace and INTERREG programmes and Unionists' anger at the IFI in its early days, all point to the necessity for putting such a policy in place. Moreover, as O'Dowd has observed,

> Any overview of the plethora of cross-border projects and initiatives cannot fail to be struck by their varied and unsystematic nature. Some projects have been noticeably dynamic, others much less so. This has led organisations like Co-operation Ireland to call regularly for a more coherent, strategic policy framework for such co-operation.[54]

At its most basic, billions of euros have been spent on transformation tools individually and collectively which could have been utilised more effectively had a strategic, long-term vision been embodied in a policy framework. A policy is needed if, at a minimum, scarce resources are not to be dissipated and the learning and practice from good projects not lost forever. In terms of the Peace programmes, for example, most commentators agree that this lack of a policy framework and institutional support for cross-border co-operation by governments in Belfast, Dublin and London severely limits its impact as a tool for long-term peacebuilding. Without such a framework the kind of shorter-term, capacity-building projects promoted by the Peace programmes will simply disappear into the sand, and much of the cross-border learning gained will go with them.[55]

When contrasted with other experiences, the policy absence is even more disquieting: in examining the peacebuilding experiences of the peoples of the German-Dutch border in the aftermath of the Second World War, Pollak notes that 'one key element that has been present in the German-Dutch drive for cross-border co-operation that is singularly absent in Ireland is some kind of overarching policy framework at government level'.[56] This lack of policy has not been lost on those at the coalface of the transformation process either. The Northern Ireland Council for Voluntary Action (NICVA) and the all-island Community Workers Cooperative (CWC), in examining the scope of a potential Peace III programme, pointed out that 'there is no body, architecture or system in place to sustain or drive north-south co-operation apart from *ad hoc* arrangements and the joint north-south bodies, which have important, but specific and limited remits'.[57] Thus, Co-operation Ireland has argued that

> a strategic and developmental approach to the building of a coherent policy for North-South co-operation across all government departments and agencies, alongside a partnership approach with civil society to policy-making, should be adopted so that funding truly addresses need, duplication is avoided and models of best practice are developed. This approach could ensure that we genuinely use the space that structural changes have created to build peace on this island.[58]

Moreover, this lack of policy presents serious consequences for the sustainability of the transformation process; while a political framework, in the form of the Good Friday Agreement (GFA), was put in place by the two governments with support from all levels of society, this constituted 'a particular institutionalisation of three sets of relationships within a constitutional agreement'[59] and as such represented only a small component of the conflict transformation process.[60] Thus, the political stalemate that surrounded the full implementation of the GFA from October 2002 until May 2007, along with the increased polarisation of Northern Ireland politics, increasing sectarianism and financial reductions in and eventual completion of the current transformation tools does not bode well for the successful sustainability of the transformation process. It has largely been driven by EU funding. Without an overarching policy to guide and indeed ground the transformation process from within, any hope of it being sustained over the long term, when the aforementioned factors are weighing heavily on it, is threatened with being extinguished or, at the every least, presents what O'Dowd has termed a 'crisis of sustainability'.[61]

Certainly, a glimmer of hope emerged in recent years with a number of key reports and plans proposing increased development and integration of horizontal and vertical relationships, notably the 2006 *Comprehensive Study on the All-Island Economy* (Department of Foreign Affairs, Dublin and the OMDFM, Belfast) and, more significantly, for the first time, a chapter on the all-island economy included in the Republic's (fourth) National Development Plan (NDP) for 2007–2013. The implementation of the NDP was predicated on the expectation that the Irish economy would 'expand at an average of around 4–4½% per annum over the period 2007–2013'.[62] However, with the Republic's economy in turmoil since, such hopes have all but dissipated, leaving a question mark over these ambitions. Furthermore, a recent assessment of the success of the Common Chapter, included since 1994 in the respective development plans North and South for EU structural funds and 'intended to act as a strategic statement or framework for agreed [cross-border] cooperation, particularly in the economic development field',[63] has found that despite government claims of an apparent strategic framework, the extent of the cooperation has been negligible. The Common Chapter, it seems, 'has not, so far, delivered'.[64]

A policy framework is therefore needed if a piecemeal approach to transformation is to be avoided, sustainability of efforts are to be ensured and maintained and clarity in terms of policy and practice is to be provided in the field. While formal research to date has not comprehensively examined the consequences of this policy omission in either the Irish or British contexts, the lack of a living peacebuilding policy from the British government has been highlighted by Smith, who, in discussing the peacebuilding practice of a number of countries including the UK, found they all 'lack[ed] single official statements of their approach to peacebuilding – having, rather, a plethora of statements about aspects of their policy approaches'.[65] The UK in particular does not have a peacebuilding policy. While this study was carried out in the context of development cooperation, thus eliminating Northern Ireland from the UK sphere of activities assessed, by not allowing for Northern Ireland to enter its frame of reference, it suggests that 'a strategic assessment approach to Northern Ireland would be very worthwhile'[66] from a theoretical perspective, as a basis for practical implementation. In the Irish context, as previously noted, a formal conflict transformation policy is also absent, reflected in the location of brief allusions to peacebuilding, mixed up with discussions on conflict resolution and prevention within the development cooperation field, again eliminating Northern Ireland from its frame of reference and once again highlighting the clear lack of specialist knowledge and understanding of the specifics of conflict transformation. Moreover, for conflict transformation to take place over the long term, it should be embedded in mainstream activities. While this is arguably taking place in Northern Ireland (in the form of the central Community Relations Unit and the community relations units of each of the local councils), 'there are doubts about the efficacy of these structures. When a separate body like the CRC, is established with a relatively small funding base, there are definite limitations on what it can achieve. Indeed, its function may be to legitimate the main departments ignoring the issue.'[67] Furthermore, the future of the SEUPB, one of six North–South implementation bodies set up under the GFA, could be described as precarious; its staff are seconded from the departments of Finance North and South, leaving a return to their respective departments a feasible option, superseding any permanent obligation to the SEUPB. Thus, the proposal has been put forward 'to rationalise all that existing effort, by demanding that all statutory bodies have a clearly defined obligation to encourage peacebuilding and reconciliation'.[68]

Strategic planning deficit

This policy requirement also highlights a further linked implication, the need for conflict transformation and related policies to be strategic and therefore part of an overall planning framework. Conflict transformation is a multi-faceted process whereby the huge range of activities involved in any such process are inter-dependent on many other national, regional and local activities. Peacebuilding activities and conflict transformation processes are not simply stand-alone actions, separate from everyday life; 'peacebuilding is strategic when resources, actors, and approaches are coordinated to accomplish multiple goals and address multiple issues for the long term'.[69]

The experiences of these three particular transformation tools has overwhelmingly demonstrated the range and depth of difficulties that can arise when clear and strategic thinking and planning are not employed to guide the process. A conflict transformation policy, in the same vein as the anti-poverty strategies, for example, strategically connected to national planning guidelines such as the Republic's NDP, would provide for the strategic planning and development of the process. Take, for example, the two-year gap that emerged between Peace I and II; the difficulties faced by project promoters may well have been avoided as a survey by NICVA found that 'without exception, all respondents commented that if their organisations had known that gap/ interim funding would have run for this length of time, things would have been different in strategic and planning terms'.[70] Moreover, it has also been observed that while bottom-up delivery mechanisms have their benefits, they require greater strategic direction.

The lack of strategic focus experienced by many of the LSPs, who were charged in Northern Ireland with administrating and managing Peace II monies, is to be expected if strategic planning is not shaped and driven at a national level by government: 'if the outcomes from the Peace II Programme are to be sustained and reconciliation initiatives are to be developed, future initiatives could benefit from greater strategic linkage and an understanding of how they are located with other government initiatives'.[71] The range of problems in the wider social, economic and cultural environment of Northern Ireland in particular[72] ensured that the Peace programmes demonstrated that 'any future peace-building programme should be capable of responding to these developments and linking with other policy responses such as the Shared Future Strategy in Northern Ireland and Anti-Poverty Strategy in Ireland'.[73] Conflict transformation by its very nature requires a multi-dimensional approach to its implementation; therefore, what makes it complex and demanding is the 'necessity for multi-layered cooperation'.[74]

Thus, while the current operational programmes (2007–2013) for Peace III and INTERREG IV claim to have taken this issue on board by highlighting the ways in which they complement 'other relevant programmes and policy initiatives ... [and] ... key strategic linkages ... with other broader government initiatives',[75] it is only that, a highlighting exercise. While the proposed operation of this phase of these particular tools can be linked (in as far as they make reference) to a range of other government policies and initiatives, this range of policies and initiatives do not strategically link themselves to the overall conflict transformation process as such and were not strategically developed with the conflict transformation process in mind (the exception being the proposed links to the IFI). In other words, they were not conflict-transformation proofed. This rhetoric is nothing new; Magennis damningly concludes of his assessment of the 'Common Chapter' that 'a more obvious weakness ... is that there is no clear framework for cooperation proposed in the British-Irish Intergovernmental Conference study beyond the fact that all the proposals are combined in one document'.[76]

Moreover, the Peace III and INTERREG IV programmes are transformation tools (although this is disputed by some in the case of INTERREG) which do not constitute a transformation policy, even less a transformation plan. The rolling out of such tools over three to seven years along with gestural references to the tools in only a couple of these policies and initiatives, goes nowhere near meeting the existing strategic planning deficit simply because such efforts are not strategically connected, within an overarching policy or plan, either to efforts in the same field or to everyday life. Such so-called strategic planning has not been properly formalised and written down. Oftentimes valuable information that could feed into strategic planning is not sourced or maintained for such purposes; 'the rotation of personnel means that strategic understanding rotates away as well. Institutional memory seems to go back about three years, four at most; peacebuilding goes on for ten at least',[77] an issue perfectly illustrated by the move from Peace I to Peace II and through the three phases of INTERREG. Practitioners and policy-makers alike should not be misled into thinking that 'an impressive degree of on-the-ground coordination ... is a valid substitute for the strategy they have not worked out. Coordination is only strategic if the actions being coordinated are serving joint strategies.'[78]

However, at the root of the strategic planning deficit is the short-sightedness of governments in general who find it virtually impossible to see past the next election, a weakness not lost on practitioners such as Pollak, who has pointed out that 'politicians, with their focus on the short term electoral cycle, usually find it difficult to understand the importance of sustaining such programmes over the necessary longer term',[79] or theorists such as Ryan, who has observed in the international context that

> it is remarkable how it [the international community] seems incapable of using this [transformation] knowledge in practice because of political expediency resulting in short term thinking and not a little arrogance ... how often are key post-conflict decisions made by governments because they have one eye on looming elections and what real effort do they make to understand the societies (they have decided to intervene in)?[80]

Conclusion

This essay has outlined some of the unnecessary difficulties that arose in Northern Ireland and the Border Counties for conflict transformation practice implemented through transformation tools such as the IFI and the Peace and INTERREG programmes. Some of these issues are not uncommon in post-conflict/ceasefire situations, Iraq being a case in point.[81] However, in the case of Northern Ireland it was argued that these difficulties emerged because of a lack of specialist knowledge and understanding of conflict transformation theoretics and concepts, a strategic planning deficit and a non-existent overarching policy framework to guide the process. The implications of these issues for successful process implementation and sustainability were examined in further detail.

The resultant implications demonstrate that it is not realistic to expect conflict transformation tools such as the IFI or the Peace programmes to resolve the problems resulting from prolonged conflict. Moreover, over-reliance on these tools has placed direct responsibility for the implementation and sustainment of the process largely on the shoulders of civil society. While this is certainly a progressive move, it provides an open invitation to both governments to shirk their responsibilities. However, a strategic policy framework needs to be put in place which ensures the responsibility for the conflict transformation process rests equally across all levels of society and beyond the narrow realm of a political framework if, at a minimum, process sustainability is to be ensured. Without such a framework, tools such as the IFI or the Peace programmes and the projects they fund can only enable such a process over the short term; for conflict transformation to succeed, it must be sustained over the long term.

Notes

1 S. Buchanan, 'Cost of Conflict, Price of Peace: Assessing Conflict Transformation through Social and Economic Development – Northern Ireland and the Border Counties as a Case Study' (University of Ulster, unpublished PhD thesis, 2008), 160–61.
2 International Fund for Ireland, *Sharing This Space: A Strategic Framework for Action 2006–2010* (Belfast/Dublin, 2006).
3 S. Buchanan, 'Transforming Conflict in Northern Ireland and the Border Counties: Some Lessons from the Peace Programmes on Valuing Participative Democracy', *Irish Political Studies* 23.3 (2008), 387–409; W. McCarter, 'Economics of Peace Making: The Case of the International Fund for Ireland', *Asia Europe Journal* 6.1 (2008), 93–99.
4 Buchanan, 'Cost of Conflict'. Levels of society are understood in terms of Lederach's peacebuilding pyramid – top, middle and bottom/grassroots.
5 See Dan Smith, *Towards a Strategic Framework for Peacebuilding: Getting Their Act Together. Overview Report of the Joint Utstein Study of Peacebuilding* (Oslo, 2004).
6 See Part III, 'The Challenge: Peace, Security and Development', Government of Ireland, *White Paper on Irish Aid* (Dublin: Department of Foreign Affairs, 2006), 56–58, and 'Ireland Offers Major Support to UN Peacebuilding Fund', 12 October 2006, http://foreignaffairs.gov.ie/home/index.aspx?id=25138 (accessed 16 March 2011).
7 S. Ryan, *The Transformation of Violent Intercommunal Conflict* (Aldershot, 2007), 2.
8 J. G. Cockell, 'Conceptualising Peacebuilding: Human Security and Sustainable Peace' in Michael Pugh (ed.), *Regeneration of War-Torn Societies* (London, 2000), 16.
9 J. Hughes, 'Paying for Peace: Comparing the EU's Role in the Conflicts in Northern Ireland and Kosovo', *Ethnopolitics* 8.3–4 (2009), 294.
10 J. P. Lederach, 'The Challenge of the 21st Century: Justpeace', in European Centre for Conflict Prevention, *People Building Peace: 35 Inspiring Stories from around the World* (Utrecht, 1999), 28.
11 See Buchanan, 'Transforming Conflict', 387–409.
12 Author's interview, mid-level actor (IFB representative), 3 December 2004.
13 Author's interview, mid-level actor (IFB representative), 28 January 2005.
14 Author's interview with a grassroots/top-level actor, 6 January 2005.
15 Author's interview with a grassroots/top-level actor, 6 January 2005.
16 House of Commons Northern Ireland Affairs Committee, *Peace II. Seventh Report of Session 2002–03 Volume 1* (London, 2003), 14.
17 Buchanan, 'Transforming Conflict', 387–409.
18 P. McGinn, 'Delivering Peace at Local Level – The Practical Experience', Community Relations Council, *Shaping and Delivering Peace at Local Level? Learning from the Experience of Peace II. Learning from Peace II, Volume 3* (Belfast, 2005), 22.
19 House of Commons Northern Ireland Affairs Committee, *Peace II*, 31.
20 NICVA have stated that 'there is evidence that many community-based peace-building projects did not apply to the [Peace II] programme because of the [administrative] difficulties involved ... The level of concern about these issues in the voluntary and community sector should not be underestimated. In its poll in late 2003, NICVA found an overwhelming conviction that the administrative arrangements for Peace II were unnecessarily complicated (91.9% took this view).' See NICVA (in association with the Community Workers Co-operative), *Designing Peace III* (Belfast, 2004), 20.

21 Author's interview with Grassroots-level actor, 13 January 2005.

22 The Community Foundation for Northern Ireland, *Taking 'Calculated' Risks for Peace II* (Belfast, 2002), 5.

23 Community Foundation for Northern Ireland, *Taking 'Calculated' Risks*, 29.

24 Community Foundation for Northern Ireland, *Taking 'Calculated' Risks*, 22.

25 Author's interview with top/mid-level actor, 6 January 2005.

26 S. Pettis, 'Round Table Reflections: Highlighting the Key Issues', Community Relations Council, *Shaping and Delivering Peace at Local Level? Learning from the Experience of Peace II. Learning from Peace II, Volume 3* (Belfast, 2005), 34.

27 PricewaterhouseCoopers (PWC), *Ex-Post Evaluation of Peace I and Mid-Term Evaluation of Peace II. Final Report* (Belfast, 2003), 226–27.

28 PWC, *Ex-Post Evaluation*.

29 Participant comment, SEUPB Peace II Extension Consultation, Derry, 7 September 2004.

30 Author's interview with mid-level actor, 14 December 2005.

31 Author's interview with grassroots actor, 6 December 2004.

32 See statement by NICVA in House of Commons Northern Ireland Affairs Committee, *Peace II*, 19.

33 Author's interview with mid-level actor, 7 January 2005.

34 Author's interview with mid-level actor, 21 July 2005.

35 Author's interview with mid-level actor, 7 January 2005.

36 Author's interview with mid-level actor, 7 January 2005.

37 Author's interview with top-level actor, 4 January 2005.

38 Author's interview with mid-level actor, 11 April 2005.

39 Author's interview with grassroots-level actor, 6 December 2004.

40 C. E. B. Brett, 'The International Fund for Ireland 1986–1989', *Political Quarterly* 61 (1990), 431.

41 *Belfast Newsletter*, 19 September 1986 and 8 May 1986.

42 See *Derry Journal*, 8 September 1995 and *Irish Times*, 3 November 1995.

43 *Sunday Independent*, 12 November 1995; five author interviews (completed 13 January, 15 February, 29 March 2005; 13 July and 15 August 2006).

44 KPMG Management Consulting, *The International Fund for Ireland: Assessment of the Fund's Impact on Contact, Dialogue and Reconciliation between the Communities and on Employment* (1995), 17, 22; Commission of the European Communities, *Report on the International Fund for Ireland Pursuant to Article 5 of Council Regulation (EC) No. 214/2000* (Brussels, 2001), 13.

45 B. Laffan and D. Payne, *Creating Living Institutions: EU Cross-Border Co-operation after the Good Friday Agreement. A Report for the Centre for Cross-Border Studies* (Dublin, 2001), 47.

46 L. O'Dowd and J. Corrigan, 'Buffer Zone or Bridge: Local Responses to Cross-Border Economic Co-operation in the Irish Border Region', *Administration* 42.4 (1995), 346.

47 Official Journal of the European Communities, Court of Auditors, *Annual Report concerning the Financial Year 1994*, C 303, 38, 14 November 1995, par. 4.68.

48 *Annual Report concerning the Financial Year 1994*, 284.

49 Laffan and Payne, *Creating Living Institutions*, 58.

50 Quoted in P. Shirlow and K. McEvoy, *Beyond the Wire: Former Prisoners and Conflict Transformation in Northern Ireland* (London, 2008), 68.

51 B. Hamber and G. Kelly, *A Place for Reconciliation? Conflict and Locality in Northern Ireland* (Belfast, 2005).

52 B. Hamber and G. Kelly, 'Reconciliation: Time to Grasp the Nettle?', *Scope: Social Affairs Magazine* (February 2007), 14.

53 Smith, *Strategic Framework*, 42

54 L. O'Dowd, 'The Future of Cross-Border Co-operation: Issues of Sustainability', *Journal of Cross Border Studies in Ireland* 1 (2006), 10.
55 A. Pollak, 'How Does Cross-Border Co-operation Contribute to Peace Building in Ireland?', in Community Relations Council, *Bordering on Peace? Learning from the Cross-Border Experience of Peace II. Learning from Peace II, Volume 4* (Belfast, 2006), 31.
56 Pollak, 'Cross-Border Co-operation'.
57 NICVA, *Designing Peace*, 8.
58 T. Kennedy and C. Lynch, 'Towards an Island at Peace with Itself: An NGO View of North-South Co-operation', in *Year 5* (Armagh, 2003), 11.
59 O'Dowd, 'Cross-Border Co-operation', 5.
60 Hamber and Kelly's definition of reconciliation includes five strands of which political/constitutional issues are only one (Hamber and Kelly, *Place for Reconciliation*, 7). This is also the case for Smith's 'peacebuilding palette' which consists of a political framework, security, reconciliation and justice and socio-economic foundations. See Smith, *Strategic Framework*, 28.
61 O'Dowd, 'Cross-Border Co-operation', 15.
62 Government of Ireland, *Ireland National Development Plan 2007–2013. Transforming Ireland. A Better Quality of Life for All* (Dublin, 2007), 17.
63 E. Magennis, 'Public Policy Cooperation: The "Common Chapter" – Shadow or Substance?', in John Coakley and Liam O'Dowd (eds), *Crossing the Border: New Relationships between Northern Ireland and the Republic of Ireland* (Dublin, 2007), 245.
64 Magennis, 'Public Policy Cooperation', 256.
65 Smith, *Strategic Framework*, 23.
66 Private correspondence with Dan Smith, 25 April 2005.
67 Area Development Management Ltd, Combat Poverty Agency, Co-operation Ireland, The Community Foundation for Northern Ireland, The Special European Union Programmes Body, *Building on Peace: Supporting Peace and Reconciliation after 2006* (Monaghan, 2003), 203.
68 Area Development Management Ltd et al., *Building on Peace*.
69 L. Schirch, *The Little Book of Strategic Peacebuilding* (Pennsylvania, 2004), 9.
70 NICVA, *Assessment of the Impact of Gap/Interim Funding on the Sustainability of Voluntary and Community Sector Organisations* (Belfast, 2002), 20.
71 NICVA, *Assessment*.
72 PWC, *Update of the Mid-Term Evaluation of Peace II 2000–2006: Final Report* (Belfast, 2005), iv; Special EU Programmes Body, *European Union Programme for Territorial Cooperation: EU Programme for Peace and Reconciliation (Peace III) 2007–2013. Northern Ireland and the Border Region of Ireland. Draft Operational Programme* (Belfast/Omagh/Monaghan, 2007), 10–17.
73 PWC, *Update*, iv.
74 Smith, *Strategic Framework*, 41.
75 Special EU Programmes Body, *European Union Programme for Territorial Cooperation. Peace III. EU Programme for Peace and Reconciliation 2007–2013. Northern Ireland and the Border Region of Ireland. Operational Programme* (Belfast/Omagh/Monaghan, 2007), 101.
76 Magennis, 'Public Policy Cooperation', 258.
77 Smith, *Strategic Framework*, 43.
78 Smith, *Strategic Framework*, 58.
79 Pollak, 'Cross-Border Co-operation', 28.
80 Ryan, *Transformation*, 155.
81 See 'No Plan, No Peace – The Inside Story of Iraq's Descent Into Chaos', BBC 1, 28–29 October 2007; F. Cochrane, *Ending Wars* (Cambridge, 2008).

11

Building Peace and Crossing Borders: The North/South Dimension of Reconciliation

Katy Hayward, Cathal McCall and Ivo Damkat

> You cannot really address the issue of the conflict without addressing the issue of cross-border communication and cross-border co-operation ... Cross-border co-operation provides an opportunity to give us a totally new perspective on what it is like to live in a region emerging from conflict.[1]

The Irish border was the thread that ran throughout the Agreement signed on Good Friday 1998 – it was there in the prime negotiating role of the British and Irish governments, in the casting line between 'unionist' and 'nationalist', and in the three strands of institutionalised cooperation between politicians divided over and by the border between Northern Ireland and the Republic of Ireland. But where should we metaphorically place the border in the task of building peace? As the well-respected public official who has played a major part in north/south cooperation since 1998 notes in the interview extract quoted above, not only is the cross-border dimension crucial to resolving conflict, it also offers a fresh vision of the post-Agreement landscape. This is the premise from which we will examine the nature of cross-border cooperation on the island of Ireland, specifically as it has been connected to the goals of peace and reconciliation.

Peacebuilding has been defined as '[a] process that establishes peace and prevents violence from continuing or re-emerging by addressing the root causes and the consequences of conflict.'[2] In this chapter we consider the role of cross-border cooperation as means of realising the goal of building peace. What makes this analysis simultaneously essential and problematic is the fact that the interpretation of the border as a 'cause' and 'consequence' of conflict is a fundamental issue of contention within Northern Ireland. This political difference of opinion was manifest in the contrasting presentations of 'Strand Two' of the 1998 Agreement, which institutionalised north/south relationships on the island of Ireland. The new North/South Ministerial Council and cross-border Implementation Bodies were characterised by pro-Agreement nationalists *and* anti-Agreement unionists as being a major step towards closer Irish unity, but presented by pro-Agreement unionists *and* anti-Agreement nationalists as being little more than tokenistic. We hope, in this essay, to go beyond this problematic by presenting an assessment of the significance of cross-border cooperation in the transition to peace from the perspective of actors at all levels of engagement in this process. In this way, we aim to apply the multi-level framework of peacebuilding outlined by John Paul Lederach,[3] it being the model most commonly advocated by third (voluntary and community) and public sector actors involved in cross-border peacebuilding measures in Ireland.[4]

The starting point for our analysis is that cross-border initiatives connected to building peace are premised on two core assumptions: (1) that the border is a root *cause* of conflict because it embodies cultural difference and alienation, and (2) that the border is a *consequence* of conflict because it embodies the harm of conflict. In this chapter we will explore the viability of these hypotheses through a critical assessment of the cross-border activities sponsored by the European Union's three Programmes for Peace and Reconciliation in Northern Ireland and the Border Region of Ireland (hereafter referred to as the Peace programmes).[5] This is not to say that the Peace programmes were the only funding source to identify cooperation across the Irish border (as well as cooperation between communities within Northern Ireland) as a crucial element of peacebuilding, nor to imply that cross-border projects funded by the Peace programmes were more significant or numerous than those funded by other sources. Rather, we consider them in particular here because such projects had the explicit purpose of uniting cross-border and peacebuilding activities.[6] This chapter will assess the connection between cross-border cooperation and peacebuilding, as particularly supported by the Peace programmes, by considering the post-Agreement and EU framework for cross-border cooperation and how this supports peacebuilding by addressing the causes and consequences of conflict. In doing so, we draw upon primary research on the subject of cross-border cooperation in Ireland through the authors' engagement in projects dating back to 2003.[7] For the purpose of this chapter, we cite data from semi-structured interviews with almost thirty actors in the third sector, private sector and public sector engaged directly in cross-border activity (particularly EU-funded) in the Irish border region conducted by Ivo Damkat in 2008/09.[8] Following analysis of this data, we conclude with a consideration of the outlook for the sustainability of north/south cooperation and its implications for building peace in Ireland's borderlands.

The post-Agreement north/south context

The post-Agreement shift in political attitudes towards the border are nowhere better reflected than in the personal journey undertaken by the Reverend Ian Paisley. In the 1960s he lambasted the north/south rapprochement efforts of Northern Ireland Prime Minister Captain Terence O'Neill: 'He is a bridge builder he tells us. A traitor and a bridge are very much alike for they both go over to the other side.'⁹ Three decades later, when speaking as Northern Ireland First Minister at a press conference in Dublin, he outlined the rationale for taking this step himself:

> Some say hedges make the best neighbours but that is not the case. I don't believe we should plant a hedge between our two countries ... I am proud to be an Ulsterman but I am also proud of my Irish roots ... Today, we can confidently state that we are making progress to ensure that our two countries can develop and grow side by side in a spirit of generous co-operation. Old barriers and threats have been, and are being, removed daily. Business opportunities are flourishing and genuine respect for and understanding of each other's differences and, for that matter, similarities, is now developing.¹⁰

It is necessary to consider here some of the core elements of the post-Agreement framework for cross-border cooperation that has enabled just such a recon-ceptualisation of north/south relations. Put simply, it is possible to identify the expansion and formalisation of what might be termed a 'north/south sphere of commonality' since the 1998 Agreement. First of all, the common institutions of the North/South Ministerial Council (including its Joint Secretariat, staffed by civil servants from Dublin and Belfast) and the Implementation Bodies have survived periods of suspension of devolved powers in Northern Ireland and some political criticism regarding their administration to become fairly well accepted, if not necessarily wholly embedded, in the political and admin-istrative culture of north and south. There are also formalised mechanisms for cooperation between institutions in each jurisdiction on particular matters of shared concern, namely agriculture, education and health, environment, transport and tourism – all but one of which notably replicate practice in the European Union.

Also in line with practice in the European Union has been a growth of multi-level governance on the island of Ireland connected to cross-border cooperation. In their analysis of the context of European integration, Bache and Flinders identify 'an emerging dynamic in the context of European integra-tion that pulls authority away from national governments and empowers sub-national and supranational actors'.¹¹ In the Irish context, one of most significant changes for dissipating the locus of power has been the formali-sation of relations between local authorities to create regional partnerships around and across the border; being cross-border they, in effect, empower both sub-national *and* supranational actors. The North West Region Cross Border Group, the East Border Region Committee and the Irish Central Border Area Network, for example, have functioned to facilitate partnership between councillors from both sides of the border, particularly in relation to the administration of EU Structural Funds in the border region. The multi-level dimensions of EU-funded cross-border cooperation are further enhanced in the third Peace programme, for which Peace and Reconciliation Action Plans have to be written by 'clusters' of Local Councils in Northern Ireland (of which there are eight) and the six County Councils in Ireland's border region.

Relating to this point, from the mid-1990s to mid-2000s, there was a growth in the common resources available for cross-border cooperation, particularly those open to community-level initiatives. This has not only taken the form of externally funded initiatives such as from the International Fund for Ireland or the EU's INTERREG or Peace programmes, but also the extension of the Republic of Ireland's National Development Plan (NDP) to include Northern Ireland. Indeed, 'all-island cooperation' was a horizontal theme of the 2007–2013 NDP, meaning that there was an all-island dimension to plans to enhance infrastructure and public investment in, for example, energy, health services, environment policy and social inclusion.[12] Whether the stated goal of generating 'economies of scale'[13] will ultimately add up to what has been envisaged as a 'mega-city region' in Ireland's east is debatable.[14] The spectre of economic recession realised in late 2008 put capital projects for Irish public investment in doubt, including those under the NDP's All-Island Cooperation rubric such as the restoration of the Ulster Canal, upgrading Derry City Airport and the Narrow Water Bridge project.[15] The issue of sustainability is addressed in the conclusion of this chapter – an issue of increasing concern given the prospective end of the EU Peace programmes, the impact of which we now turn to consider.

The Peace programmes

Promoting economic, political and cultural networks of cooperation across state borders is an enterprise intimately associated with the process of European integration. Building a European transnational market and polity is widely recognised as the primary objective of the European integration project founded by Jean Monnet, Robert Schumann and Konrad Adenauer. State borders configured as barriers or 'lines of exclusion' served as major obstacles to this project. Yet, half a century of European inter-governmental cooperation, plus the subsequent expansion of transnational networks across borderlands, has helped to reconfigure the European Union's internal borders as 'lines of inclusion' – meeting points between states rather than divisions among them. This has had the effect of reducing the obstructions to European cooperation and integration posed by the mere existence of national state borders.

The absence of inter-state conflict in Europe for two generations means that the greater objective of the European project – building peace – has faded, except perhaps in regions where old national conflicts continue and/or new intra-state conflicts explode.[16] In such circumstances, borders and border regions tend to become focal points for violence. However, in a peace process context, they can also be transformed into vital political spaces and cultural landscapes for conflict transformation initiatives. According to Brian Graham, 'a cultural landscape can be visualised as a powerful medium in expressing feelings, ideas and values, while simultaneously being an arena of political discourse and action in which cultures are continuously reproduced and contested'.[17]

In the context of the island of Ireland, the main EU cross-border programmes address these twin objectives of economic development and peacebuilding. From their inception in 1989, the EU-wide INTERREG programmes have been primarily concerned with promoting economic integration and coopera-tion across EU borders, including the Irish border. Meanwhile, the EU Peace programmes for Northern Ireland and the Border Counties of the Republic of Ireland remain arguably the most concrete embodiment of the EU's peace-building objective. At the outset of the Irish peace process, the EU launched its first Peace programme in Ireland to help secure the loyalist and republican paramilitary ceasefires of 1994. The Peace programmes were also emblematic of renewed interest within the EU in addressing conflict, an interest undoubt-edly stirred by intra-state, ethno-national conflicts in the Balkans during the 1990s.[18] A second Peace programme was launched in 2000 to help support a grassroots process to accompany the top- and middle-level institutions and initiatives of the 1998 Agreement. Following an extension of Peace II, a third Peace programme was initiated in 2007.

The Peace programmes have constituted a major regime of public funding. Peace I (1995–99) was allocated EU funding totalling €500 million. Between 2000 and 2004 Peace II received €531 million from the EU.[19] Peace II was extended until 2006 with an additional €160 million in funding.[20] Finally, Peace III (2007–13) was worth €333 million for the period (with just under a third of this funding coming from national contributions).[21] In total, therefore, the Peace I–III programmes will have drawn €1,524 million from EU Struc-tural Funds and Community Initiatives over the course of two decades. For the first two programmes at least 15 per cent of the total package was allocated to specifically cross-border projects. The strategic aim of Peace I was defined as follows: 'To reinforce progress towards a peaceful and stable society and to *promote reconciliation by* increasing economic development and employ-ment, promoting urban and rural regeneration, *developing cross-border co-operation* and extending social inclusion.'[22] Cross-border cooperation (economic, social and cultural) was one of the five priorities of the second Peace programme. A specific cross-border priority is absent in the third Peace programme, although it does appear as a 'crosscutting' theme.

To help ensure that local communities and actors are integrated into and benefit from this peace initiative, the third sector has been heavily involved in the implementation of the Peace programmes, for example, through such all-island organisations as Co-Operation Ireland and Pobal (formerly Border Action). Such bodies have provided development support to existing commu-nity groups, helping them with applications for funding and adopting experi-mental approaches with particular groups such as ex-prisoners, victims of violence and their families.[23] The community-level impact of the Peace programmes has been direct and substantial; one interviewee representing a north/south Implementation Body heavily involved in the Peace II and III programmes calculated that

> Over 450,000 people have taken part in Peace II activities, well over 200,000 people have taken part in cross-border activities. A very high percentage of those will be reconciliation-type of activities. That is a lot of activity. That is a lot of movement, a lot of energy put into creating links across the border, between communities that probably never spoke to each other.[24]

The next two sections of this chapter assess the relationship between participation in such projects and the wider peacebuilding goals of redressing the causes and consequences of conflict.

Reconciliation: addressing the border as a cause of conflict

> We are very clear if you are building peace and reconciliation, you [must] take cognisance of the role that the border has played and still plays in probably preventing certain relations.[25]

As noted at the beginning of this chapter, the border between Northern Ireland and the Republic of Ireland is presented in the 1998 Agreement as being fundamental to the conflict that the parties to the Agreement sought to redress. The task of peacebuilding, as performed by actors at all levels, must also incorporate recognition of the border as being a root cause of conflict. From interviews with such actors specifically engaged in cross-border work, it is notable how readily they make a connection between the border and sources of conflict, although sometimes this connection is made more directly than others. This discourse is particularly prevalent among actors in the third sector and, importantly, connects to their belief that it is not the existence of the border *as such* but the effects it has had on communication and contact between people who live on either side of it:

> the border, and attitudes towards the border, go to the root of the conflict. A lot of people died attacking it and a lot of people died defending it. You could say in a sense the border was the cause, an arena of the conflict ... That is not to say that to engage in peacebuilding you are trying to get rid of the border.[26]

Another actor, this time from the public sector, makes loose connections between the task of overcoming several centuries of conflict in Ireland and the role of cross-border cooperation, which he describes as 'essential for the welfare of our citizens; it is essential for the future, for our children and for our communities to come beyond the terrible experience that this region has experienced for many, many years – thirty years, eight hundred years, three hundred years'.[27]

Thus, the development of a cross-border cultural landscape is seen as providing opportunities to escape what has been termed 'the cage of ethno-national conflict' in Northern Ireland.[28] Cross-border, cross-community group engagement and communication in that landscape involves the expression of feelings, fears, ideas and values – challenging nationalist and unionist cultural monoliths in the process. Examples of cross-border projects funded by Peace programmes that may be seen as linking a borderland cultural landscape to building peace include group discussions on Irish histories with the aim of increasing mutual understanding, for example consideration of the significance of 1916 for nationalists (the Easter Rising) and unionists (the Battle of the Somme), or enabling locally focused 'storytelling' groups. Other such inclusive cultural events include music and sports activities for young people, often with conflict resolution and cultural diversity awareness discussions appended, or open-access use of the arts, for example local carnivals or art in public spaces. Funding has also been given to local initiatives involving the use of media, such as film-making as a shared initiative among women's groups or documenting the life stories of paramilitary ex-prisoners. One project that exemplifies the connection between creating a shared cultural landscape in the border region with efforts to build social capital is the Cross-Border Orchestra of Ireland. The 160 members (aged between 12 and 24) are drawn from both sides of the border and rehearse weekly in the border town of Dundalk. The orchestra has performed across Europe and in the USA and has benefited from Peace-funding support. With accompanying youth choirs often numbering 500 singers at a time, the Orchestra touches the lives of many more than the core group. Its potential effect on individuals as well as group relations is illustrated by the following tableau:

> ... a group of pipers and a Lambeg drummer have joined the orchestra. Among them are the Walker brothers from Portaferry, Jamie and eight-year-old Jake, who is attending his first rehearsal today. 'Jamie, can you play Amazing Grace?' the conductor demands. The tiny head moves uncertainly, somewhere between a nod yes and a shake no. 'I'll help him,' his brother offers. They play it together – but [the conductor] persists. 'Try the first bit by yourself,' he urges the little piper. Jake does so – and gets a round of spontaneous applause from the whole orchestra. It sums up, instantly ... what the Cross-Border Orchestra of Ireland is all about.[29]

Building relationships

The classic motivating logic of peace activism – seeing opportunity today to address sources of past conflict *and* potential future conflict – is evident in some of the discourses around such cross-border projects among what Lederach calls 'grassroots leaders':[30]

> The main reason to be involved in cross-border co-operation ... is that people north and south still don't understand each other. They don't interact with each other. The failure to understand each other could lead possibly, 10 years down the line, to the return of violence.[31]

Given the fundamental connections made by many actors between the border and the conflict, it is a fairly small step, then, to associate cross-border cooperation with reconciliation. Drawing again on Hamber and Kelly's definition of reconciliation, we note that – although variously defined – reconciliation brings *relationships* to the fore, that is, a process of reconciliation must involve person-to-person contact.[32] This is a difficult area to investigate, not least because reconciliation is interpreted differently within sectors and even within organisations. Analysis of our interview data, supported by findings of other researchers in this field,[33] suggests that 'reconciliation' is not generally presented as an end-point or goal of cross-border activity by those involved (even by leaders of Peace-funded projects) but more typically as a by-product of the work they do. As the brief extracts below reflect, these notions are upheld by actors from north and south and third and public sectors:

> anything we can do to bring people together to get to know each other and understand each other is a small contribution to peacebuilding.[34]

> The peace laid the bedrock and then we have some [cross-border] co-operation that can lead to reconciliation and that reconciliation in due course can cause other people to do co-operation where they previously wouldn't have. They are so utterly intermingled.[35]

Much of this appears to reflect assumptions about the benefits and implications of contact and communication as relating to peacebuilding – assumptions which, it could be said, are generally reinforced by the requirements and operation of EU Peace programme funds and, indeed, EU integration more generally.

Cross-border and/or cross-community?

This leads, naturally, to the wider question as to whom such reconciliation should be between. It is notable that, although it would be most clear to suggest that cross-border cooperation builds relationships between people north and south of the border, few interviewees would purport that the conflict is straightforwardly about north/south difference. The choice of phrasing in an interview with a southern civil servant is worth highlighting here, given his revealing conflation of territorial jurisdiction with cultural tradition: 'Doing things on a north/south basis, cross-border, whatever way you want to look at it – it helps reconciliation between *two traditions on the island.*'[36] However, this is a notable exception; generally interviewees are careful not to equate cross-border cooperation with cross-community work – this is not because they do not perceive there to be a close connection between them, but rather because of the complexity of relationships and sensitivity of definitions around and *about* the border: 'I cannot think of a single example where cross-border work is not also cross-community work. [But] ... If you were to amalgamate the two and [say that], by definition, cross-border work is cross-community work, you only create problems – because it is not.'[37] The differences between cross-border and cross-community cooperation can be subtle, not least because of the need for cross-community work in the southern border region as well as in the north,[38] but they remain significant. This is where we come back to the effects of the border over ninety years of division: the existence of different political, economic and social jurisdictions have created a certain degree of unfamiliarity, alienation even, which are seen (in accordance with the vision of Monnet, Schumann and Adenauer) to have negative effects. Yet this type of back-to-back development and mutual wariness is substantially different from the type of fractured relationships seen between communities in Northern Ireland. Nevertheless, cross-border cooperation can, according to actors involved, positively contribute to improving both north/south *and* unionist/nationalist or Catholic/Protestant relationships. Cross-border cooperation has proven to be attractive for individuals and groups coming from both an Irish Catholic nationalist and an Ulster Protestant unionist background. Protestant unionist groups have engaged with nominally nationalist groups south of the border because they represent the less threatening Irish nationalist 'other' due to their existence outside the territorial cage of the Northern Ireland conflict. This is important because of sometimes misplaced perceptions held by those on one side of the border about those on the other: 'Any good cross-border work can benefit peace. It breaks down barriers, it reassures [participants] that people on the other side are not whatever monster or demons they imagine them to be.'[39]

Yet cultural engagement in this Irish border landscape does not necessarily preclude engagement with groups from another community background *within* Northern Ireland. Indeed, the perception that north/south contact can be less 'in your face', as one interviewee puts it,[40] means that it is seen as being a crucial first step in a wider process of reconciliation: cross-border cooperation can be easier than local cross-community work but it can also ultimately make it 'easier to do internal Northern Ireland co-operation'.[41] Thus, for many, cross-border engagement is an essential first step towards cross-community contact and communication within Northern Ireland. 'I think cross-border work will probably lead to increased cross-community work ... I think that cross-border is probably more important in the first instance and hopefully that will lead to cross-community.'[42] Nevertheless, other respondents warn that cross-community work cannot be neglected:

> You have to keep an eye on cross-community, you cannot leave it to itself. There could be a tendency to see cross-border as important, all-island is important, and north/south is important and that is easier than the cross-community internally. It can be easier to work on the easy stuff rather than on the difficult stuff, so that is the danger, but they are both equally important.[43]

Another interviewee, this time from the private sector (whose business is actively cross-border but based in Northern Ireland), makes a similar point, although rather more bluntly (the use of the phrase 'other people', ostensibly referring to those south of the border, being noteworthy): 'I think you have to learn to live with one another before we start trying to improve our relationship with other people.'[44] The processual nature of reconciliation, therefore, must be reiterated. Whilst most interviewees made points along the lines of those outlined above, i.e. that cross-border and cross-community work were compatible and complementary, others claim that cross-community work is a prerequisite for useful cross-border cooperation:

> Unless you have good cross-community contact in the north you are not going to get healthy cross-border co-operation.[45]

> Peace and reconciliation is [sic] an essential precondition for good cross-border co-operation to emerge. You need to deal with the reconciliation issue before you get long term sustainable co-operation.[46]

Although different respondents place different emphases on different aspects of the border's connection to the experience of conflict, none suggest that cross-border cooperation can substitute for reconciliation within Northern Ireland. This connects to our next argument, that is, that when it comes to redressing the consequences of conflict, cross-border cooperation seems to be most usually connected to functional priorities: meeting practical needs and benefitting mutual interests previously hidden or harmed by conflict.

Functionalism: addressing conflictual consequences of the border

Benedict Anderson famously argued that national communities are imagined communities wherein 'the members of even the smallest nation will never know most of their fellow-members, meet them, or even hear of them, yet in the minds of each lives the image of their communion'.[47] Culturally, the Irish nationalist version of imagined community has remained intact – drawing on the cultural resources of the Catholic Church, the Gaelic Athletic Association, Irish traditional music, and the Irish language – although partition created political and social schisms that engendered north/south estrangement. The conflict in Northern Ireland and ensuing manifestation of the Irish border as security barrier heightened estrangement because the mere idea of crossing the border became a truly daunting prospect, especially for 'southerners'. 'The main inhibiting factor is a mental one in terms of co-operating with a jurisdiction that a lot of people may not have trusted, or a lot of people not have thought secure and safe.'[48]

Separate state development and the post-1969 IRA campaign of violence led some southern politicians and newspaper columnists to suggest that an Irish 'Free State' national community was now the reality and 'the North' was 'a place apart'. However, the evidence for this 'reality' is thin on the ground

today. A large-scale qualitative research project on 'intergenerational trans-
mission and ethno-national identity in the border area' (2004–06) found that
quite the opposite was true for respondents in the southern border counties:
'North and South – it's all the same, we're all the same' reflected general
opinion.[49] The decline of violent conflict and a minimised security presence,
as well as cross-border engagement and communication, have begun to
address degrees of estrangement caused by partition, separate state development and ethno-national conflict along the north/south axis for this imagined
community, as some of our respondents noted:

> I think a lot of people in the south have overcome reluctance and a timidity,
> and in some quarters there is a curiosity. [Yet] Remarkably few people from
> the south come north regularly.[50]

> ... even my relatives down south wouldn't come up to see me, they just
> didn't want to come up here. When the peace process came of course
> everybody then hopped on the bandwagon.[51]

It is important to ask whether a top-down peace process really has changed
the context for, and approach to, cross-border peacebuilding in Ireland.

The 1998 Agreement described the purpose of the North/South Ministerial Council as being 'to develop consultation, co-operation and action within
the island of Ireland – including through implementation on an all-island
and cross-border basis – on matters of mutual interest'.[52] As noted above,
the North/South Ministerial Council and its Implementation Bodies created
a potentially valuable transnational institutional infrastructure for cross-
border engagement, and for linking advances in political elite cooperation
to cultural cooperation among local communities and people. The Special
EU Programmes [Implementation] Body was credited in particular with
'promoting cross-border co-operating and creating an atmosphere and
environment within which you can speak about cross-border co-operation in
a way that you might not have been able to do before'.[53] The typical analysis of
respondents from across sectors and levels confirms a 'functionalist' belief in
the trickle-down benefits of formalising cross-border cooperation in political
institutions:[54]

> The broad institutional setting is the framework for co-operation. That
> journey is set out at the macro-level. You can have cross-border co-opera-
> tion on the provision of infrastructure ... We set up institutions that further
> cross-border co-operation and that has impact at a certain level.[55]

The emphasis on mutual interest and practical benefit found at the top-
and middle-range levels of leadership is also a theme in our interviews with
actors working from all sectors in the field of cross-border cooperation. The
justification for the expansion of cross-border cooperation into multi-level,
multi-sectoral arenas thus becomes a plea to commonsense:

> Regardless of whether you are north or south of the border or what organi-
> sation you are working for, we are basically faced with the same challenges
> and opportunities.[56]

> The only reason that we do cross-border co-operation is that it contributes
> to making life better for people in the region.[57]

Such a stress on pragmatics is apparently made with an eye to those seen most reluctant to engage with cross-border cooperation, namely unionists and southern officials:

> When you talk with people in the south, they don't see cross-border work
> in political terms, they see it more in functional terms.[58]

> ... we certainly have to bear in mind that the Northern Ireland unionist,
> although he would claim that he has no real time for the Republic of
> Ireland, he is a pragmatist.[59]

Some respondents acknowledge that, although cross-border cooperation did not begin with the Agreement, the peace process itself (not just the north/south institutions) added a degree of stability and consistency that was previously absent.[60] It is also for such reasons that cross-border cooperation is viewed as the practical groundwork for the ephemeral goals of building peace: 'Hopefully as people see those benefits of north south co-operation [they see] that reconciliation is a happy by-product, that peace is bedded down.'[61]

This relates to the perennial tension within the Peace programmes in particular, namely whether it helps to have reconciliation as a stated goal of cross-border cooperation. Some critics contend that measures of the Peace programmes 'seem to be more pious than actual practical implementation measures', and such perceptions have a detrimental effect on their impact.[62]

Respondents can also be quick to point out the size of the gap between top-level cooperation on specific matters of mutual concern and the greater goal of peacebuilding around the border (both as a territorial region and a political concern). Voices of caution, we note from our interview material, often come from civil servants based in Northern Ireland, as in the case of this official, who argued, 'I think you can have as much formal north south co-operation as you like, and it won't make a blind bit of difference to fundamental human attitudes towards things like identity, which is really what the issue in Ireland, north and south, is about.'[63] Although the same person was willing to acknowledge the functionalist logic of such cooperation ('the more evidence you have that two jurisdictions, two administrations can cope, exist harmoniously and in the interest of both jurisdictions, that can help perhaps to dispel myths and correct misapprehension'), he was also very conscious of the practical restrictions on the 'trickle down' effect: 'The general knowledge that the average citizen in Northern Ireland and the Republic has about what north/south co-operation takes place is so limited that it will only be at the very margins that it will have a manifest effect.'[64] It could be said, however, that public awareness of cross-border cooperation may be limited for one of the same reasons that the border region still suffers the consequences of conflict today, namely that the border is (literally) marginal to the centres of power in Ireland and the United Kingdom. As one respondent summarised, 'North/south co-operation ... will always have a peripheral part to play.'[65]

Conclusion: is cross-border peacebuilding sustainable?

Although measuring the success of the 'reconciliation' aspect of the Peace programmes is problematic, evaluations of Peace I and II found that they facilitated increased engagement on a cross-border, cross-community basis.[66] Such engagement at the local community level, it has been argued, is likely to have helped bolster the Irish peace process, especially between 2002 and 2007 when the main institutions of the 1998 Agreement were suspended and an elite-level political void opened.[67] With this in mind, sustainability appears to be a key element in the pursuit of long-term reconciliation. Since the first Peace programme, this has been an abiding issue of concern for cross-border, cross-community groups: the sustainability of the group, its project(s) and the work of the project(s). The problem of a 'funding gap' between programmes, or the discontinuation of funding when one programme ends or changes remit, was further exacerbated following the enlargement of the EU in 2004 and 2007. With most of the new EU states qualifying for Objective One funding from a limited EU Structural Funds budget, continuing generous levels of EU Structural Funding for Ireland was untenable. That this included the 'Peace and Reconciliation' objectives particularly attached to the Irish case was made clear when the Peace III programme (2007–13) was allocated an amount that was less than half the value of its predecessor.[68] To add insult to injury, some third-sector respondents perceive Peace III to be 'extremely difficult for local communities to access' in comparison with past experience – although this may be disputed by architects of the programme.[69]

In the past, hopes were pinned on the 'mainstreaming' of funding for cross-border peacebuilding projects as external funding sources diminished.[70] However, the commitment of the Irish government and Northern Ireland Executive to building social capital across the border has been placed in question in the post-2008 context of severe economic downturn. In addition to cuts in public spending, it is of some concern that there appears to be some uncertainty in the Irish civil service as to which department will ultimately be responsible for peacebuilding in the border region:

> There is a question whether that function will ultimately end up in the Department of Foreign Affairs or whether it will end up in Rural, Community and Gaeltacht Affairs or the Department of the Taoiseach. There was a lot of money for the groups and there certainly won't be anything near that level of government intervention, particularly in the current economic situation. There definitely is a role for OFMDFM [Office of the

First and Deputy First Ministers in the Northern Ireland Executive] and us in exploring how we might approach that in a co-ordinated fashion. I think there will be a lot of attention focusing on that in particular when the end of the EU programmes are approaching.[71]

Yet, despite this note of optimism for north/south top-level institutional cooperation (one echoed by assessments from Britain as well),[72] it seems likely that the multi-level approach to conflict transformation in Ireland – involving a variety of actors ranging from the European Commission, to British and Irish governments and their respective government departments, private business and the community sector – will wane.[73] Even common discursive themes of the 'island economy' and 'mutual benefit' in cross-border cooperation could come under pressure if competition between north and south, for foreign direct investment for instance, re-emerges. Although the existence of the transnational institutions of the 1998 Agreement, such as the Implementation Bodies, is not in question at the moment, they remain relatively weak and appear wholly dependent on the inter-governmental framework and certainly not able to take up the slack of a gap in funding or top-level disinterest. For such reasons, with the benefit of hindsight, one respondent argues that an inter-governmental approach should have been adopted at the outset:

> Two very wealthy countries, Ireland and the United Kingdom, have depended on the EU and the IFI [International Fund for Ireland] to fund their peacebuilding programmes: why? It should actually have been the responsibility of the states and they should have stepped forward and do it. For me it has always been too easy for them ... It may increase the pressure when money gets tight, cutting down our activities and increasing our lobbying and trying to get more out of *InterTrade Ireland* [an Implementation Body] ... because they are going to stay, no matter what. There is an element of north/south co-operation that has moved forward and that will never go back again. People see that it makes sense, business can make money out of it. That will remain. But what will happen is that a number of [community-based, peacebuilding] projects will fall off.[74]

When commitments to building 'hard' cross-border physical infrastructure are undermined in the context of severe economic downturn, then prospects are gloomy for 'soft' factors such as enhancing social capital and trust. In straitened times, inter-governmental support for supporting local, small-scale reconciliation projects in the Irish border region may appear to some unnecessary, irrelevant and even extravagant. However, peacebuilding on the island of Ireland is a process that, as confirmed throughout this volume, is still at an early stage. To lose the momentum behind a community-based process of reconceptualising the border as a meeting point would be short-sighted and potentially disastrous for the wider process of reconciliation on the island of Ireland. Peace can only be built by crossing borders.

Notes

1 Author's interview with an official from a North/South Implementation Body, 1 September 2008.
2 B. Hamber and G. Kelly, 'A Working Definition of Reconciliation', Occasional paper for Democratic Dialogue (Belfast, 2004), http://cain.ulst.ac.uk/dd/papers/ddo4recondef.pdf (accessed 18 May 2010), 8.
3 J. P. Lederach, *Building Peace: Sustainable Reconciliation in Divided Societies* (Washington, DC, 1997), and *The Moral Imagination: The Art and Soul of Building Peace* (Oxford, 2005).
4 For example, Lederach's model of peacebuilding is heavily drawn upon by the Special EU Programmes Body (SEUPB, the Implementation Body responsible for monitoring the running of EU programmes on a cross-border basis) in *A Monitoring and Evaluation Framework for Peacebuilding* (Belfast, 2007), http://www.seupb.eu/Libraries/PEACE_Programme_Evaluations/PWC.sflb.ashx (accessed 18 May 2010).
5 For more on the origins of the Peace programmes as a stream of external aid to peacebuilding within Northern Ireland, see E. Atashi, 'Peace Dividends: The Role of External Aid in Peacebuilding' in this volume.
6 A detailed comparison of the potential for conflict transformation in cross-border activity funded by the International Fund for Ireland and the EU on the island of Ireland has been conducted by Sandra Buchanan. See S. Buchanan, 'Cost of Conflict, Price of Peace – Assessing Conflict Transformation through Social and Economic Development; Northern Ireland and the Border Counties as a Case Study' (PhD thesis, University of Ulster, 2008).
7 The authors acknowledge the funding of the Royal Irish Academy's Third Sector Research Programme, EU Fifth Framework Programme (*EUBorderConf* project), Peace II (via the Higher Education Authority [Ireland] in the *Mapping Frontiers, Plotting Pathways* project), the Irish Research Council for the Humanities and Social Sciences, and the Department for Employment and Learning (Northern Ireland) that has enabled our research in this field.
8 Interviewees were assured of anonymity in citation, hence the manner of reference to these interviews herein. Full interview transcripts are held by the interviewer.
9 M. Mulholland, *Northern Ireland at the Crossroads: Ulster Unionism in the O'Neill Years, 1960–9* (Basingstoke, 2000), 84.
10 Extract from the speech by First Minister Ian Paisley on meeting Taoiseach Bertie Ahern in Dublin on 4 April 2007, at which the two first shook hands in public, http://borderireland.info/info/mdetail.php?mref=99 (accessed 18 May 2010).
11 I. Bache and M. Flinders, 'Multi-level Governance: Conclusions and Implications', in I. Bache and M. Flinders (eds), *Multi-Level Governance* (Oxford, 2004), 197.
12 Ireland, *National Development Plan 2007–2013: Transforming Ireland* (Dublin, 2007).
13 Ireland, *National Development Plan*, 96.
14 J. Yarwood (ed.), *The Dublin-Belfast Development Corridor: Ireland's Mega-city Region?* (Aldershot, 2006).
15 'Narrow Water Bridge Building in Doubt', 26 March 2010, http://www.4ni.co.uk/northern_ireland_news.asp?id=108970 (accessed 18 May 2010).
16 H. Anastasiou, 'The EU as a Peacebuilding System: Deconstructing Nationalism in an Era of Globalization', *International Journal of Peace Studies* 11.2 (2008), 31–50.
17 B. Graham, *In Search of Ireland: A Cultural Geography* (London, 1997), 4.
18 M. Braniff, 'The Transformative Capacity of Integration with the European Union on Conflict in Croatia and Serbia' (PhD thesis, Queen's University Belfast, 2008).

19 European Commission, 'Peace Programme – A Brief Guide', http://ec.europa. eu/unitedkingdom/about_us/office_in_northern_ireland/funding/peaceii.pdf (accessed 18 May 2010).

20 SEUPB, *Peace III*, 5.

21 Department of Finance and Personnel (Northern Ireland), 'PEACE III Programme 2007–2013', http://www.dfpni.gov.uk/index/finance/european-funding/eu-funding-2007-2013/peace_iii_programme_2007-2013.htm (accessed 18 May 2010).

22 Special EU Programmes Body (SEUPB), *PEACE III – EU Programme for Peace and Reconciliation 2007–2013 Northern Ireland and the Border Region of Ireland: Operational Programme* (Belfast, 2007), emphasis added, http://www.seupb.eu/ Libraries/PEACE_III_Reports_Pubs/PEACE_III_Operational_Programme.sflb.ashx (accessed 18 May 2010).

23 C. McCall and L. O'Dowd, 'Hanging Flower Baskets, Blowing in the Wind? Third Sector Groups, Cross-Border Partnerships and the EU Peace Programs in Ireland', *Nationalism and Ethnic Politics* 14.1 (2008), 29–54.

24 Author's interview with an official from a North/South Implementation Body, 1 September 2008.

25 Author's interview with a leader of a cross-border third-sector organisation, 10 September 2008.

26 Author's interview with a leader of a southern-based cross-border third-sector organisation, 8 August 2008.

27 Author's interview with an official from a North/South Implementation Body, 1 September 2008.

28 L. O'Dowd and C. McCall, 'Escaping the Cage of Ethno-national Conflict in Northern Ireland? The Importance of Transnational Networks', *Ethnopolitics* 7.1 (2008), 81–99.

29 *Irish Times*, 13 October 2009.

30 Lederach, *Building Peace*, 39.

31 Author's interview with a leader of a cross-border third-sector organisation, 10 September 2008.

32 Hamber and Kelly, 'Working Definition', 4.

33 S. Byrne, C. Thiessen, E. Fissuh and C. Irvin, 'The IFI and EU Peace II Fund: Respondents' Perceptions of Funded Project Success in Promoting Peacebuilding and Community Development in Northern Ireland', *Peace and Conflict Studies* 16.1 (2009), 44–67; S. Buchanan, 'Transforming Conflict in Northern Ireland and the Border Counties: Some Lessons from the Peace Programmes on Valuing Participative Democracy', *Irish Political Studies* 23.3 (2008), 387–409.

34 Author's interview with an official from a cross-border institution, 31 October 2008.

35 Author's interview with a Republic of Ireland civil servant, 30 September 2008b.

36 Author's interview with a Republic of Ireland civil servant , 30 September 2008a, emphasis added.

37 Author's interview with an official from a cross-border network, 25 September 2008.

38 H. Donnan and K. Simpson, 'Changing Relationships in the Irish Borderlands', *Anthropology in Action* 13.1–2 (2006), 69–77.

39 Author's interview with a leader of a cross-border third-sector organisation, 21 August 2008.

40 Author's interview with an official from a cross-border network, 25 September 2008.

41 Author's interview with a leader of a cross-border third-sector organisation, 10 September 2008.

42 Author's interview with an official from a Northern Ireland border region council, 25 September 2008.

43 Author's interview with a Republic of Ireland civil servant, 30 September 2008a.

44 Author's interview with a businessman in the cross-border private sector, 15 August 2005, conducted for *Mapping Frontiers, Plotting Pathways* project.

45 Author's interview with a Northern Ireland civil servant, 22 May 2009.

46 Author's interview with an official from a North/South Implementation Body, 1 September 2008.

47 B. Anderson, *Imagined Communities: Reflections on the Origin and Spread of Nationalism* (rev. edn, London, 1991), 5–6.

48 Author's interview with a Republic of Ireland civil servant, 30 September 2008b.

49 J. Todd, O. Muldoon, K. Trew, L. C. Bottos, N. Rougier and K. McLaughlin, 'The Moral Boundaries of the Nation: The Constitution of National Identity in the Southeastern Border Counties of Ireland', *Ethnopolitics* 5.4 (2006), 365–82.

50 Author's interview with a Northern Ireland civil servant, 14 November 2008.

51 Author's interview with a businessman in the cross-border private sector, 15 August 2005.

52 *The Agreement: Agreement Reached in the Multi-party Negotiations* (Belfast, 1998).

53 Author's interview with an official from a North/South Implementation Body, 1 September 2008.

54 For a critique of the application of the (neo)functionalist logic to understanding cross-border cooperation in Ireland, see E. Tannam, 'Cross-Border Co-operation between Northern Ireland and the Republic of Ireland: Neo-functionalism Re-visited', *British Journal of Politics and International Relations* 8.2 (2006), 258–78.

55 Author's interview with a southern civil servant in a border region authority, 3 November 2008.

56 Author's interview with an official from a cross-border network, 2 September 2008.

57 Author's interview with an official from a North/South Implementation Body, 1 September 2008.

58 Author's interview with a Northern Ireland civil servant, 22 May 2009.

59 Author's interview with a Northern Ireland civil servant, 14 November 2008.

60 For example, this opinion was expressed by a Republic of Ireland council official when interviewed, 21 August 2008.

61 Author's interview with a Republic of Ireland civil servant, 30 September 2008.

62 Author's interview with a representative of a cross-border third-sector organisation, 1 April 2009.

63 Author's interview with a civil servant in Northern Ireland department, 14 November 2008.

64 Author's interview with a civil servant in Northern Ireland department, 14 November 2008.

65 Author's interview with a Northern Ireland civil servant, 14 November 2008.

66 Channel Research for Border Action, 'Review of Peace II project evaluations' (Ohain, 2007), www.seupb.eu/Libraries/Peace_Network_Meetings_and_Events/PN__Review_of_Peace_Evaluation__020210.sflb.ashx (accessed 18 May 2010); HELM for SEUPB, 'Community Uptake Analysis – Peace II' (Belfast, 2007), www.seupb.eu/Libraries/PEACE_Programme_Evaluations/UPTAKE_REPORT.sflb.ashx (accessed 18 May 2010).

67 O'Dowd and McCall, 'Escaping the Cage', 81–99.

68 Department of Finance and Personnel, 'PEACE III Programme'.

69 Author's interview with a representative of a cross-border third-sector organisation, 1 April 2009.

70 K. Hayward, 'Building on the EU's Legacy: Cross-border Cooperation in Ireland', *Administration* 55.3 (2007), 51–74.

71 Author's interview with a Republic of Ireland civil servant, 30 September 2008b.

72 As in the report on criminal justice inter-governmental cooperation published by the Northern Ireland Affairs Committee of the House of Commons, *Cross-border Co-operation between the Governments of the United Kingdom and the Republic of Ireland* (London, 2009), www.parliament.the-stationery-office.co.uk/pa/cm200809/cmselect/cmniaf/78/7808.htm (accessed 18 May 2010).

73 For more on the approach of the British and Irish governments to peacebuilding, see S. Buchanan, 'Examining the Peacebuilding Policy Framework of the Irish and British Governments' in this volume.

74 Author's interview with a leader of a cross-border third-sector organisation, 10 September 2008.

12

Peace Dividends: The Role of External Aid in Peacebuilding

Elham Atashi

During the Cold War, external aid was a significant component of East–West rivalries with each side influencing their allies through economic support and resources. With the new World Order and increase in the number of protracted intra-state conflicts, external aid was increasingly considered as integral to peacebuilding.[1] Peacebuilding, a term popularised in the 1990s, went beyond the dominant model of managing conflicts and instead focused on addressing their root causes.[2] The changing pattern of conflicts required the international community to focus on new intervention strategies to end violent conflicts based on negotiated agreements, leading to a peace process and followed by peacebuilding strategies to transform them.[3] A peace process can be considered as a mechanism or a set of processes whereby the parties involved attempt to avoid destructive conflict by using different techniques such as diplomacy, mediation and negotiation. Defining the concept, Saunders argues that a peace process is more than conventional diplomacy and negotiation. It encompasses a full range of political, psychological, economic, diplomatic and military actions woven together into a comprehensive effort to establish peace.[4] The term 'peace dividend' has been broadly defined as social, political and psychological benefits that accrue as an outcome of a peace process. From this view, external aid is channelled into peace dividends to transform a conflict by social and economic development and therefore a significant component of peacebuilding. It is also hoped that economic growth and prosperity can create incentives on the ground by convincing people that they are stakeholders in the peace process, thereby increasing public support.[5]

Often, the signing of a peace agreement is followed by promises and pledges of aid by various donors as a way to create incentives, enhancing the sustainability of a peace process.[6] However, opinions on the relationship between external aid and its role in peacebuilding are varied. In various literatures it has been argued that external aid can be a key contributor to peacebuilding and preventing the renewal of conflict.[7] Several studies have explored the role of economic and social peace dividends based on external aid and the potential to bring about positive results in different stages of a conflict.[8] For example, in the Israel–Palestine peace process, external aid was considered necessary as leading to a peace agreement.[9] The Oslo Accord was followed by promises and delivery of substantial international aid which played a major role in the Israeli–Palestinian peace and reconstruction process in the period of 1993–2000.[10] Similarly, external aid played a significant role in the Salvadoran peace process. Boyce argues that a sustainable peace process must include measures to end political violence as well as deal constructively with social and economic deprivations.[11] Peacebuilding efforts must also focus on restoring relations on the ground after years of divisions and violence with a well-designed and achievable set of confidence-building measures that could lead to a change in community relations. He concludes that external aid can assist local institutions in implementing strategies to reduce fear, mistrust and hostility on the ground.[12]

However, not everyone agrees to external aid being a necessary condition for peacebuilding. External aid from the international community and donor organisations can actually escalate conflicts and have a negative impact on peacebuilding efforts.[13] Menkhaus discusses the challenges in evaluating the positive contribution of external aid projects in peacebuilding due to the diverse contextual nature of post-conflict situations which differ in each case.[14] In Sri Lanka, for example, external aid has been ineffective in peacebuilding and the advancement of parties towards a sustainable peace process.[15] On the contrary, in Somaliland, lack of external aid created a sense of local ownership and had a positive impact on the development of political institutions accountable to people rather than donor agencies. It also contributed to an increased willingness among political parties to engage constructively in state-building.[16]

Within this background, Northern Ireland provides an interesting context in examining the role of external aid in peacebuilding. In Northern Ireland, contrary to other cases, peace dividends were substantial, thanks to the European Union delivering sizeable amounts of money to support the peace process. Several studies on Northern Ireland explore the role of foreign investment, economic growth and particular projects funded by external aid.[17] Yet, most do not address the connection between public perceptions on the distribution of external aid and the impact on peacebuilding. Furthermore, less attention has been given to whether external aid has led to improvements in community relations, not just at a macro-elite level, but also on the ground particularly in interface areas.

This essay examines perceptions of the European Union's Peace and Reconciliation Fund as leading to peace dividends and improving relations after the Good Friday Agreement. It focuses on exploring public perceptions in several interface areas. Perceptions of external aid and its role in improving community relations in these areas are significant. They were the bedrock of violence throughout the conflict, highly affected, marginalised and with high levels of socio-economic deprivation.[18] The primary source of data for this study was through a series of 45 in-depth interviews. The interviews were conducted with 33 residents living in interface zones of Belfast (North and West), Derry-

Londonderry (Bogside and Waterside) and 12 individuals involved in community relations work in these areas.[19] Community perceptions in the mentioned
interface areas are examined, regarding the distribution of external aid,
whether it addressed local needs and led to improvements in community
relations. Finally, interviews results are analyzed as to the impact of external
aid in peacebuilding and a contributing factor leading to the sustainability of
the peace process. I provide a critical assessment and argue that external aid
has contributed to political institution-building, development and economic
recovery at a macro-national level, but not everyone has equally benefited.
People that live in areas that have historically experienced the direct impact
of violence and unrest known as interfaces have not seen practical improvements on their daily lives. As a result, external aid is considered to have been
unevenly distributed with very little impact as far as improving relations as
a result of peacebuilding in these areas. While community relations needs to
focus on levels of mistrust, fear and addressing deep divisions that continue
to separate communities, this work has not been realistic. It has not addressed
class divisions, economic deprivation, social exclusion and access to resources.
I conclude with implications for peacebuilding based on divisions between
those that have benefited from external aid and those that have been left out.

Community relations

On 10 April 1998, following two years of intense negotiations, an Agreement on the social, political and economic future of Northern Ireland was
signed and became known as the 'Belfast' or the 'Good Friday' Agreement.
The Agreement was hailed as a success and considered as the most important event in the recent political history of Ireland. From the outset, the
Agreement appeared comprehensive, addressing many issues from political
needs that would promote political inclusiveness, cross border cooperation
between the Republic of Ireland and Northern Ireland, to the institutions that
would address the protection of human rights and equality and measures to
deal with the impact of conflict that were important on the ground.[20] In an
attempt to transform the conflict from bottom up, some policy initiatives in
Northern Ireland pursued attempts to improve community relations, reduce
segregation, economic deprivation and inequality.[21] For three centuries or
three decades, depending on how far one wants to look back into the history
of the conflict (or whose version of history), the Unionists and Nationalists
in Northern Ireland have been living with conflict and the majority of the
population demographically segregated. Years of fear, mistrust and resentment cannot be forgotten about overnight or solved by an Agreement on paper.
Even though with the peace process the overt political violence was over,
the underlying causes that led to the conflict remained unresolved. Political
negotiations can establish Agreements, yet in the post-Agreement phase focus

was directed to peacebuilding strategies with the goal of improving relations between communities on the ground. From this perspective external aid can increase collaboration between the government and society, create local ownership, empower communities' capacity for peacebuilding and support of the peace process.

While gaining a new momentum, the adoption of such strategies were not entirely new. Prior to the Agreement, and as early as the 1960–1970s, efforts by individuals and community-based groups were made to address hostilities between communities by focusing on improving relations on the ground. Such bottom-up approaches are broadly considered as 'community relations' work and based on the notion that increased and direct contact between the communities can lead to positive relationships to reduce fear, mistrust and hostility.[22]

A structural attempt to formalise such efforts was led by the 'Community Relations Commission (CRC)'. The Commission was initially set up by the British government to improve relations between the two communities but it eventually dissolved in 1975. Knox and Quirk argue that the failure of the Stormont and introduction of Direct Rule led to disillusionment among community activists regarding the Commission's real commitment to addressing divisions on the ground.[23] Despite this setback, the establishment of Community Relations was an acknowledgement by the British government that addressing the conflict in Northern Ireland required an integrative and bottom-up approach that addresses prejudices and divisions politically as well as among communities.[24] Improving economic and social structures as well as increasing contact between communities was considered as essential in leading to a new set of relationships and ending political strife. In 1987 the Government established the Central Community Relations Unit (CCRU) followed by the Community Relations Council (CRC). Built as an independent agency, the goals of the CRC were to increase local community contact and understanding with projects that address a broader scope in peacebuilding such as human rights, conducting political dialogues, social and economic cooperation, enhancing cultural diversity and ending sectarian violence. The CRC also expanded its stakeholders. It focused on including local community organisations (some already active) such as trade unions, businesses and churches previously left out of peacebuilding efforts. As a result, the 1990s witnessed a growth in the number and diversity of groups engaged in peacebuilding work as well as an increase in financial support with the help of external aid.

External aid from the International Fund for Northern Ireland began flowing into Northern Ireland as early as 1989, after the Anglo Irish Agreement. Funding by the EU followed in 1995 as a gesture of support for the Downing Street Joint Declaration and the promise of a ceasefire by the main paramilitary groups on both sides. The substantial external aid that followed was a direct recognition of the EU's support for social and economic dividends to enhance the peace process. Furthermore, external funding by the EU was to be directed towards investment and development of deprived areas, particularly in interfaces, highly impacted by conflict.[25]

Jarman and O'Halloran define interfaces as the boundaries where the two main communities live close to each other.[26] Across Northern Ireland these interfaces were more prone to outbreaks of sectarian violence during the conflict. Smyth adds that the effects of 'the Troubles' were not distributed on an equal basis as there was a considerable variation between areas, in terms of both death rates of residents and death rates for those killed within specific areas.[27] Similarly, groups within the Northern Ireland population had suffered from the effects of the 'Troubles' at different rates. On both counts, Belfast and Derry-Londonderry had the highest death rate of any area in Northern Ireland. Smyth also states that within Belfast not all communities have been equally affected. In the city of Belfast, the highest amount of violence had occurred in 'interface zones' scattered in west, east, north and south Belfast.[28] In Derry-Londonderry the separation between communities is less scattered as the Unionist and Nationalist areas are divided in two, separated by the river Foyle. The Bogside is where most Nationalists live (with the exception of Fountain area with a community of 200 Unionists) and the Waterside is where the Unionists reside.[29] In exploring perceptions of external aid and its connection to peacebuilding and improving community relations, this essay focuses on three interface areas. The next section explores perceptions of community workers and residents of west and north Belfast and the Bogside, Waterside in Derry-Londonderry.

Defining community relations post-Peace Agreement

Immediately after the Agreement, community development workers were faced with several challenges. First, they had to shift their goals and strategies to address the specific needs of people on the ground and conform to the demands of peace instead of conflict. In the wake of the new Agreement, external aid was directed towards projects with a focus on cross-community instead of single-community relations. Community workers needed to explore new ideas and ways of working more effectively not just within their communities as they had done in the past, but in cooperation with other communities.[30] One interviewee working in various projects addressing community relations in west Belfast responded that 'initially it was difficult to have an inclusive vision of community relations, when community workers had worked in segregated and separate communities addressing specific localized needs'.[31]

Another problem was associated with specific definition of community relations. What exactly did the term entail? Perceptions of what community relations represented differed widely.[32] On the ground, community workers had to define the nature of their work in terms of cross-community relations to comply with the request of external aid funders. Furthermore, throughout the conflict, there had always been certain members from both communities who had met in informal gatherings and formed friendships.[33] However, these meetings were locally (neighbourhoods) organised and their agenda was not imposed through an institution and did not involve external aid or distribution of funds. Gatherings among women of different communities are one example; participation was voluntary and based on willingness and enthusiasm among certain people regardless of religious identity, to talk about common concerns such as health or domestic abuse. When community relations became institutionalised, it changed the nature and the framework of community relations.[34] According to some, 'this made the process superficial and imposed'.[35] External funding for community gatherings as well as monetary incentives for participation also posed challenges in the voluntary nature of civil society.

Initially, some people, among them community workers, rejected the idea of working with other communities. Perhaps a better analogy of this would be to say they thought that there were enough problems within their communities to resolve, hence, urgency or priority of cross-community work was questioned. The idea of cross-community relations was not a concept everyone was ready to embrace, due to suspicious and cynical perceptions on both sides. Many also considered participation to be in conflict with their strong political ideology, that is, to meet or have dialogue with people from the other community could be translated as a weakness or impertinent to strongly held identities. Hence, to sit with a Nationalist would mean that one did not care strongly about being a Unionist. Many perceived that to partake in cross-community programmes would also place one's position in society in danger as one could be seen as acting reconciliatory and sympathetic to the cause of the 'other' and giving up one's position or being soft.

> Why should we do that when we got enough problems to think about in our own areas? There must be priorities. First we have to solve our own problems, before we can sit and talk to them about our problems. These days nobody is even sure what being a Loyalist means. So if we don't know that ourselves, how can we explain it to them? It would make us feel weak.[36]

Therefore, at the outset, the term 'cross-community relations' and its relationship to peacebuilding was vague, leading to assorted and often misleading perceptions. People working or involved at the community level needed to think of ways to educate their communities and provide a definition of what the term entails and how it can be utilised positively.

Another reason why communities were suspicious of the term was its historical context. Some members of community considered the historical context in which this terminology developed to have a political motive. A community worker argued, 'Like everything else in Northern Ireland, everything is politicized, so of course when people heard the word cross community or community relations, they got suspicious.'[37] The use of the term was perceived by some as a deliberate attempt by the British government and civil servants in Northern Ireland to find a way of redefining the conflict. Arguments began to surface that the British government wanted to present the cause of conflict in Northern Ireland to be of sectarian nature and therefore a problem to be solved through community relations.[38] The term was perceived by some as a way to obscure the true nature of conflict that was embedded in a sense of injustice and discrimination of the Nationalist minority. This poses a challenge in the relationship between community relations and peacebuilding. As a strategy, cross-community work is based on the belief that improved relations will be likely to lead to less tension and violence and therefore a major component of peacebuilding since the peace Agreement. However, it raises a question on whether such efforts can have a positive impact if the very nature of such work, goals and objectives are questioned by some community members and seen as moving away rather than addressing root causes of conflict. In other words, for some the underlying causes of the conflict have yet to be addressed.

Peace money and dividends

A year after the Agreement, some 33,000 people were employed in cross-community relations and various community organisations. Conflict resolution and dealing with community relations had become a business employing a large sector of the community. This amounts to five per cent of a total population of 1.5 million that live in Northern Ireland. According to a community worker, 'Everyone was trying to benefit from rewards offered by various funders, so overnight we had half of our community converting their jobs to work in this field.'[39]

EU funding in the form of a 'Peace and Reconciliation' package, otherwise known in the community as 'Peace Money I', was delivered in 1995-99. It provided around €500 million directed at community projects. In 1999 the EU agreed to a new peace programme known as Peace Money II for Northern Ireland committing another €500 million over a period 2000-2004.[40] The aim of 'Peace Money I' was to move both communities towards a peaceful and stable society by getting involved in inclusive projects to promote cross-community contact and dialogue, reconciliation, business development, employment, rural development and cross-border communication.[41] Some of the money was directly aimed at supporting projects to bring together people from both sides of the community.

It was hoped that external economic assistance and dividends could lead to a positive role in decreasing deep communal divisions by providing incentives for people to support the peace process in return for dividends of peace.

However, community development had its limitations and priority was given to projects that promoted cross-community relations rather than addressing real needs, particularly in areas that had been affected directly. Some community organisations had managed to translate cross-community relations positively and were engaged in various projects.[42] One example is various educational programmes working with youth to end segregated schooling, some taking children from both communities on various holiday schemes. Schubotz and Robinson highlight that increased contact among the children and youth who participated in such projects led to a positive impact in changing perceptions of the other's community.[43] Another example is the mobile network schemes. These are members of community in both groups who work across interface areas. Through liaison with each other over mobile phones they advise each other of possible trouble in communities and attempt to reduce tensions before they escalated. Racioppi and O'Sullivan have conducted a detailed study of the various cross-community and economic development programmes initiated by Peace Money I and II.[44] They highlight the EU's success in its objective to engage mid-level elite groups in peacebuilding by providing community organisations with funds as well as the opportunity to design and implement projects in their communities.

Other community projects had a focus on dialogues and interchurch meetings.[45] Initially, some organisations were pleased with the availability of funding, especially considering the history of the poorly funded civil society sector. However, soon after EU funds began to be delivered, aimed at diverse projects, questions were raised as to the efficiency and direction of funds. Many residents, particularly in interface areas, regarded funds as being misused and their communities exploited. Furthermore, many residents perceived that decision-makers were not directing funds to their specific needs but were imposing projects according to misguided judgements on wrong issues. In an interview with a resident of west Belfast she commented,

> I think people in our area have real needs and other types of worries than to think about community relations issues. You go and tell the women with kids, she can't pay her bills to go and do what? Funders come in and say we are doing 'empowerment and equality' workshop, what is that? How is that relevant to what is going on in our areas to address unemployment?[46]

Who has benefited from the dividends?

The perception of people interviewed is that they have not seen the effects of peacebuilding. This suggests that access to funding within deprived communities, particularly in interface areas, remained limited and many in these areas consider that money has been wasted on projects that do not have a tangible effect on their lives. A community worker commented,

People were angry because they thought a lot of these projects were a waste of money and to be honest, a lot of them were. What we got was a lot of training to train people that would do conflict resolution, but what happened, is that this created problems. These people that were now trained were coming to these areas, telling them how they should run their lives, they would sit and lecture them but often their language appeared alien to people who had real problems.[47]

Many also consider that the middle and business classes have largely benefited from allocation of funds, leaving out the working-class areas. Therefore, within interface areas competition between communities for scarce funding has resulted in increasing bi-communal polarisations. Considering that the expectation among people in these areas involved provision of opportunities, many consider that 'peace money' has not been used appropriately in these communities.

There is a significant factor in these assumptions. Funders assume that they need to direct resources to address sectarian divisions in society which, throughout the history of conflict, has been defined as based on religious/ ethnic identity rather than on socio-economic factors. Identity is also embedded within socio-economic aspects, because experiences impact upon identity. Among the causes of conflict in many interface areas is socio-economic deprivation. Also, as Jarman argues, despite the peace Agreement, many residents in interface areas continue to live amidst constant violence, which needs to be dealt with.[48] Therefore, in interface areas, the issue of community relations is linked to other themes such as socio-economic conditions, segregation, violence and inequality. Community relations may not be a priority in certain communities and should not be applied as a universal strategy in peacebuilding. Peacebuilding strategies may benefit from a needs-based approach. Interview results indicate that in certain areas residents may not be ready to begin addressing identity and relationship-building issues, before addressing their localised needs within their community. Unless local problems such as levels of violence, unemployment and economic deprivation are addressed within communities, cross-community work may be premature and counter-productive. Defining problems by funders may also be considered as an imposition. Superiority associated with the knowledge of 'experts' within community relations and civil servants can add to perceptions of disempowerment rather than empower communities.

Community development should form the basis for community relations; the latter should not be a substitute for the former. As two community workers commented,

Since the peace process, 'people up there' (middle class, politicians and civil servants) look down at us in these areas. Their attitude is that they are tolerant and we are not. Sectarianism here means you will have a brick through your window. So how can you expect them to know what goes on in our areas, their lives is so different.[49]

I don't think just because we have an assembly it means they don't have differences. What gets to me is that they think we down here are the problem, but look at their [politicians'] mess.[50]

The interview results shed light on the challenges of implementing peacebuilding. This raises the question of how external aid can be better utilised in its contribution to peacebuilding. External funding directed at economic development and community relations does not guarantee that dividends reach and address local needs. Despite a fair share of projects dedicated to improving community relations, residents of interface areas remained frustrated with the allocation of resources. Distribution of dividends can also polarise and lead to increased divisions within communities because of perceptions of inequality in fund allocation, creating obstacles to peacebuilding.

Peace money: improving relations or further division?

Deep divisions between communities in Northern Ireland while being sectarian in nature are also embedded along class lines, between 'haves' and 'have-nots'. This is not to divert attention away from political and sectarian divisions that obviously do exist, but rather to draw attention to diverse and complex dynamics of social identity and group categorisation in Northern Ireland's communities. Hence, interview results suggest that Unionist residents were more likely to have similar perceptions and concerns as Nationalist residents living in interface areas than with their own in-group members. This appeared to be an issue related to deprivation, inequality in power, privilege and access to resources. Therefore, while separated by sectarianism and walls, residents in interface areas share the same social class. While conducting interviews with residents living in interface areas it became evident that when they refer to the 'other', the 'other' is not just someone from the other community. It could also be someone from a different demographic area. This is because divisions in society can also be based on socio-economic class lines and it would be misleading to ignore this meta-culture that surpasses sectarian identities. This is an important finding as it provides opportunities for peacebuilding to address commonalities between the two communities despite divisions. Sadly, community workers and funders rarely acknowledge this or challenge assumptions regarding sectarian divisions.

For years we have been told your lives are different, it's harsh, we don't want to deal with you. The government sent us a message that police won't come to your area to deal with your problems [during conflict]. So we have been forced to take care of our own problems, rely on ourselves to be able to survive.[51]

Well you look at these walls, until we have these walls; they are walls that will separate us forever, inside our hearts and outside in our lives. So we are getting a mixed message, form relations and then come back inside your walls and live your life.[52]

Although the 'peace money' was to contribute to better relations between communities, it has led to tension because of diverse perceptions between Unionists and Nationalists as well as conflict within communities. The main reason for this has been the perception that allocation of resources is inequitable, unfair and is creating divisions. While this perception is mostly held among Unionists, Nationalists remain critical overall of the focus of funds and consider that they have in many cases lost their cohesiveness as a community. One interviewee described this as follows:

> Before you would walk around, everyone was there for each other and there was a sense of community. We all helped each other out, not because of money, but because we were in this together and now you don't see that anymore, we are more divided and want self interest. Our people are changing and our society has changed for the worse.[53]

It should also be noted that not everyone is equally aware of these funds, as information about monetary aid and assistance remains limited to certain segments of society. The people more likely to be aware of the availability of funds are usually those working on the community level, limited to community organisations, academics, business owners and professionals. While most people welcomed and supported the funds, there was an increasing perception, particularly in Unionist communities, that the distribution of funds was benefiting the Nationalists.

'Who got what' often became dependent on who had more information as to what funding was available, had mastered the rigid requirements of donors and knew how to write better grant proposals, rather than who could do the best work that addressed the real concerns of the community. Northern Ireland is a small country and news often travels fast through community members. Therefore, as soon as a certain organisation receives money, others know about it and begin to feel deprived if they do not receive any. Funding given to aid was creating competition rather than cooperation. 'All the money went to Nationalist organizations of course. So now tables have turned, everybody wants to give them money.'[54]

Many Unionist community organisations were new and reactive, set up to respond to the needs of their communities after the Agreement. Traditionally they had not been accustomed to assembling community support based on a spirit of community volunteership and relied heavily on state assistance, compared to many Nationalist communities in which traditionally a spirit of volunteership and community mobilisation was strong. Reacting to the need to get involved in order to benefit from the available funding and furious at the allocation of resources being directed to the Nationalist communities, the Unionists decided to take action. However, civil society groups and grassroots organisations were unprepared to respond to the new challenges in getting funding to support the needs of their communities. The main reason for this was that, within deprived Unionist communities in interface areas, there had traditionally been a lack of community infrastructure compared to the Nationalist communities.

> They have always had a community structure, while we never had that. So when the money was given out, they got together, arranged meetings and of course the funders are also to blame because they had to be seen to be giving more money to them, because of their suffering mentality, but we have suffered too. It was then that we had to wake up and start resistance. Enough was enough.[55]

Many community workers considered that the overall decisive principles for funding proposed projects was determined by the grandeur of the writing skills which had to include elements of relationship-building between the two communities. This meant whatever project proposed would have to include Unionist and Nationalist participants in order to qualify for funding. This criterion frustrated and eventually marginalised many smaller organisations that simply did not have the skills or resources to comply with rules enforced by funders. Some community organisations perfected the art of 'tailored' grant writing. Hence, some organisations became the darling of funders, causing resentment, while others were left out.[56]

Since community organisations writing grants would have to include some dynamic of inter-community dialogue, they needed participants. In the years following the Agreement, some members of the community remained enthusiastic in participating in such projects. However, what became clear was that many of these projects were not based on the needs of the community, the desire to take part in such projects or their real effect.

Participants were often selected based on their willingness to show up, rather than on their abilities to be open to the process of dialogue. The following interviews revealed this pattern:

> We avoided talking about the real issues, the important stuff. We avoided it, because we thought what is the point? So we would get together and talk about our relationships. We did all get along and it was interesting but we never discussed anything that would divide us. We were told to concentrate on the positive stuff. It was superficial.[57]

> What is really sad is some people have really benefited from the money, but it has also divided us. Years back you did this type of work because of passion and love. But now those people who were genuinely involved in their communities, volunteered their time and did this work from the bottom of their heart have been marginalized. So we have lost a sense of volunteership.[58]

Often there was a danger that such initiatives are only reaching out to people who already share a commitment to dialogue, peace and reconciliation and are therefore prepared to engage with the other community. Those in interface areas, who are more radical and hard-line opponents of any compromise, often do not participate and are hostile towards those that do. As a consequence they do not share the same views as people that participate and benefit from such programmes. O'Halloran highlights that activists are often caught in a dilemma: if they enter inter-community dialogue they risk retribution from their own communities, yet if they do not they risk further inter-community violence.[59] Unless these programmes begin to reach out to residents of interface areas and be more inclusive, significant inter-communal divides will remain. For example, Burgess, Ferguson and Hollywood argue that there has been a growing sense of intergroup identity rather than a shared one as a result of segregation in interface areas since the Agreement. They observed that residents were 'especially unlikely to interact with members of the other community'.[60] Inadequate needs-assessment in addition to accusations of unfairness in the allocation and distribution of money have also added to tensions. During an interview with a member of the Unionist community in Waterside, frustration with reasoning as to why her project was rejected and others were not became evident. She showed me her proposal, which she said took her months to write:

> I don't understand how they could do this. I had to cut short my full time job to become involved in youth projects in my community, because I really care about the future of these youth. We are not like them [Catholics]; we don't have a strong interest among the members of our community to get involved. So I thought it's worth it, one should get involved and now this, a real slap on my face and a real disappointment.[61]

Allocation of money has become a source of bitterness and division among civil society groups. Unionists are increasingly feeling victimised due to growing dissatisfaction and perceptions of inequality in funding. However, some members of the Unionist community argued that lack of funding is not due to inequality in distribution but consequential to lack of motivation, organisation and unity within Unionist communities.

> We would set up community meetings to tell and inform people about what is going on and how they can benefit from it, but very few people would show up and if they did, they would just moan, they did not want to get involved. Since the Agreement, we been invited to go to Nationalist communities and have dialogue with their community workers and what I saw was that they are much more involved and engaged in community work than we are. It's difficult to say why that is, also traditionally we are not used to mobilising support, so very few people are willing to give us their time to come and get involved.[62]

> Since the peace money started coming, it quickly became evident that we have not seen any real benefits from funding. This is mainly our fault because many people in our communities did not know how to go about getting funding; we did not have the right skills. At first we as a community

were trying to adapt to all the new changes that were happening politically, everything was happening too fast.[63]

Outside of Derry, in the small Unionist community of 'TullyAlley', an inspiring member of the TullyAlley community and the head of the Youth Community Center had a different perspective:

> I am tired of people in my community nagging about how much the others are getting, how they are getting everything ... because it won't get us anywhere. If they are unhappy with the way things are they should get up, get organized and do something about it rather than constantly complain. The Unionists need to wake up and realize that they need to get mobilized to change things they are not happy about rather than rely on the traditional methods of waiting for the government to support their ways. Things have changed, if we don't wake up and learn new skills, manage our communities and respond to our new environment, we would be left behind. When I saw what was happening in my community with youth violence and intimidation from paramilitary groups, I decided to do something. I set up a youth centre.[64]

Unionist communities are particularly vulnerable to the perception that they have not been treated fairly by funders and were often left out of allocation of resources. This has added a layer of insecurity to a population that already considers the Nationalists as the main political beneficiary of the Agreement.[65] As a result, perceptions of victimhood were on the increase. Furthermore, similar to other conflicts, a peace process may lead to peace benefits for some, but the end of conflict also means a loss to others who had benefited from conflict. Conflict generates jobs in certain sectors related to security. The end of overt violence often leads to a decrease in the number of people employed in these areas. Considering that the majority of security forces were historically Unionist, there was also the insecurity over loss of employment and availability of future opportunities. Given the changes in the political environment, Unionists feel abandoned and isolated by state and security forces. This created added tensions and led to disunity in their already fragile communities.

Conclusion: assessment of external aid and peace dividends

Do the majority of interviewees feel satisfied that peace dividends have led to socio-economic development, reduction of violence and improved community relations as a result of peacebuilding efforts supported by external aid? The short answer is no, the majority of residents in interface areas remain extremely dissatisfied with tangible improvements in their lives and do not consider having better relations with members of the other community. Peace dividends have been uneven, particularly in dealing with specific problems such as unemployment in interface areas. It is also clear, as highlighted by

O'Hearn, that benefits have occurred at a macro level as far as economic and business development is concerned.[66] Cragin and Chalk argue that since the Agreement peace dividends have led to the emergence of new middle- and business-elite classes that have directly benefited from economic development programmes.[67]

Efforts have been made to address some of the problems associated in interface areas with housing, education and employment. However, due to various factors such as unemployment, poverty, segregation and ongoing crime and youth violence, residents have not been able to benefit from initiatives aimed at economic development that have revived other areas in Northern Ireland.[68] The community relations sector has created jobs as seen in the increasing number of people employed. However, this has not had a major effect in interface areas. The long-term impact of constructive community work and development is likely to be overshadowed by the negative aspects associated with allocation of funds.

The term 'community relations' continues to lead to confusion and different perceptions as far as what it means to people. It is difficult to define success as far as the goal of many projects aimed at improving relations through economic and relationship development. In the short term, it is clear that people tend to define the goal of such programmes as having a direct tangible impact on their lives, which remains elusive. From a long-term perspective, it is difficult to assess whether these programmes can contribute to improving relations and lessening the divisions. In assessing success, as far as implementing the specific requests of various projects as defined by funders, the programmes have been successful in that they have been implemented. However, if success is evaluated according to the contribution of programmes based on specific needs of communities, then much remains to be done.

From the interview results, it becomes clear that both the Unionist and the Nationalist communities in interface areas remained marginalised from distribution of Peace money funded by the European Peace and Reconciliation Fund. Poor management of funds is partly responsible for this. Furthermore, funding appears to have contributed to deepening of divisions over competition, allocation and distribution, which many consider to be based on inadequate guidelines. The main benefactors of funding have been professionals, conflict resolution specialists and middle-class business owners. Second, community relations have not focused on levels of mistrust, fear and addressing deep divisions that continue to separate communities, but this work needs to be realistic and address class divisions as well as power and access to resources. Without this acknowledgment, it is likely that the term could lead to greater divisions, and given the existing hostility between communities, yet another division should not be welcome.

If the current destructive pattern regarding allocation of money is not stopped, competition for resources could escalate and communities already divided along many lines could become further fragmented. What is largely being ignored is that the main problems in interface areas are not the fact that people do not get along and therefore need cross-community relations. The term 'community relations' has been utilised to focus on one form of societal division while wrongly excluding the other. Both divisions need to be addressed equally. This could also be an opportunity for these communities to realise that they do share common concerns along class lines that go beyond religious divides.

The conflict in Northern Ireland has largely persisted because of negative attitudes and perceptions forming the foundation of community relations. Despair and an unwillingness to hope that the situation can be overcome are common among residents of interface areas. This is unlikely to be just a problem of perceptions. Much is also dependent on perceptions of equality in access to resources. First, significant levels of deprivation, poverty and violence have to be dealt with as a priority. Once again, this theme is intertwined with others. If dividends are not distributed equally, peacebuilding strategies may continue to be challenged based on those people benefiting from them and others who feel left out.

Notes

1 B. B. Ghali, *An Agenda for Peace: Preventive Diplomacy, Peacemaking and Peace-keeping*, Document A/47/277 – S/241111 (New York, 17 June 1992).
2 C. T. Call and S. E. Cook, 'On Democratization and Peacebuilding', *Global Governance* 9 (2003), 233–34.
3 J. Darby and R. McGinty, *Contemporary Peace Making: Conflict, Violence and Peace Processes* (New York, 2002).
4 H. Saunders, *A Public Peace Process: Sustained Dialogue to Transform Racial and Ethnic Conflicts* (New York, 1999).
5 E. Atashi, 'Challenges to Conflict Transformation from the Streets', in *B. Dayton and L. Kriesberg (eds), Conflict Transformation and Peacebuilding: Moving from Violence to Sustainable Peace* (New York, 2009).
6 C. Bigdon and B. Korf, 'The Role of Development Aid in Conflict Transformation: Facilitating Empowerment Processes and Community Development', in A. Austin, M. Fischer and N. Ropers (eds), *Transforming Ethnopolitical Conflict: The Berghof Handbook* (Wiesbaden, Germany, 2004), 341–70.
7 M. Leonhardt, 'The Challenge of Linking Aid and Peacebuilding', in L. Reychler and T. Paffenholz (eds), *Peacebuilding: A Field Guide* (Boulder, 2001), 238–45.
8 A. Regan, 'External versus Internal Incentives in Peace Processes: The Bougainville Experience', in A. Griffiths and C. Barnes (eds), *Powers of Persuasion: Incentives, Sanctions and Conditionality in Peacemaking, Accord* 19 (London, 2008); O. Seliktar, 'The Economy of Israel and the Peace Process', in I. Peleg (ed.), *The Middle East Peace Process: Interdisciplinary Perspectives* (Albany, NY, 1998), 223–35; R. Vayrynen, 'Economic Incentives and the Bosnian Peace Process', in D. Cortright (ed.), *Price of Peace: Incentives and International Conflict Prevention* (Lanham, 1997), 155–81.
9 R. Brynen, *A Very Political Economy: Peacebuilding and Aid in the West Bank and Gaza* (Washington, DC, 2000).

10 M. Keating, A. Le More and R. Lowe (eds), *Aid, Diplomacy, and Facts on the Ground: The Case of Palestine* (London, 2005).

11 J. K. Boyce (ed.), *Economic Policy for Building Peace: The Lessons of El Salvador* (Boulder, CO, 1996).

12 Boyce (ed.), *Economic Policy for Building Peace.*

13 O. J. Sending, 'Learning to Build a Sustainable Peace-Ownership and Everyday Peacebuilding', in *CMI Report* (Bergen, Norway, R2000: 14); M. B. Anderson, *Do No Harm: How Aid Can Support Peace or War* (Boulder, CO, 1999).

14 M. Menkhaus, *Impact Assessment in Post-Conflict Peacebuilding: Challenges and Future Directions* (Geneva, July 2004).

15 H. Peiris, 'The Limits of External Influence', in Griffiths and Barnes (eds), *Powers of Persuasion.*

16 N. Eubank, *Peace-building without External Assistance: Lessons from Somaliland*, CGD Working Paper 198 (Washington, DC, 2010).

17 D. O'Hearn, '*Peace Dividend,* Foreign Investment and Economic Regeneration: The Northern Irish Case', in *Social Problems* 47.2 (2000), 180–200; S. Byrne and C. Irvin, 'A Shared Common Sense: Perceptions of the Material Effects and Impacts of Economic Growth in Northern Ireland', *Civil Wars* 5.1 (2002), 55–86; S. Byrne and M. Ayulo, 'External Economic Aid in Ethno-Political Conflict: A View from Northern Ireland', *Security Dialogue* 29.4 (1998), 421–34; J. Coakley, 'Has the Northern Ireland Problem Been Solved?', *Journal of Democracy* 19.3 (2008), 98–112; A. J. Wilson, 'Doing the Business: Aspects of the Clinton Administration's Economic Support for the Northern Ireland Peace Process, 1994–2000', *Journal of Conflict Studies* 23.1 (2003), 155–76.

18 For a description and location of interface areas, see Interface Communities and the Peace Process Report, Belfast Interface Project: Belfast, http://www.belfastinterface.project.org (accessed 16 March 2011).

19 Interviews were conducted over a one-year period in 2003–04. Unless permission was given to state their names and date of interview, all respondents remain anonymous and are identified according to the month they were interviewed, their demographic residential or community work areas. In Derry-Londonderry the interviews were conducted in the interface areas of 'Fountain, TullyAlley, Bogside and Waterside'.

20 See K. Hayward, C. McCall and I. Damkat, 'Building Peace and Crossing Borders: The North/South Dimension of Reconciliation' in this volume, and The Agreement (Belfast, 1998).

21 See S. Buchanan, 'Examining the Peacebuilding Policy Framework of the Irish and British Governments' in this volume.

22 G. W. Allport, *The Nature of Prejudice* (Reading, MA, 1954).

23 C. Knox and P. Quirk, *Peacebuilding in Northern Ireland, Israel and South Africa: Transition, Transformation and Reconciliation* (New York, 2000).

24 H. Frazer and M. Fitzduff, 'Improving Community Relations', in *Community Relations Council Report* (Belfast, 1994).

25 Interface areas were to be the specific target of Peace II money as stated by the European Union Structural Funds Programme in Northern Ireland. See European Union Structural Funds Report (2000–2006), PPMC13, Paper 3, Appendix 1-090519, http://ec.europa.eu/ (accessed 10 February 2009).

26 N. Jarman and C. O'Halloran, *Peace Lines or Battlefields: Responding to Violence in Interface Areas* (Belfast, 2000).

27 M. Smyth and F. M. Therese, *Personal Accounts from Northern Ireland's Troubles: Public Conflict, Private Loss* (London, 2000); M. T. Fay, M. Morrissey and M. Smyth, *Northern Ireland's Troubles: The Human Costs* (London, 1999).

28 They are also known as 'flashpoint' or 'frontline' areas. See C. Heatley, *Interface: Flashpoints in Northern Ireland* (Belfast, 2004); M. Morrissey and M. Smyth, *Northern Ireland after the Good Friday Agreement: Victims, Grievance and Blame* (London, 2002).

29 It is important to point out that Derry is the name used by Nationalists and Londonderry is the name used by Unionists. When referring to the city both terms are included.

30 F. Cochrane, '*Unsung Heroes?* The Role of Peace and Conflict Resolution Organizations in the Northern Ireland Conflict', in J. McGarry (ed.), *Northern Ireland and the Divided World* (Oxford, 2001).

31 Author's interview with a Nationalist, community worker, Belfast, February 2003.

32 G. Robinson and F. Foley, *Politicians and Community Relations in Northern Ireland* (Coleraine, November 2004).

33 C. McCartney, 'The Role of Civil Society', in C. McCartney (ed.), *Striking a Balance: The Northern Ireland Peace Process, Accord* 89 (London, 1999).

34 F. Cochrane and S. Dunn, *People Power? The Role of the Voluntary and Community Sector in the Northern Ireland Conflict* (Cork, 2002).

35 Author's interview with a Nationalist, community worker, Bogside, Derry-Londonderry, March 2003.

36 Author's interview with a Unionist, Belfast, February 2003.

37 Author's interview with a Nationalist community worker, Belfast, March 2003.

38 M. Hall, *Community Relations – An Elusive Concept: An Exploration by Community Activists from North Belfast* (Newtownabbey, 2001).

39 Author's interview with a Nationalist community worker, Belfast, February 2003.

40 Peace Money III will be implemented from 2007–13.

41 EU Programme for Peace and Reconciliation in Northern Ireland and Border Region of Ireland, 2000–2004, Operational Programme, 'Reinforcing Progress towards a Peaceful and Stable Society and Promoting Reconciliation', *CCI 2000, RG.16.1.PO.2001, http://*www.delni.gov.uk/ *(accessed 23 January 2009)*.

42 See D. Morrow, 'Towards a Shared Society', a report on the community relations, Council Policy Development Conference (May 2004), http://arrts.gtcni.org.uk (accessed 17 February 2007).

43 D. Schubotz and G. Robinson, *Cross Community Integration and Mixing: Does it Make a difference?*, *Research Update* 43, Ark publications, http://www.ark.ac.uk/publications/updates/update43.pdf (accessed 10 February 2009).

44 L. Racioppi and K. O'Sullivan, 'Grassroots Peacebuilding and Third-Party Intervention: The European Union's Special Support Programme for Peace and Reconciliation in Northern Ireland', *Peace and Change* 32.3 (2007), 361–90.

45 C. Knox and J. Hughes, 'Crossing the Divide: Community Relations in Northern Ireland', *Journal of Peace Research* 33.1 (1996), 83–98.

46 Author's interview with a Unionist, March 2003.

47 Author's interview with a Nationalist community worker, Belfast, January 2003.

48 N. Jarman, 'From War to Peace? Changing Patterns of Violence in Northern Ireland, 1990–2003', *Terrorism and Political Violence* 16.3 (2004), 420–38.

49 Author's interview with a Unionist, Belfast, March 2003.

50 Author's interview with a Nationalist, Belfast, April 2003.

51 Author's interview with a Nationalist community worker, Derry-Londonderry, March 2003.

52 Author's interview with a Unionist youth worker, Belfast, February 2003.

53 Author's interview with a Nationalist, community worker, Derry-Londonderry, April 2003.

54 Author's interview with a Unionist community worker, Waterside, Derry-London-derry, March 2003.

55 Author's interview with a Unionist community activist, TullyAlley, Derry-London-derry, March 2003.

56 See S. Buchanan's essay in this volume.

57 Author's interview with a Unionist participant in dialogue workshops, Belfast, February 2003.

58 Author's interview with a Nationalist, community worker, Belfast, March 2003.

59 C. O'Halloran, *Inner East/Outer West: Addressing Conflict in Two Interface Areas*, Belfast Interface Project (Belfast, 1999).

60 M. Burgess, N. Ferguson and I. Hollywood, 'Rebels Perspectives of the Legacy of Past Violence and of the Current Peace in Post-Agreement Northern Ireland: An Interpretative Phenomenological Analysis', in *Political Psychology* 28.1 (2007), 85.

61 Author's interview with a community worker, Waterside, Derry-Londonderry, March 2003.

62 Author's interview with a Unionst community worker, Waterside, Derry-London-derry, March 2003.

63 Author's interview with a Unionist community worker, Belfast, January 2003.

64 Author's interview with a Unionist, TullyAlley, Derry-Londonderry, March 2003.

65 J. Coakley, 'Has the Northern Ireland Problem Been Solved?', *Journal of Democracy* 19.3 (2008), 98–112.

66 O'Halloran, *Inner East/Outer West*.

67 K. Cragin and P. Chalk, *Terrorism and Development: Using Social and Economic Development to Inhibit a Resurgence of Terrorism* (Santa Monica, CA, 2003).

68 N. Jarman, *No Longer a Problem? Sectarian Violence in Northern Ireland* (Belfast, March 2005); G. Horgan and M. Monteith, *What Can We Do to Tackle Child Poverty in Northern Ireland?* (New York, 2009).

Index

Printed and bound by CPI Group (UK) Ltd, Croydon, CR0 4YY

09/06/2025

14685961-0002